CRITICAL THINKING HANDBOOK
K-3

A Guide for Remodelling Lesson Plans
in
Language Arts, Social Studies, & Science

by
Richard Paul, A.J.A. Binker, and Marla Charbonneau

Center for Critical Thinking and Moral Critique
Sonoma State University
Rohnert Park, CA 94928
707-664-2940
© 1986

K-3 Advisory Committee

Shirley Collins, Penngrove School
Marion Fairbank, St. John the Baptist School
Teresa Ruhl, St. John the Baptist School

CONTENTS

*Those lessons short enough, are included with the remodels. The rest of the originals which we were given permission to use, are reprinted in this appendix. They are numbered in accord with the first page of the remodel. For instance, the original for "Places to Play" (which begins on p. 53) is numbered 'O-53.' The original for "Air Has Weight" (p. 183) is numbered 'O-183.'

Critical Thinking Handbook, K-3: A Guide For Remodelling Lesson Plans in Language Arts, Social Studies, and Science

Preface

The Design of the Book

This Handbook has a two-fold goal and everything it contains can be seen as aiming at one or both of these objectives: 1) to make the concept of critical thinking and the principles that underlie it clear, and 2) to show how critical thinking can be taught. The second goal has two forms: a) presenting general strategies which can be used at any time to foster critical thinking, and b) demonstrating how lesson remodelling can be used as a process of bringing critical thinking into the heart of everyday classroom activities. Most sections of the book attempt to do both 1 and 2.

This preface, besides explaining the structure of the Handbook as a whole, introduces the reader to the concept of critical thinking, and how it affects education. The Introduction explains and justifies lesson plan remodelling. This method of infusion is the main concern of this book. The chapter "Global Critical Thinking Strategies" combines the objectives of clarifying critical thinking and suggesting general teaching strategies. It does not directly address remodelling. The first section explains the necessity for critical thinking across the curriculum, and circumstances the child faces in school and everyday life. The second section introduces the technique of Socratic questioning first in general terms, then by illustration in a transcript of a Socratic discussion. The next section briefly introduces another general technique: Role playing and reconstructing opposing views.

The second chapter, "How to Use This Book," begins the remodelling thrust of our approach, and describes some of the most common problems we found when examining K-3 texts. The third chapter, "Strategies," clarifies the idea of critical thinking further, and discusses how it can be taught, by introducing and explaining the twenty-eight specific teaching strategies at the heart of the remodelling process. The rest of the book contains examples of our use of the remodelling process on lessons, lesson fragments, and units, extracted from the teacher's editions of textbooks. For reference, the original lessons are listed in order in an appendix.

Our Concept of Critical Thinking

The term 'critical,' as we use it, does not mean thinking which is negative or finds fault, but rather thinking which evaluates reasons, and brings thought and action in line with our evaluations, our best sense of what is true. The ideal of the critical thinker could be roughly expressed in the phrase 'reasonable person.' Our use of the term 'critical' is intended to highlight the intellectual autonomy of the critical thinker. That is, as a critical thinker, I do not simply accept conclusions (uncritically.) I evaluate or critique reasons. My critique enables me to reject poor reasoning, and accept strong reasoning. To do so to the greatest extent possible, I make use of a number of identifiable and learnable skills. I discount reasons and evidence irrelevant to the conclusion; make assumptions explicit and evaluate them; reject unwarranted inferences, or 'leaps of logic;' use the best and most complete evidence available to me; make relevant distinctions, clarify; avoid inconsistency and contradiction; reconcile apparent contradictions; and distinguish what I know from what I merely suspect to be true.

The uncritical thinker, on the other hand, doesn't reflect on or evaluate reasons for his beliefs, he simply agrees or disagrees, accepts or rejects conclusions, often without understanding them, and often on the basis of egocentric attatchment or unassessed desire. Lacking skills to analyze and evaluate, he allows irrelevant reasons to affect his conclusions; doesn't notice assumptions, and therefore fails to evaluate them; accepts any inference that "sounds good;" is unconcerned with the certainty and completeness of evidence; can't sort out ideas, confuses different concepts, is an unclear thinker; is oblivious to contradictions; feels certain, even when not in a position to know. The classic uncritical thinking line is, "I've made up my mind! Don't confuse me with facts." Yet, critical thinking is more than evaluation of simple lines of thought.

As I evaluate beliefs, by evaluating the evidence or reasoning that supports them (that is, the 'arguments' for them,) I notice certain things. I learn that sometimes I must go beyond evaluating small lines of reasoning; that to understand an issue, I may have to think about it for a long time, and weigh many reasons and clarify basic ideas. I see that evaluating a particular line of thought often forces me to re-evaluate another. A conclusion about one case forces me to come to a certain conclusion about another. I find that often, my evaluation of someone's thinking turns on the meaning of a concept, which I must clarify. Such clarification affects my understanding of other issues. I notice previously hidden relationships between beliefs about different issues. I see that some beliefs and ideas are more fundamental than others. In short, I must orchestrate the skills I have learned into a longer series of moves. As I strive for consistency and understanding, I discover opposing sets of basic assumptions which underlie those conclusions. I find that, to make my beliefs reasonable, I must evaluate, not individual beliefs, but rather, large sets of beliefs. Analysis of an issue requires more work, a more extended process, than that required for a short line of reasoning. I must learn to use my skills, not in separate little moves, but together, coordinated into a long sequence of thought.

Sometimes, two apparently equally strong arguments or lines of reasoning about the same issue come to contradictory conclusions. That is, when I listen to one side, the case seems strong. Yet when I listen to the other side, that case seems equally strong. Since they contradict each other, they cannot both be right. Sometimes it seems that the two sides are talking about different situations, or speaking different languages, even living in different 'worlds.' I find that the skills which enable me to evaluate a short bit of reasoning do not offer much help here.

Suppose I decide to question two people who hold contradictory conclusions on an issue. They may use concepts or terms differently; disagree about what terms apply to what situations, and what inferences can then be made, or state the issue differently. I may find that the differences in their conclusions rest, not so much on a particular piece of evidence, or on one inference, as much as on vastly different perspectives; different ways of seeing the world, or different conceptions of, say, human nature. As their conclusions arise from different perspectives, each, to the other, seems deluded, prejudiced, or naive. How am I to decide who is right? My evaluations of their inferences, uses of terms, evidence, etc., also depend on perspective. In a sense, I discover that *I* have a perspective.

I could simply agree with the one whose overall perspective is most like my own. But how do I know I'm right? If I'm sincerely interested in evaluating beliefs, should I not also consider things from other perspectives?

As I reflect on this discovery, I may also realize that my perspective has changed. Perhaps I recall learning a new idea or even system of thought that changed the way I see myself and the world around me in fundamental ways, perhaps changed my life. I remember how pervasive this change was. I began to interpret a whole range of situations differently, continually used a new idea, concept or phrase, paid attention to previously ignored facts. I realize that I now have a new choice regarding the issue under scrutiny.

I could simply accept the view that most closely resembles my own. But, thinking further I realize that I cannot reasonably reject the other perspective unless I understand it. To do so would be to say: I don't know what you think, but, whatever it is, its's false. The other perspective, however strange it seems to me now, may have something both important and true, which I have overlooked and without which my understanding is incomplete. Thinking along these lines, I open my mind to the possibility of change of perspective. I make sure that I don't subtly ignore or dismiss these new ideas; I realize I can make my point of view richer, so it encompasses more.

One of the most important stages in my development as a thinker, then, is a clear recognition that I have a perspective, one that I must work on and change as I learn and grow. To do this, I can't be inflexibly attatched to any particular beliefs. I strive for a consistent 'big picture.' I approach other perspectives differently. I ask how I can reconcile the points of view. I see variations between similar but different perspectives. I use principles and insights flexibly, and do not approach analysis as a mechanical, 'step one, step two' process. I pursue new ideas in depth, trying to understand the perspectives from which they come. I am willing to say, "This view sounds new and different, I don't yet understand it. There's more to this idea than I realized, I can't just dismiss it."

Or, looked at another way, suppose I'm rethinking my stand on an issue. I re-examine my evidence. Yet, I cannot evaluate my evidence for its completeness, unless I consider evidence cited by those who disagree with me. I find I can discover my basic assumptions by considering alternative assumptions, alternative perspectives. I use fairmindedness, or 'reciprocity' to clarify, enhance, and improve my perspective.

A narrow minded critical thinker, lacking this insight, says, not, "This is how *I* see it," but, "This is how it *is*." He works on pieces of reasoning, separate arguments, and individual beliefs, but not on his perspective as such. His thinking consists of separate or fragmented ideas. He examines beliefs one at a time, failing to appreciate connections between them. He may be conscious and reflective about particular conclusions, but is unreflective about his own point of view, how it affects his evaluations of reasoning, and how it is limited. When confronted with alternative perspectives or points of view, he assesses them by their degree of agreement with his own view. He lumps together similar, though different perspectives. He is given to sweeping acceptance or sweeping rejection of points of view. He is tyrannized by the words he uses. Rather than trying to understand *why* another thinks as she does, he dismisses new ideas. He assumes the objectivity and correctness of his own beliefs and responses.

As I strive to think fairmindedly, I discover resistence to questioning my beliefs and considering those of others. I find a conflict between my desire to be fairminded, and my desire to be right. I realize that without directly addressing the obstacles to critical thought, people tend to seek its appearance, rather than its reality, that I tend to accept rhetoric rather than fact, that without noticing it, I hide my own hypocrisy, even from myself.

By contrast, the critical thinker lacking this insight, though a good arguer, is not a truly reasonable person. He gives good sounding reasons, can find and explain flaws in opposing views, and has well thought out ideas, but he never subjects his own ideas to scrutiny. Though he gives lip service to fairmindedness, and can describe views opposed to his own, he doesn't truly understand, or seriously consider them. He often uses reasoning to get his way, cover up hidden motives, defend himself, or make others look stupid or deluded. He uses skills to reinforce his views and desires, not to subject them to scrutiny.

To sum up, the kind of critical thinker we are concerned to foster contrasts with at least two other kinds of thinkers. The first kind has few intellectual skills of any kind and tends to be naive, easily manipulated and controlled, and so easily 'defeated' or 'taken in.' The second has skills but only of a restricted type: able to pursue his narrow selfish interests and to effectively manipulate the naive and unsuspecting. The first we call 'uncritical thinkers' and the second 'weak sense' or selfish critical thinkers. What we aim at, therefore, are 'strong sense' critical thinkers, those who use their skills in the service of sincere, fairminded understanding and evaluation of their beliefs.

Critical Thinking and Education

The foundation for fairminded as against self-serving critical thinking, is laid in the early years of one's life. The same is true of uncritical thought. We can raise children from the earliest years to passively accept authority figures and symbols. We can systematically manipulate and inculcate children so they are apt to become adults highly susceptible to manipulation.

Or we can foster the development of intellectual skills while ignoring the ultimate use to which the learner puts them. We can ignore the problems of egocentrism, the natural tendencies of the mind toward self-deception and ego-justification. We can assume that students will use those skills fairmindedly. In this case we ignore the problem of integrating cognitive and affective life. And so we make likely that our more successful students will become intelligent manipulators rather than fairminded thinkers. They will gain intellectual empowerment at the expense of a likely selfish use of that power to further egocentric ends.

But there is a legitimate third option on which we should focus our efforts: fostering the development of intellectual skills in the context of rational dispositions and higher critical thinking values. We can emphasize the intimate interplay of thought and feeling, not set them off as separate or oppositional. We can recognize the existence of both rational and irrational passions and cognitions. We can accentuate the insight that only through the development of rational passions can we prevent our intelligence from becoming the tool of egocentric emotions.

The earlier the foundation for intellectual fairness is laid, the better our chance for success. If we want children to develop into adults with a passion for clarity, accuracy, and fairmindedness, a fervor for exploring the deepest issues, a propensity for listening sympathetically to opposition points of view; if we want children to develop into adults with a drive to seek out evidence, with an aversion to contradiction, sloppy thinking, and inconsistent applications of standards; then we had better pay close attention to the affective dimension of their lives from the beginning. We had better recognize the need to unite cognitive and affective goals.

The highest development of intelligence and conscience creates a natural marriage between the two. Each is distinctly limited without the other. Each requires special attention in the light of the other.

In this workbook we provide something more than a set of remodelled lessons which accentuate needed intellectual skills. We have tried to keep in mind our vision of the conscientious, fair-minded, critical person. Many of the strategies for remodel that we use explicitly call for a blending of the skills of critical thinking with the dispositions that foster critical thinking values. All of the strategies have been used with this overall end in mind.

The following strategies should be viewed, therefore, not as isolated intellectual activities, but as insight builders that mutually support each other and work toward a unified end. Wherever possible there is a cognitive/ affective integration.

Three Modes of Mental Organization
(expressed in exclusive categories for purposes of theoretical clarity)

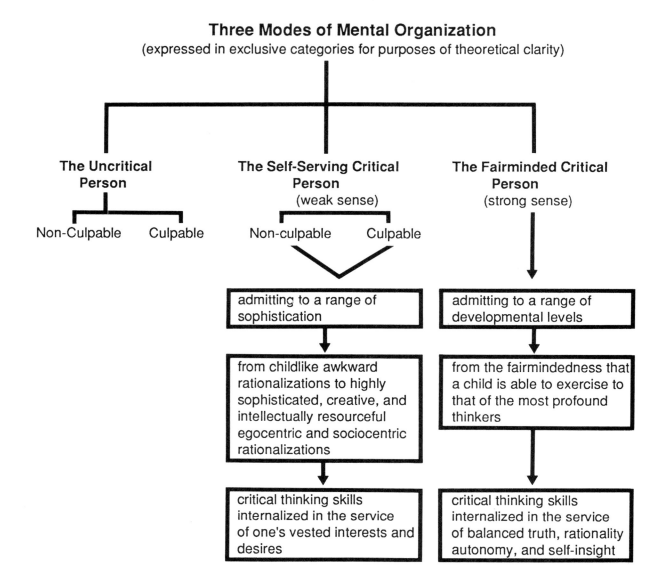

The Uncritical Person

Non-Culpable   Culpable

The Self-Serving Critical Person
(weak sense)

Non-culpable   Culpable

The Fairminded Critical Person
(strong sense)

admitting to a range of sophistication

admitting to a range of developmental levels

from childlike awkward rationalizations to highly sophisticated, creative, and intellectually resourceful egocentric and sociocentric rationalizations

from the fairmindedness that a child is able to exercise to that of the most profound thinkers

critical thinking skills internalized in the service of one's vested interests and desires

critical thinking skills internalized in the service of balanced truth, rationality autonomy, and self-insight

Note

Children enter school as fundamentally non-culpable uncritical and self-serving thinkers. The educational task is to help them to become, as soon as possible and as fully as possible, responsible, fairminded, critical thinkers, empowered by intellectual skills and rational passions. Most people are some combination of the above three types; the proportions are the significant determinant of which of the three characterizations is most appropriate. For example, it is a common pattern for people to be capable of fairminded critical thinking only when their vested interests or ego-attachments are not involved, hence the legal practice of excluding judges or jury members who can be shown to have such interests.

Diagram #1
VII

Critical Thinking Lesson Plan Remodelling

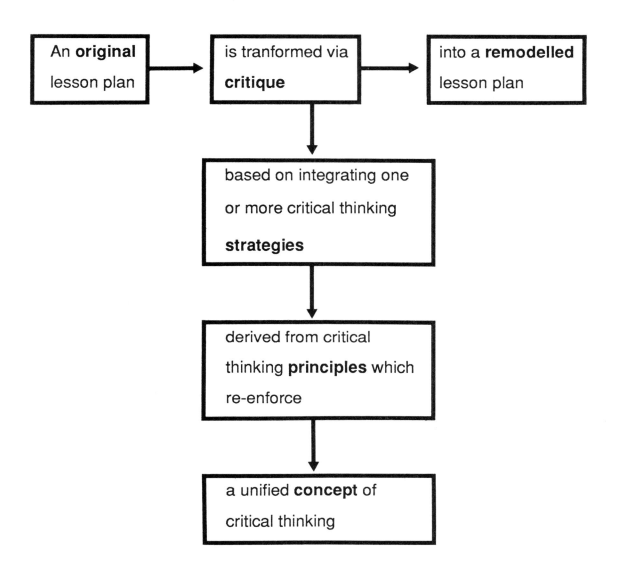

Diagram #2

VIII

INTRODUCTION

Remodelling: A Strategy For Infusing Critical Thinking

The basic idea behind lesson plan remodelling as a strategy for staff development in critical thinking is simple. Every practicing teacher works daily with lesson plans of one kind or another. To remodel lesson plans is to critique one or more lesson plans and formulate one or more new lesson plans based on that critical process. It is well done when the person doing the remodel understands the strategies and principles used in producing the critique and remodel, when the strategies and principles are well thought-out, when the remodel clearly follows from the critique, and when the remodel teaches critical thought better than the original. The idea behind our particular approach to lesson plan remodelling is also simple. A group of teachers or staff development leader who has a reasonable number of examplary remodels with accompanying explanatory principles can design practice sessions that enable teachers to begin to develop new teaching skills as a result of experience in lesson remodelling.

When teachers are provided with clearly contrasting 'befores' and 'afters,' lucid and specific critiques, a set of principles clearly explained and illustrated, and a coherent unifying concept, they can increase their own skills in this process. To put this another way, one learns how to remodel lesson plans to incorporate critical thinking only through practice. The more one does it the better one gets, especially when one has examples of the process to serve as models.

Of course, a lesson remodelling strategy for critical thinking inservice is not tied to any particular handbook of examples, but it is easy to indicate the advantages of having such a handbook, assuming it is well executed. Some teachers do not have a clear concept of critical thinking. Some think of it as negative, judgmental thinking, which is a stereotype. Some have only a vague notions, such as 'good thinking,' or 'logical thinking,' with little sense of how such ideals are achieved. Others think of it simply in terms of a laundry list of atomistic skills, and lack a clear sense of how these skills need to be orchestrated or integrated or of how they can be misused. Rarely do teachers have a clear sense of the relationship between the component micro-skills, the basic, general concept of critical thinking, and the obstacles to using it fully. It is theoretically possible, but practically speaking unlikely that teachers will sort this out for themselves as a task in abstract theorizing. In the first place most teachers have very little patience with abstract theory and little experience in developing it. In the second place it is doubtful that very many school districts could free-up the time for them to take on this task, even if they were qualified and motivated enough themselves.

But getting the basic concept sorted out is not the only problem. There is also the problem of translating that concept into 'principles,' linking the 'principles' to application, and implementing them in specific lessons.

On the other hand, if we simply present the teacher with pre-packaged finished lesson plans, ones designed by the critical thinking of someone else, someone who used a process that is not clearly understood by the teacher, then a major opportunity for the teacher to develop her own critical thinking skills, insights, and motivations will have been lost. Furthermore, a teacher who is unable to learn how to use basic critical thinking principles so as to critique and remodel some of her own lesson plans probably won't be able to implement someone else's effectively. Providing teachers with the scaffolding for carrying out the process for themselves, and examples of its application, opens the door for continuing development of critical thinking skills and insights. It begins a process which gives the teacher more and more expertise and more and more success in critiquing and remodelling the day-to-day practice of teaching.

Lesson plan remodelling can become a powerful tool in critical thinking staff development for other reasons as well. It is action oriented, puts an immediate emphasis on close examination and critical assessment of what is being introduced into the classroom on a day-to-day basis. It makes the problem of critical thinking infusion more manageable by paring it down to the critique of particular lesson plans and the progressive infusion of particular principles. It is developmental in that, over time, more and more lesson plans are remodelled, and what has been remodelled can be remodelled again. It provides a means of cooperative learning for teachers. Its results can be collected and shared, both at the site and district levels, so that teachers can learn from and be encouraged by what other teachers do. The dissemination of plausible remodels provides recognition for motivated teachers. It forges a unity between staff development, curriculum development, and student development. It provides a simple demonstrable refutation of the contradictory, but equally popular, crude excuses that 1) every good teacher naturally teaches critical thinking, and that 2) it is too hard to teach because students aren't ready for it. It avoids recipe solutions to critical thinking instruction. And, finally, properly conceptualized and implemented, it unites cognitive and affective goals as well as integrating the curriculum.

Of course it is no panacea. It will not work for those who are deeply complacent or cynical or for those who do not put a high value on students learning to think for themselves. It will not work for those who have a low command of critical thinking skills coupled with low self-esteem. It will not work for those who are 'burned out' or have given up on change. Finally, it will not work for those who want a quick and easy solution based on recipes and formulas. It is a long-term solution that transforms teaching by degrees as the critical thinking insights and skills of the teachers develop and mature. If teachers can develop the art of critiqing the lesson plans they use, and learn how to use that critique to remodel those lesson plans more and more effectively, they will progressively 1) refine and develop their own critical thinking skills and insights, 2) re-shape the actual or 'living' curriculum (what is as a matter of fact taught day-to-day in the classroom,) and 3) develop their teaching skills. (see diagram #2)

2

The Center For Critical Thinking Approach

The approach to lesson remodelling developed by the Center for Critical Thinking and Moral Critique is based on the publication of Handbooks, such as this one, which illustrate the remodelling process, unifying well though-out critical thinking theory with practical application. The goal is to explain critical thinking by translating general theory into specific teaching strategies. The strategies are multiple allowing the 'novice' critical thinkers to begin with more elementary strategies, while the more 'advanced' critical thinkers can use more complex strategies. This is especially important since the skill at and insight into critical thought vary.

This approach, it should be noted, respects the autonomy and professionality of the teacher. He chooses which strategies to use in a particular situation, and controls the rate and style of integration. It is a flexible approach, maximizing the decision-making and thinking of the teacher. The teacher can apply the strategies to any kind of material: text lesson, lessons or units the teacher has created, discussion outside of formal lessons, discussion of movies, etc.

Teaching for Critical Thinking

In teaching for critical thinking in the strong sense we are committed to teaching in such a way that children learn as soon and as completely as possible how to become responsible for their own thinking. This requires that they learn how to take command of their thinking which in turn requires that they learn how to notice and think about their own thinking, as well as the thinking of others. Consequently, we teach so as to help children to talk about their thinking in order to be mindful and directive in it. We want them to study their own minds and how they operate. We want them to gain tools by which they can probe deeply into and take command of their own mental processes. Finally, we want them to gain this mentally skilled self-control with a view to becoming more honest with themselves and more fair to others, not simply to 'do better' in school. We want them to develop mental skills and processes in an ethically responsible context. This is not a "good-boy/bad-boy" approach to thinking, for everyone must think his own way to the ethical insights that underlie becoming a fair-minded thinker. We are careful not to judge the content of the student's thinking. Rather, we facilitate a process whereby the student's own insights can be developed.

The global objectives of critcal thinking-based instruction are intimately linked to specific instrumental objectives. It is precisely becuase we want students to learn how to think for themselves in an ethically responsible way that we use the strategies we do; why we help them to gain insight into their tendency to think in narrowly self-serving ways (egocentricity;) why we stimulate them to empathize with the perspectives of others; to suspend or withold judgment when they do not have the evidence to justify making a judgment; to clarify issues and ideas, to evaluate sources, solutions, and actions; to notice when they make assumptions, how they make inferences and where they use or ought to be using evidence; why we stimulate them to consider the implications of their ideas, the possible contradictions or inconsistencies in their thinking, the qualifications or lack of qualifications in their generalizations; and why we do all of these things in encouraging, supportive, non-judgmental ways.

To help teachers generalize from specific remodelling moves, and so facillitate their grasp of strong sense critical thinking, and how it can be taught, we have devised a list of teaching strategies. Each strategy highlights an aspect of critical thought. Each use illustrates how that aspect can be encouraged in students. In the chapter, "Strategies," we explain the twenty-eight strategies illustrated in the remodels. Each is linked to the idea of strong sense critical thinking, in the 'principle.' And for each we explain some ways the aspect of critical thought can be encouraged, in the 'application.' When a strategy is used in a remodel, we have drawn attention to it by putting its strategy symbol in the remodel, e.g., "*S-13.*"

To make the list more manageable, we have divided the strategies into three types: those which emphasize the affective side of critical thought, Affective Strategies, promoting autonomy, empathy, and understanding of obstacles to critical thought; those which generally require extended use of cognitive skills, Cognitive-Macro-abilities, emphasizing extended exploration of ideas, perspectives, and basic issues; and those which highlight a specific, usually brief, critical move, Cognitive-Micro-skills. These divisions are not absolute, however. Crtical thought requires integration of the affective and cognitive dimensions of thinking. Macro-abilities usually require use of micro-skills. And micro-skills are pointless unless used to some end.

A.   Affective Strategies

S-1   fostering independent thinking
S-2   developing insight into egocentricity
S-3   fostering reciprocity
S-4   exploring thoughts underlying feelings
S-8   discouraging stereotyping
S-26   suspending judgment

B.   Cognitive Strategies - Macro-Abilities

S-5   fostering insight into mechanical skills
S-6   exploring underlying purposes
S-7   recognizing reasons underlying categories
S-11   clarifying issues
S-12   clarifying ideas
S-15   developing criteria for evaluation
S-19   evaluating source credibility

S-23	evaluating arguments
S-24	evaluating solutions
S-25	evaluating actions
S-28	critiquing text

C.   Cognitive Strategies - Micro-Skills

S-9	distinguishing facts from ideals
S-10	integrating critical vocabulary
S-13	distinguishing ideas
S-14	making assumptions explicit
S-16	distinguishing relevant from irrelevant facts
S-17	making inferences
S-18	supplying evidence for a conclusion
S-20	recognizing contradictions
S-21	exploring implications
S-22	evaluating assumptions
S-27	using probablity qualifiers

Some Staff Development Design Possibilities

Let us now consider how we can incorporate these general understandings into inservice design. There are five basic goals, or, if you like, five basic understandings, that we need to aim forin helping teachers to learn the art of lesson remodelling. Each can be the focus of some stage of inservice activity:

1) **Clarifying the global concept**

   What is it to think critically? How is the fair-minded critical thinker unlike the self-serving critical thinker and the uncritical thinker?

2) **Understanding component teaching strategies that parallel the component critical thinking values, processes and skills**

   What are the basic values that (strong sense) critical thinking presupposes? What are the micro-skills of critical thinking? What are the macro-processes?

3) **Seeing a variety of ways in which the various component strategies can be used in classroom settings**

   What do critical thinkers do? Why? What do they avoid doing? Why? When can each aspect of critical thought be fostered? What questions or activities foster it?

4) **Getting experience in lesson plan critique**

   What are the strengths and weaknesses of this lesson? What critical principles, concepts, or strategies apply to it?

5) **Getting experience in lesson plan remodelling**

   How can I take full advantage of the strengths of this lesson? How can this material best be used to foster critical insights? Which questions or activities should I drop, use, alter or expand upon? What should I add to it?

Let us emphasize at the outset that these goals or understandings are interrelated and that the achievement of any, or all, of them is a matter of degree. We would therefore recommend against trying to achieve 'complete' understanding of any one of these in some absolute sense, before proceeding to the others. Furthermore, we emphasize that understanding in each case should be viewed practically or pragmatically. One does not learn about what critical thinking is by memorizing a definition or a set of distinctions. The teachers' mind must be actively engaged at each point in the process -- concepts, principles, application, critique, and remodel. At all of these levels, 'hands-on' activities should immediately follow any introduction of explanatory or illustrative material. If, for example, teachers are shown a handbook formulation of one of the principles, they should then have an opportunity to brainstorm application of the principle, or an opportunity to try out their own formulations of another principle. When they are shown the critique of one lesson plan, they should be given an opportunity to remodel it or critique another. If they are shown a complete remodel -- original lesson plan, critique, and remodel -- they should be given an opportunity to do a full critique of their own, individually or in groups. This back and forth movement between example and practice should characterize the staff develpment process overall. These practice sessions should not be rushed, and the products of that practice should be collected and shared in some form with the group as a whole. Teachers need to see that they are fruitfully engaged in this process; dissemination of the products of the process demonstrates this fruitfulness. Of course, it ought to be a common understanding of staff development participants that initial practice is not the same as final product, that what is remodelled today by critical thought can be re-remodelled tomorrow and imporved progressively thereafter as experience, skills, and insights grow.

In any case, be careful not to spend too much time on the general formulations of what critical thinking is, before moving to the level of particular principles and strategies. The reason for this is simple. People tend to have trouble assimilating general concepts unless they are made accessible by concrete examples. Furthermore, we want teachers to develop an *operational* view of critical thinking, to understand it as particular intellectual behaviors derivative of basic insights, commitments, and principles. Crticial thinking is not a set of high sounding platitudes, but a very real and practical way to think things out and to act upon that thought. We want teachers therefore to make realistic translations from the general to the specific as soon as possible. Most importantly, we want teachers to see how acceptance of the general concept of critical thinking translates into clear and implementable critical thinking teaching and learning strategies.

For this reason, all the various strategies explained in the handbook are couched in terms of behaviors. The principles express and describe a variety of behaiors of the 'ideal' critical thinker; they become applications to lessons when teachers canvass their lesson plans to find appropriate places where those behaviors can be fostered. The practice we recommend helps guard against teachers using these strategies as recipes or formulas, since in each case good judgment is required in the application process.

The process we have described thus far presupposes motivation on the part of the teacher to implement changes. Unfortunately we cannot presuppose this motivation. We must address it directly. This can be done by focusing attention on the insights that underlie the strategies in each case. We need to foster discussion of them so that it becomes clear to teachers not only *that* critical thinking requires this or that kind of activity but *why*, that is, what desirable consequences it brings about. If, for example, teachers do not see why thinking for themselves is of high importance for the well-being and success of their students, they will not take the trouble to implement activities that foster it, even if they know what these activities are.

To meet this motivational need, we have formulated 'principles' so as to suggest important insights. For example, consider the brief introduction which is provided in the strategy chapter for the strategy "fostering reciprocity:"

Principle: To think critically about issues we must be able to consider the strengths and weaknesses of opposing points of view. Since critical thinkers value fair-mindedness, they feel that it is especially important that they entertain positions with which they disagree. They realize that it is unfair either to judge the ideas of another until they fully understand them, or act on their own beliefs without giving due consideration to relevant criticisms. The process of considering an opposing point of view aids critical thinkers in recognizing the logical components of their beliefs, (e.g. key concepts, assumptions, implications, etc.) and puts them in a better position to amend those beliefs. Furthermore, critical thinkers recognize that their behavior affects others, and so consider their behavior from the perspective of those others.

If teachers reflect on this principle in the light of their own experience, they should be able to come up with their own reasons why reciprocity is important. They might reflect upon the personal problems and frustrations they faced when others --spouses or friends, for example -- did not or would not empathically enter their point of view. Or they might reflect on their frustrations as children when their parents, siblings, or schoolmates did not take their point of view seriously. Through examples of this sort, constructed by the teachers themselves, insight into the need for reciprocity can be developed.

Once the insight is in place, we are ready to put the emphasis on discussing the variety of ways that students can practice reciprocity. As always, we want to be quite specific here, so that teachers are clear about the kinds of behaviors they are fostering. The Handbook, in each case, provides a start in the application section following the principle. For further examples, one can look up one or more remodelled lesson plans in which the strategy was used. For example,

7

sixteen examples of remodels are referenced under 'fostering reciprocity.' Remember, it is more important for teachers to think up their own examples and applications than to rely on the Handbook examples, which are intended as illustrative only.

Lesson plan remodelling as a strategy for staff and curriculum development is not a simple one-shot approach. It requires patience and commitment. But it genuinely develops the critical thinking of teachers and puts them in a position to understand and help structure the inner workings of the curriculum. While doing so, it builds confidence, self-respect, and professionality. With such an approach, enthusiasm for critical thinking strategies will grow over time. It is an approach worth serious consideration as the fundamental thrust of a staff development program. If a staff becomes proficient at critiquing and remodelling lesson plans, it can, by redirecting the focus of its energy, critique and 'remodel' any other aspect of school life and activity. In this way the staff can become increasingly less dependent on direction or supervision from above and increasingly more activated by self-direction from within. Responsible, constructive critical thinking, developed through lesson plan remodelling, is a vehicle for this transformation.

Global Critical Thinking Strategies:
Beyond Compartmentalized Subject Matter
Teaching

I. The Role of the Teacher

A teacher committed to teaching for critical thinking must think beyond subject matter teaching to ends and objectives that transcend subject matter classification. To teach for critical thinking is, first of all, to create an environment in the class and in the school that is conducive to critical thinking. It is to help make the classroom and school environment a mini-critical society, a place where the values of critical thinking (truth, open-mindedness, empathy, autonomy, rationality and self-criticism) are encouraged and rewarded. In such an environment students come to believe in the power of their own minds to identify and solve problems. They come to believe in the efficacy of their own thinking. Thinking for themselves is not something they fear. Authorities are not those who tell them the "right" answers, but those who encourage and help them to figure out answers for themselves, who encourage them to discover the powerful resources of their own minds.

The teacher is much more a questioner than a preacher on this model. The teacher learns how to ask questions that probe meanings, that request reasons and evidence, that facilitate elaboration, that keep discussions from becoming unhelpfully confusing, that provide incentive for listening to what others have to say, that lead to fruitful comparisons and contrasts, that highlight contradictions and inconsistencies, and that elicit implications and consequences.

The teacher committed to critical thinking realizes that the primary purpose of all education is to teach students how to learn. Since there are more details than can be taught, and no way to predict which the student will use, she emphasizes thinking about basic issues and problems. Thus, details are learned as a necessary part of the process of settling questions, and so are functional and relevant. The teacher who teaches students how to learn and think about many basic issues gives them knowledge they can use the rest of their lives. This teacher realizes that subject matter divisions are arbitrary and a matter of convenience. She realizes that the most important problems of everyday life rarely fall neatly into subject matter divisions; that understanding a situation fully usually requires a synthesis of knowledge and insight from several subjects. She also sees that an in-depth understanding of one subject requires an understanding of others. One cannot answer questions in History, for example, without asking and answering related questions in psychology, sociology, etc. She realizes that the students must discover the value of "knowledge" "evidence," and "reasoning"

9

by finding significant payoffs in dealing outside of school with their own everyday life problems. She realizes the universal problems we all face, and that each should find personal solutions through their self-reflective experience and thought processes:

> Who am I? What is the world really like? What are my parents, my friends, and other people like? How have I become the way I am? What should I believe in? Why should I believe in it? What real options do I have? Who are my real friends? Whom should I trust? Who are my enemies? Need they be my enemies? How did the world become the way it is? How do people become the way they are? Are there any really bad people in the world? Are there any really good people in the world? What is good and bad? What is right and wrong? How should I decide? How can I decide what is fair and what is unfair? How can I be fair to others? Do I have to be fair to my enemies? How should I live my life? What rights do I have? What responsibilities?

The teacher who believes in personal freedom and thinking for yourself does not spoon-feed her students with pre-digested answers to those questions. Neither does she encourage students to believe that the answers to them are arbitrary and a matter of sheer opinion. She raises probing questions whenever they are natural to a subject under discussion. She realizes that as a student thinks her way to answers to such questions the student will be forging an over-all perspective into which subject matter discoveries will be fit. She does not force the discussion, nor attempt to force a student to conclusions that do not seem to the student to follow.

The teacher committed to teaching for critical thinking is aware that the child has two sources of "belief": beliefs that the child forms as a result of her personal experience, inward thinking, and interaction with her peers and environment, and beliefs that the child learns through instruction by adults. The first could be called real or operational beliefs. They are what define the child's real world, the foundation for her action, the source of her acted-upon values. They are a result of the child making sense of or figuring out the world. They are heavily influenced by what has been called pleasure-principle thinking. They are in large measure egocentric, unreflective, and unarticulated.

The child (and most adults too for that matter) believes in many things for egocentric, irrational reasons: because those around her hold the belief, because her desires are justified by the belief, because she is more comfortable with the belief, because she is rewarded for the belief, because she has ego-identified with the belief, because she will not be accepted by her peers without acting on the belief, because the belief helps her to justify her feelings toward people she likes or dislikes.

The child of course also has spontaneously formed reasonable beliefs. Some of those are inconsistent with the expressed beliefs of her parents and teachers. As a result of this contradiction with authority she rarely raises these beliefs to what Piaget calls "conscious realization." The totality of these real beliefs is unsynthesized and contains many contradictions which the child will discover only if she is encouraged to freely express herself in an atmosphere that is mutually supportive and child-centered.

The other source of belief, didactic instruction from adult authority figures, is an adult's interpretation of reality, not the child's. It is something the child learns to verbalize, but does not synthesize with operational real belief. Therefore the child typically does not recognize contradictions between these two belief systems. The teacher concerned with this problem, then, provides an environment wherein students can discover and explore their beliefs. Such teachers don't rush students who are struggling to express their beliefs, allow a lot of discussion, don't allow anyone to attack students for their beliefs, reward students for questioning their own beliefs, and support students when they consider many points of view.

Unless the teacher provides conditions in which the child can discover her operational beliefs through reflective thinking, these two systems of beliefs will exist in separate dimensions of her life. The first will control her deeds, especially her private deeds. The other will control her words, especially her public words. The first will be used when she acts for herself. The other when she perfoms for others. Neither, in a sense, will be taken seriously. Neither will be subjected to rational scrutiny. The first because it isn't openly expressed and challenged verbally; the second because it is not tested in the crucible of action and practical decision-making. This dichotomy, when embedded in an individual's life, creates a barrier to living an "examined life." She lacks the wherewithal to explore her contradictions, double standards, and hypocrisies. Critical thinking skills, if learned at all, will only be used as weapons in a struggle to protect herself from exposure while the contradictions of the "other," the "enemy," are laid bare. When integrated into this dichotomous thinking, the uncritical thinker becomes the self-serving, not the fairminded, critical thinker.

II. A Sample Socratic Discussion

Socratic instruction can take many forms. What these forms have in common is that someone develops his thought as a result of the probing, stimulating questions asked him. The "Socratic" questions can come from the teacher or from students. Socratic questions can be used in a large group discussion, in small groups, one-to-one, or, even, with one's self.

In one sense, any discussion, any thinking, that is guided by Socratic questioning is structured. The discussion, the thinking, is structured to take students from the unclear to the clear, from the unreasoned to the reasoned, from the implicit to the explicit, from the unexamined to the examined, from the inconsistent to the consistent, from the unarticulated to the articulated. To learn how to participate in it, one has to learn how to listen carefully to what others say, to look for reasons and evidence, to recognize and reflect upon assumptions, to discover implications and consequences, to seek examples, analogies, and objections, to seek to discover, in short, what one really knows and to distinguish it from what one merely believes.

Toward the beginning of the year, Socratic questioning can be used to get students thinking about a subject, and to probe what students already know about it. Socratic discussion about a subject can also be used at the end of the year to reinforce what students have learned, and highlight any remaining questions or problems. Such general discussions give students a chance to organize details within a given subject, and explore the relationship of the subject to other knowlege. A teacher probing students' ideas about a subject could ask questions like the following (for Social Studies):

> What is Social Studies? If students have difficulty, ask: When you've studied Social Studies, what have you studied/talked about? (If students list topics, put them on the board. Then have students discuss the items and try to group them.) Do these topics have something in common? Are there differences between these topics? (Encourage students to discuss details they know about the topics. If, instead of listing topics, they give a general answer or definition, or if they are able to give a statement about what the topics listed have in common, suggest examples that fit the definition, but are not Social Studies, e.g., if a student says, "It's about people" suggest a subject in medicine or health. Have them modify or improve their definition.) How is Social Studies like and unlike other subjects? Why study Social Studies? Is it important? Why or why not? How can we use what we learn in Social Studies?

With practice, teachers can learn when and how to probe key concepts, explore implications, uncover assumptions, etc.

Similar questions can be asked at the beginning and end of any particular unit. More important, however, is that the teacher can conduct Socratic discussions anytime, on any topic. Use topics the students find interesting, or would find useful. Here are some possible opening questions: What is a friend? What is education/Why learn? What is most important? What is right and wrong? Why be good? What is a good person? What is the difference between living and non-living things?

The teacher must use care and caution in introducing students to Socratic questioning. The level of the questions should match the level of the students' thought. It should not be assumed that students will be fully successful with it except over a considerable length of time. Nevertheless, properly used, it can be introduced in some form or other at virtually any grade level. It can be introduced spontaneously, in any lesson or activity. It need not be pre-planned. It should be available to the teacher at all times.

The following is a transcript of a 4th grade Socratic discussion. The Socratic discussion leader was with these particular students for the first time. The purpose was to determine the status of the children's thinking on some of the abstract questions whose answers tend to define our broadest thinking. The students were eager to respond and often seemed to articulate responses that reflected potential insights into the character of the human mind, its relation to the body, the forces that shape us, the influence of parents and peer group, the nature of morality and of ethnocentric bias. The "insights" are disjointed of course but the questions that elicited them and the responses that articulated them could be used as the basis of future discussions or simple assignments with these students.

While reading the transcript which follows, you may want to formulate questions that could have been asked, but weren't: student responses that could have been followed up, or other directions the discussion could have taken. Another way to approach the manuscript would be to explain the function of each question. Or you could group the questions.

Transcript
4th Grade Socratic Discussion

How does your mind work?
Where's your mind?

Student: "In your head." (numerous students point to their heads)

Does your mind do anything?

Student: "It helps you remember and think."

Student: "It helps, like, if you want to move your legs. It sends a message down to them."

Student: "This side of your mind controls this side of your body and that side controls this other side."

Student: "When you touch a hot oven it tells you whether to cry or say ouch!"

Does it tell you when to be sad and when to be happy?
How does your mind know when to be happy and when to be sad?

Student: "When you're hurt it tells you to be sad."

Student: "If something is happening around you is sad."

Student: "If there is lightning and you are scared."

Student: "If you get something you want."

Student: "It makes your body operate. It's like a machine that operates your body."

Does it ever happen that two people are in the same circumstance but one is happy and the other is sad? Even though they are in exactly the same circumstance?

Student: "You get the same toy. One person might like it. The other gets the same toy and he doesn't like the toy."

Why do you think that some people come to like some things and some people seem to like different things?

Student: "'Cause everybody is not the same. Everybody has different minds and is built different, made different."

Student: "They have different personalities?"

Where does personality come from?

Student: "When you start doing stuff and you find that you like some stuff best."

Are you born with a personality or do you develop it as you grow up?

Student: "You develop it as you grow up."

What makes you develop one rather than another?

Student: "Like, your parents or something."

How can your parent's personality get into you?

Student: "Because you're always around them and then the way they act if they think they are good and they want you to act the same way then they'll sort of teach you and you'll do it."

Student: Like, if you are in a tradition. They want you to carry on something that their parents started."

Does your mind come to think at all the way the children around you think? Can you think of any examples where the way you think is like the way children around you think? Do you think you behave like other American kids?

Student: "Yes"

What would make you behave more like American kids than like Eskimo kids?

Student: "Because you're around them."

Student: "Like, Eskimo kids probably don't even know what the word 'jump-rope' is. American kids know what it is."

And are there things that the Eskimo kids know that you don't know about?

Student: "Yes"

Student: "And also we don't have to dress like them or act like them and they have to know when a storm is coming so they won't get trapped outside."

O.K., so if I understand you then, parents have some influence on how you behave and the kids around you have some influence on how you behave... Do you have some influence on how you behave? Do you choose the kind of person you're going to be at all?

Student: "Yes"

How do you do that do you think?

Student: "Well if someone says to jump off a five-story buidling, you won't say O.K. You wouldn't want to do that..."

Do you ever sit around and say, "Let's see shall I be a smart person or a dumb one?"

Student: "Yes"

But how do you decide?

Student: "Your grades"

But I thought your teacher decided your grades. How do you decide?

Student: "If you don't do your homework you get bad grades and become a dumb person but if you study real hard you'll get good grades."

So you decide that, right?

Student: "And if you like something at school like computers you work hard and you can get a good job when you grow up. But if you don't like anything at school you don't work hard.

Student: "You can't just decide you want to be smart, you have to work for it."

Student: "You got to work to be smart just like you got to work to get your allowance."

What about being good and being bad, do you decide whether you're good or you're bad? How many people have decided to be bad? (3 students raise their hands) To first student: Why have you decided to be bad?

Student: "Well, I don't know. Sometimes I think I've been bad too long and I want to go to school and have a better reputation but sometimes I feel like just making trouble and who cares."

Let's see, is there a difference between who you are and your reputation? What's your reputation? That's a pretty big word. What's your reputation?

Student: "The way you act. If you had a bad reputation people wouldn't like to be around you and if you had a good reputation people would like to be around you and be your friend."

Well, but I'm not sure of the difference between who you are and who people think you are. Could you be a good person and people think you bad? Is that possible?

Student: "Yeah, because you could try to be good. I mean, a lot of people think this one person's really smart but this other person doesn't have nice clothes but she tries really hard and people don't want to be around her."

So sometimes people think somebody is real good and they're not and sometimes people think that somebody is real bad and they're not. Like if you were a crook, would you let everyone know you're a crook?

Students: Chorus of "NO!"

So some people are really good at hiding what they are really like. Some people might have a good reputation and be bad; some people might have a bad reputation and be good.

Student: "Like, everyone might think you were good but you might be going on dope or something."

Student: "Does reputation mean that if you have a good reputation you want to keep it just like that? Do you always want to be good for the rest of your life?"

I'm not sure...

Student: "So if you have a good reputation you try to be good all the time and don't mess up and don't do nothing?"

Suppose somebody is trying to be good just to get a good reputation -- why are they trying to be good?

Student: "So they can get something they want and they don't want other people to have?"

Student: "They might be shy and just want to be left alone."

Student: "You can't tell a book by how it's covered."

Yes, some people are concerned more with their cover than their book. Now let me ask you another question. So if its true that we all have a mind and our mind helps us to figure out the world and we are influenced by our parents and the people around us, and sometimes we choose to do good things and sometimes we choose to do bad things, sometimes people say things about us and so forth and so on... Let me ask you: Are there some bad people in this world?

Student: "Yeah"

Student: "Terrorists and stuff"

Student: "Nightstalker"

Student: "The TWA highjackers"

Student: "Robbers"

Student: "Rapers"

Student: "Bums"

Bums, are they bad?

Student: "Well, sometimes."

Student: "The Klu Klux Klan"

Student: "The Bums... not really cause they might not look good but you can't judge them by how they look. They might be really nice and everything."

O.K., so they might have a bad reputation but be good, after you care to know them. There might be good bums and bad bums.

Student: "Libyan guys and Machine gun Kelly"

Let me ask you, do the bad people think they're bad?

Student: "A lot of them don't think they're bad but they are. They might be sick in the head."

Yes, some people are sick in their heads.

Student: "A lot of them (bad guys) don't think they're bad.

Why did you say Libyan people?

Student: "'Cause they have o' lot a terrorists and hate us and bomb us..."

If they hate us do they think we are bad or good?

Student: They think we are bad."

And we think they are bad? And who is right?

Student: "Usually both of them."

Student: "None of us are really bad!"

Student: "Really, I don't know why our people and their people are fighting. Two wrongs don't make a right."

Student: "It's like if there was a line between two countries, and they were both against each other, if a person from the first country crosses over the line, they'd be considered the bad guy. And if a person from the second country crossed over the line he'd be considered the bad guy."

So it can depend on which country you're from who you consider right or wrong, is that right?

Student: "Like a robber might steal things to support his family. He's doing good to his family but actually bad to another person."

And in his mind do you think he is doing something good or bad?

Student: "It depends what his mind is like. He might think he is doing good for his family or he might think he is doing bad for the other person."

Student: "It's like the underground railroad a long time ago. Some people thought it was bad and some people thought it was good."

*But if lots of people think something is right and lots of people think
something is wrong, how are you supposed to figure out the difference
between right and wrong?*

Student: "Go by what you think!"

But how do you figure out what to think?

Student: "Lots of people go by other people."

But somebody has to decide for themselves, don't they?

Student: "Use your mind?"

*Yes, let's see, suppose I told you: "You are going to have a new classmate. Her name is
Sally and she's bad." Now, you could either believe me or what could you do?*

Student: "You could try to meet her and decide whether she was bad or good."

*Suppose she came and said to you: "I'm going to give you a toy so you'll
like me." And she gave you things so you would like her, but she also
beat up on some other people, would you like her because she gave you
things?*

Student: "No, because she said I'll give you this so you'll like me. She wouldn't be very
                nice."

So why should you like people?

Student: "Because they act nice to you."

Only to you?

Student: "To everybody!"

Student: "I wouldn't care what they gave me. I'd see what they're like inside."

But how do you find out what's on the inside of a person?

Student: "You could ask but I would try to judge myself."

Socratic questioning is flexible. The questions asked at any given point will depend on what the students say, what ideas the teacher wants to pursue, and what questions occur to the teacher. Generally, Socratic questions raise basic issues, probe beneath the surface of things, and pursue problematic areas of thought.

The above discussion could have gone in a number of different directions. For instance, rather than focusing on the mind's relationship to emotions, the teacher could have pursued the idea 'mind' by asking for more examples of its functions, and having students group them. The teacher could have followed up the response of the student who asked, "Does reputation mean that if you have a good reputation you want to keep it just like that?" He might, for instance, have asked the student why he asked that, and asked the other students what they thought of the idea. Such a discussion may have developed into a dialogical exchange about reputation, different degrees of goodness, or reasons for being bad. Or the idea 'bad people' could have been pursued and clarified by asking students why the examples they gave were examples of bad people. Students may then have been able to suggest tentative generalizations which could have been tested and probed through further questioning. Rather than exploring the influence of perspective on evaluation, the teacher could have probed the idea, expressed by one student, that no one is 'really bad.' The students could have been asked to explain the remark, and other students could have been asked for their responses to the idea. In these cases and others the teacher has a choice between any number of equally thought provoking questions. No one question is the 'right' question.

III. Role Playing and Reconstructing Opposing Views

A fundamental danger for human thought is narrowness. We do not naturally and spontaneously open our minds to the insights of those who think differently from us. We have a natural tendency to use our native intelligence and our cognitive skills to protect and maintain our system of beliefs rather than to modify and expand it, especially when ideas are suggested that have their origin in a very different way of thinking. We can never become fairminded unless we learn how to enter sympathetically into the thinking of others, to reason from their perspective and eventually to try seeing things as they see them.

Learning how to accurately reconstruct the thinking of others and how to role play their thinking (once reconstructed) are fundamental goals of critical thinking instruction. Very little work has yet been done in giving students opportunities to role play the reasoning of others. So it is not now clear to what extent or in what forms role-playing to enhance critical reciprocity is possible in K-3.

But imagine some possible experiments. Suppose after some Socratic discussion a list of reasons was put on the board that supported the children's views, as against their parent's views, on what the children should be allowed to do. A "let's pretend" game might be devised in which some students would pretend that they were parents and were asked, in that role, to give their reasons why children should not be allowed to do x or y or z (stay up past 10:00 p.m., play outside after it gets dark, etc.) It would be interesting to see how accurately the children could reconstruct the reasoning of their parents. Then one might experiment with a "let's pretend" discussion between a student playing "parent" and another student playing "child." The class might subsequently discuss what the best reasons were on each side.

Early history lessons might also provide opportunities for initial role playing experiences. For instance, students could role-play discussions between Indians and settlers on disputed questions.

In any event, we should always keep in mind global, as well as more specific, strategies in fostering critical thinking. When we habitually play the role of Socratic questioner and habitually seek opportunities to have students reconstruct and role play the thinking of others, we will discover new possibilities for critical thinking instruction and will develop global insights that help guide us in understanding and applying the strategies illustrated more specifically in the lesson remodels that follow.

How To Use This Book

You may choose to read the rest of this book as you would any other book, but if you do you will probably miss a good deal of the benefit that can be derived from it. If you are a K-3 teacher and you want to improve your ability to teach for critical thinking, what you doubtless want to do is to develop the ability to do the kinds of things that the writers of this handbook have done: to remodel your own lesson plans, your own teaching strategies. If so, it is very important to get a sense of your present ability to critique and redesign lesson plans. The critiques and remodels that follow, and the principles and strategies that precede them, may provide an immediate catalyst for you to take your lesson plans and redesign them. But more than likely the critiques and remodels here will seem deceptively simple to you and you may bog down as soon as you attempt to redesign your own.

We therefore suggest an alternative approach. Read through the strategies and a couple of remodels, then write critiques and remodels of your own after reading an original lesson or its abstract. After you have attempted a critique and remodel, read our critique and remodel. By using this procedure you will soon get a sense of the difficulties in the critique-remodel process. You will also have initiated the process of developing your own skills in this important activity. When comparing your work to ours, keep in mind that this is a flexible process; our remodel is not the only right one.

Another way of testing your understanding of the critical insights is to read the principle section of a strategy, and write your own application section.

When remodelling your own lessons you will probably find that sometimes you can make more drastic changes by applying several strategies, while at others you may make only minor adjustments by applying one or two.

Within each subject area, our remodels are organized by the grade of the original lesson. If you teach 2nd or 3rd grade, and your students have had no critical thinking, you may want to use our Kindergarten or 1st grade lessons as models for introduction and practice, before doing more difficult lessons. If students don't grasp an idea or skill when you introduce it, don't give up. Critical insight must be developed over time. For instance, suppose the first attempt to foster reciprocity fails. It is likely that students are not in the habit of restating each other's positions, and hence may not listen carefully to each other. You should make restating opposing views a routine part of discussion. Students will eventually learn to prepare themselves by listening more carefully.

If, when reviewing a remodel, you find a particular strategy confusing, review the principle and application in the strategy chapter. If, when reading the strategy chapter a strategy confuses you, review the critiques and remodels of the lessons listed below it. If you are still confused, do not use the strategy. Review it periodically until it becomes clear.

Although the main function of this book is to help you remodel your own lesson plans, we have not restricted our suggestions to the remodelling process. We strongly urge you to apply the insights embedded in the strategies to all aspects of classroom experience (including discussions, conflicts, and untraditional lessons -- say, a movie.) You can also use any remodels you like. Though many of our lessons are too long for one class period, we did not suggest where to break them up. Experiment with the materials; use ideas from all grades.

However you use what follows in this book, your understanding of the insights behind the strategies will determine the effectiveness of the remodels. Despite the detail with which we have delineated the strategies, they should not be translated into mechanistic, step-by-step procedures.

One crucial aspect of remodelling remains to be discussed: that of choosing which lessons to remodel. It is our view, after examining hundreds of K-3 lesson plans, that many of them ought to be abandoned rather than remodelled. Many of them are exercises in what might be called "trival pursuit," the student is presented with or led to discover random facts and esoteric vocabulary. The object behind many K-3 lesson plans seems to be to expose the student to a wide variety of unassessed "facts," on the assumption that, since this constitutes new information for her, it is a good in itself.

We, however, feel that school time is too precious to spend any sizeable portion of it on random facts. The world, after all, is filled with an infinite number of facts. No one can learn more than an infinitesimal portion of them. Random fact collecting is therefore pointless. True, we need facts and information, but there is no reason why we cannot gain facts as part of the process of learning how to think, as part of broader cognitive-affective objectives. Problem-solving, for example, is a most effective way to find and use facts, and to discover why "facts" interest us in the first place. This is true because facts are essential to solving virtually all problems. However, there are trivial and there are significant facts. Furthermore, facts significant for one problem may be insignificant for another problem. We ought not to overburden the child's mind with facts that the child cannot put to use in her thinking. If we don't apprehend the relevance and significance of facts, we tend to forget them rather quickly. We encourage the reader therefore to develop a skeptical eye for lesson plans that fall into the category of "trivial pursuit" or "fact-for-fact's sake." Keep a waste basket handy.

Beyond the lessons that need to be abandoned for their trivial pursuit character, there are also lesson plans that focus exclusively on mechanical skills, e.g.: counting, letter identification, letter-writing, spelling, telling time, knowing name and address, recognizing symbols, learning school rules, rules of grammar, etc. Clearly, it may be difficult at times to integrate these learnings into the process of learning to think critically. Still it is important to be on the alert for occasions where such integration can be achieved. For example, learning the school rules should be integrated into a process in which the child learns to think critically about what a rule is: that they have a purpose, advantages and disadvantages, are constructed by people, can be assessed and changed by people, can be good or bad, better or worse, etc. This integration should be viewed, not as slowing down, but as deepening the understanding of rules. We should view the critical thinking that the student is engaging in as providing the student with powerful concepts which she will be able to use in a host of circumstances thereafter and laying the foundation for the "I-can-figure-things-out-for-myself" attitude essential for education.

Strategies

This chapter is crucial. Any remodelling you do should reflect your grasp both of strategies like those described in this chapter, and the faults in and shortcomings of the originals you use.

Each strategy section has three parts. The 'principle' provides the theory of critical thinking on which the strategy is based. The 'application' explains when the strategy can be used, and how to use it. In some cases, our lists of possible questions are larger and more detailed here, than in the remodels. Each section concludes with a list of lesson plans (and their page numbers) in which we use the strategy.

Some strategies can be applied in more than one way. Under 'application' we explain when each specific method can be used. Most questions in the applications can be applied in any discussion, whether part of a remodel, unremodelled plan, or neither. For instance, any disagreement can be used to foster reciprocity.

As we mentioned before, the strategies and remodels should be used to illuminate each other. If puzzled by a remodel (ours, or your own) see the strategies. If puzzled by a strategy, see the originals, and our critiques and remodels for clarification.

The reader should keep in mind the connection between the principles and applications, on the one hand, and the character traits of a fairminded critical thinker, on the other. Our aim, once again, is not a set of disjointed skills, but an integrated, committed, thinking person.

In teaching for critical thinking in a strong sense, the affective dimension of thinking is fully as important as the cognitive. The strategies listed below are divided into three categories, one for the affective and two for the cognitive. This of course is not to imply that the cognitive dimension of critical thinking should be given twice as much emphasis, because in any given case, whatever dimension is emphasized, the other dimension should be integrated. We want students to continually use their emerging critical thinking skills and abilities in keeping with the critical spirit and the critical spirit can be nurtured only when actually practicing critical thinking in some cognitive way. One cannot develop one's fairmindedness, for example, without actually thinking fairmindedly. One cannot develop one's intellectual independence, without actually thinking independently. This is true of all the essential critical thinking traits, values, or dispositions. They are developmentally embedded in thinking itself.

We have divided the cognitive strategies into two groups to emphasize the importance of distinguishing critical thinking *micro-skills*, the most elementary critical thinking skills, from critical thinking *macro-abilities* or processes, the actual orchestration of skills in an

25

extended activity of thought. For example, the ability to clarify a basic issue typically requires an extended sequence of thought. In that sequence, one may use a variety of micro-skills: one might distinguish ideas, make inferences, explore assumptions, suspend a judgment, use qualifiers, and explore implications. Of course, the reader is well advised to remember that in some cases what we are calling a micro-skill might require an extended sequence of thought while in other cases what we are calling macro-abilities might seem to come down to one intellectual move. It is not important to keep these somewhat arbitrary descriptions firmly restricted to one category, but rather to realize that no set of micro-skills defines critical thinking as such, because the thinker must also learn to orchestrate them.

Macro-practice is almost always more important than micro-drill. We need to be continually vigilant against the misguided tendency to fragment, atomize, mechanize, and proceduralize thinking.

Keeping the above remarks in mind, the teacher should think about the strategies as tools for sometimes helping students develop particular micro-skills, sometimes helping students to orchestrate those skills in extended ways, and sometimes helping students to gain insight into the traits, values, and dispositions essential for strong sense critical thinking.

A.   Affective Strategies

S-1   fostering independent thinking
S-2   developing insight into egocentricity
S-3   fostering reciprocity
S-4   exploring thoughts underlying feelings
S-8   discouraging stereotyping
S-26   suspending judgment

B.   Cognitive Strategies - Macro-Abilities

S-5   fostering insight into mechanical skills
S-6   exploring underlying purposes
S-7   recognizing reasons underlying categories
S-11   clarifying issues
S-12   clarifying ideas
S-15   developing criteria for evaluation
S-19   evaluating source credibility
S-23   evaluating arguments
S-24   evaluating solutions
S-25   evaluating actions
S-28   critiquing text

C.   Cognitive Strategies - Micro-Skills

S-9   distinguishing facts from ideals
S-10   integrating critical vocabulary
S-13   distinguishing ideas
S-14   making assumptions explicit
S-16   distinguishing relevant from irrelevant facts
S-17   making inferences
S-18   supplying evidence for a conclusion
S-20   recognizing contradictions
S-21   exploring implications
S-22   evaluating assumptions
S-27   using probablity qualifiers

S-1 FOSTERING INDEPENDENT THINKING

Principle: Critical Thinking is autonomous thinking. Many of our beliefs are acquired at an early age, when we have a strong tendency to accept beliefs for irrational reasons (because we want to believe, because we are rewarded for believing). As soon as possible, the child should be encouraged to use critical skills to reveal and eradicate beliefs to which he cannot rationally assent. In formulating new beliefs, the critical thinker does not passively accept the beliefs of others; rather he analyzes issues himself, rejects unjustified authorities, and recognizes the contributions of justified authorities. He does not accept as true, or reject as false, beliefs he does not understand. He is not easily manipulated.

Application: A critical education respects the autonomy of the student. It appeals to rationality. Students should be encouraged to discover information for themselves. Whenever possible, for example, students should be given a chance to develop scientific experiments on their own. Merely giving students 'facts' or telling them the 'right way' to solve a problem, or do an experiment, hinders the process of critiquing and modifying pre-existing beliefs with new knowledge. The teacher can have students brainstorm ideas and argue among themselves about problems and solutions to problems. He can also have students develop their own categories instead of providing them with categories. Thus, students can recognize the reasons underlying categories and see how their purposes determine appropriate categories.

Sometimes text questions are formulated in a way that forces a questionable conclusion. In such cases teachers can replace the question with a neutral one. For example, in "Splash! Splash!" we suggest replacing the original question, "Why is 'Splash! Splash!' a good title?" with "Is 'Splash! Splash!' a good title?"

Students should develop the habit of asking themselves "What do I believe? How did I come to believe it? Do I really accept this belief?"

Lesson Plans in which the strategy is used:

S-2 DEVELOPING INSIGHT INTO EGOCENTRICITY

Principle: Egocentricity is the confusion of immediate perception with reality. It manifests itself as an inability or unwillingness to consider others' points of view, to accept ideas or facts which would conflict with the immediate gratification of desire. In the extreme, it is characterized by a need to be right about everything, a lack of interest in consistency and clarity, an 'all or nothing' attitude ("I am 100% right; you are 100% wrong."), and a lack of self-consciousness of one's own thought processes. The egocentric individual is concerned only with the appearance of truth, fairness, and fairmindedness; not with actually being correct, fair, or fairminded. Egocentricity is the opposite of critical thought.

Though everyone is both egocentric and critical (or fairminded) to some extent, the purpose of education in Critical Thinking is to help students move away from egocentricity, toward increasingly critical thought.

If egocentricity is the disease, self-awareness is the cure. In cases in which his own egocentric commitments are not supported, hardly anyone accepts another's egocentric reasoning. Yet when we are thinking egocentrically, it seems right to us at least at the time. Our belief in our own rightness is easier to maintain because we suppress the faults in our thinking. We automatically hide our egocentricity from ourselves. We fail to notice when our behavior contradicts our self-image. We base our reasoning on false assumptions we are unaware of making. We fail to make relevant distinctions, though we are otherwise aware of, and able to make them (when making such distinctions does not prevent us from getting what we want). We deny or   conveniently 'forget' facts inconsistent with our conclusions.   We often misunderstand or distort what others say.

The solution, then, is to reflect on our reasoning and behavior; to make our assumptions explicit, critique them, and, when they are false, stop making them; to apply the same concepts in the same ways to ourselves and others; to consider every relevant fact, and to make our conclusions consistent with the evidence; and to listen carefully and open-mindedly to those with whom we disagree. We can change these tendencies when we see them for what they are: irrational and unjust. Therefore, the development of students' awareness of their egocentric patterns of thought is a crucial part of education in critical thinking.

Application: The teacher can facilitate discussions of egocentric thought and behavior when-ever such discussions seem relevant. Such discussions can be used as a basis for having students think about their own egocentric tendencies. The class can discuss conditions under which people are most likely to be egocentric, and how egocentricity gets in the way of our ability to think and listen. Students should be encouraged to recognize common patterns of egocentric thought. The class can discuss some of the common false assumptions we all make at times (e.g., "Anyone who disapproves of anything I do is wrong or unfair. I have a right to have everything I want. Truth is what I want it to be.") Teachers can also have students point out the contradictions of egocentric attitudes. ("When I use something of yours without permission, it is 'borrowing'; when you use something of mine, it is 'stealing.' Taking something without asking is O.K. Taking something without asking is wrong.")

Lesson Plans in which the strategy is used:

S-3 FOSTERING RECIPROCITY

Principle: To think critically about issues we must be able to consider the strengths and weaknesses of opposing points of view. Since critical thinkers value fair-mindedness, they feel that it is especially important that they entertain positions with which they disagree. They realize that it is unfair either to judge the ideas of another until they fully understand them, or act on their own beliefs without giving due consideration to relevant criticisms. The process of considering an opposing point of view aids critical thinkers in recognizing the logical components of their beliefs, (e.g. key concepts, assumptions, implications, etc.) and puts them in a better position to amend those beliefs. Furthermore, critical thinkers recognize that their behavior affects others, and so consider their behavior from the perspective of those others.

Application: The teacher can encourage students to show reciprocity when class and playground disputes arise or when the class is discussing issues, evaluating the reasoning of story characters, or discussing people from other cultures.

When disputes naturally arise in the course of the day, the teacher can ask students to state one another's positions. Students should be given an opportunity to correct any misunderstanding of their positions. The teacher can then ask students to explain why their fellow student might see the issue differently than they do.

When discussing issues or evaluating the reasoning of story characters, students can state what someone with an opposing point of view might say or think. For students who can write at least at a second grade level, the teacher can assign a written dialogue in which they argue about an issue from opposing points of view, or contrast a story character's reasoning with an opposing point of view. The teacher can ask students to role play discussions. In the earlier grades, the teacher may need to facilitate the process by taking one role himself. Students should be encouraged, as much as possible, to consider evidence and reasons for positions they disagree with, as well as those with which they agree. Similarly, have students consider positions from their parents' or siblings' points of view.

When the class is discussing different cultures the teacher can encourage students to consider why people choose to do things differently or why other people think that their country is best (see "Pledge of Allegiance").

Lesson plans in which the strategy is used:

S-4 EXPLORING THOUGHTS UNDERLYING FEELINGS

Principle: Critical thinking requires self-understanding. A critical thinker realizes that his feelings are his response but not the only possible, or even necessarily the most reasonable response to a situation. He knows that his feelings would be different if he had a different understanding or interpretation of a situation. He recognizes that thoughts and feelings, far from being different kinds of 'things,' are two aspects of his responses. The uncritical thinker sees no relationship between his feelings and his thoughts.

We can better understand our feelings by asking ourselves "What are the thoughts behind this feeling? To what conclusion have I come? What is my evidence? What assumptions am I making? What inferences am I making? Are they good inferences?" We can learn to seek patterns in our assumptions, and so begin to see the unity behind our separate emotions. Understanding one's self is the first step toward self-control and self-improvement.

Application: Whenever a class discusses someone's feelings, the teacher can ask students to consider what the person might be thinking to have that feeling in that situation. Students can learn to generalize about the assumptions behind a particular emotion. It is especially important for students to practice recognizing the thoughts implicit in their feelings.

Lesson plans in which the strategy is used:

S-5 FOSTERING INSIGHT INTO MECHANICAL SKILLS

Principle: Critical education develops insight into the functions that various mechanical skills (e.g., use of grammar, sorting, counting, measuring) serve. Students need to learn, as early as possible the relationship of human purposes to the function of such skills, and the ways in which mechanical skills can be modified as human purposes change. Students will be more adept at using techniques and skills, when they see them as tools whose appropriate use depends on human purposes. They will learn to see when to apply them, and when not.

Application: Rather than asking students to perform mechanical skills merely for their own sake, the teacher can first give a reason for using the skill. State the function of the skill, e.g., "We will count the chairs in this room, to see if there are enough." Next, the teacher can encourage students to consider whether the method being used is the only, or the best way to solve the problem. Ask, "Can anyone think of another way to solve this problem? Which way do you think is best? Why?" Teachers can also point out any arbitrary aspects of mechanical skills, such as using a particular length as a standard of measurement.

Lesson Plans in which the strategy is used:

S-6 EXPLORING UNDERLYING PURPOSES

Principle: An independent thinker doesn't simply accept the necessity or usefulness of human creations. There is often another way of doing what we do. And some other ways are better. In some cases the purpose itself should be rejected. All human activity presupposes some purpose or purposes. The independent thinker understands those purposes, and so is better able to understand, and critique the activity or the way the activity is carried out.

Application: When a class discusses rules, institutions, or activities, the teacher can facilitate a discussion of their purposes. For instance, when discussing a lesson about the Health Department, we recommend that the teacher focus student attention on the reasons for having a Health Department. Students should be encouraged to see the institution as a creation of people, designed to fulfill certain functions, not as something that is 'just there.' They will be in a better position, when they are adults, to see that it fulfills its goals.

Lesson plans in which the strategy is used:

S-7 RECOGNIZING REASONS UNDERLYING CATEGORIES

Principle: The critical thinker recognizes that categories serve human purposes. Rather than merely accepting and unreflectively applying categories previously formed by others, critical thinkers compare their own purposes to the function that existing categories serve, and formulate new categories when needed. They can choose the most appropriate set of categories for the job at hand.

Application: Rather than asking students to place objects into pre-existing categories, the teacher can encourage students to form their own categories. (See *S-1*) Students can then discuss the reasons they had for forming each category. (See "Words That Go Together".) When different students have used different sets of categories to form groups, the teacher can ask such questions as: When would this set of categories be most useful? When would that set be best? Why would someone else make different groups?

Lesson plans in which the strategy is used:

S-8 DISCOURAGING STEREOTYPES

Principle: The fairminded thinker is wary of stereotypes. He hesitates before assigning a characteristic to a group of people. His thinking is flexible; he does not hold unchangeable beliefs about people, but is ready to consider new evidence. He is self-reflective enough to realize that some of his attitudes arise from stereotypes. He is sensitive to the tendency to distort evidence and dismiss examples which don't fit the stereotype.

Application: Teachers should be on the lookout for stereotypes their students have. Have students discuss their ideas, and exchange any information they have. The teacher could also have students consider what it would be like to be stereotyped by others. Sometimes textbooks inadvertently encourage stereotyping. For instance, one text has a chapter entitled "Schools in India," yet it has pictures and discussion of only poor village schools. In our remodel we suggest that the teacher ask students to think about schools in Indian cities.

Lesson plans in which the strategy is used:

S-9 DISTINGUISHING FACTS FROM IDEALS

Principle: Critical thinking requires an effort to see ourselves, others, and the world accurately. This requires a recognition of the gap between facts and ideals. The fairminded thinker values truth and consistency and hence works to minimize this gap. The confusion of facts with ideals prevents us from taking steps to minimize the gap. Self-improvement and social improvement are presupposed values of critical thinking. A critical education is one which strives to highlight discrepancies between facts and ideals, and proposes and evaluates methods for minimizing them.

Application: Since many texts consistently confuse ideals about the country with facts about the country the teacher can use them as objects of analysis. When reading about or discussing the country, the teacher can ask, "Is this a fact about the country or an ideal? Are things always this way, or is this statement an expression of what we are trying to achieve?" If it is an ideal ask, "How have people attempted to achieve this ideal? When did they not meet the ideal? What problems did they have? How could those problems be confronted? What ideals do we have today that are facts for some people, but not others?" (See "Our Country's Birthday and Martin Luther King, Jr.'s Birthday")

The teacher can ask similar questions when discussing discrepancies between individual ideals and facts, and should facilitate a general discussion of the value of achieving consistency of thought and action. Ask, "Have you ever thought something was true about yourself, but acted in a way that was not consistent with your ideal? Did you see yourself differently then? Did you make efforts to change the behavior? Is it good to have accurate beliefs about yourself, and your country? Why do you think so? Can anyone think of ways to be more consistent? (Pay attention to behavior, i.e., facts about self, country; recognize differences between facts and values; change behavior.)

Lesson plans in which the strategy is used:

S-10 INTEGRATING CRITICAL VOCABULARY

Principle: An essential requirement of critical thinking is the ability to think about thinking. The analytical vocabulary in the English language, with such terms as 'assume', 'infer', 'conclude', 'criteria', 'point of view', 'relevance', 'issue', 'contradiction', 'credibility', 'evidence', 'distinguish', enables us to think more precisely about our thinking. We are in a better position to assess reasoning, our own, as well as that of others, when we can use analytic vocabulary with accuracy and ease.

Application: When students are reasoning or discussing the reasoning of others, the teacher can encourage them to use critical vocabulary. Teachers can take advantage of students' enjoyment in learning new vocabulary to teach them very useful vocabulary.

When introducing a term the teacher can speak in pairs of sentences: first, using the critical vocabulary; then, rephrasing the sentence without the new term, e.g., "What facts are relevant to this issue? What facts ought we to consider in deciding this issue? What information would we pay attention to?" The teacher can also rephrase students' statements to incorporate the vocabulary.

Since most language is acquired by hearing words in context, the teacher should try to make critical terms part of his working vocabulary.

Lesson plans in which the strategy is used:

S-11 CLARIFYING ISSUES

Principle: In order to think critically about issues we must first be able to state the issue clearly. The more completely, clearly, and accurately the issue is formulated, the easier and more helpful the discussion of its settlement. Given a clear statement of the issue, and prior to evaluating conclusions or solutions, it is important to recognize what is required to settle the issue. The critical thinker recognizes problematic concepts, objects and standards of evaluation, the purpose of evaluation and relevant facts.

Application: Teachers should encourage students to slow down and reflect on issues before discussing conclusions. When discussing an issue the teacher can ask students first, "Is the issue clear? What do you need to know to settle the issue? What would someone who disagreed with you say about the issue?" Students should be encouraged to continually reformulate the issue in light of new information. They should be encouraged to see how the first statement of the issue or problem is rarely the most accurate, clear, complete, and that they are in the best position to settle questions only after they have developed as clear a formulation as possible.

When discussing an issue, teachers can have students ask themselves such questions as: Do I understand the issue? Do I know how to settle it? Have I stated it fairly? (Does my formulation assume one answer is correct? Would

35

everyone involved accept this as a fair and accurate statement of the issue?) Are the ideas clear? Do I have to analyze any ideas? Do I know when the terms apply and don't apply? Am I evaluating anything? What? Why? What criteria should I use in the evaluation? What facts are relevant? How can I get the evidence I need?

Lesson plans in which the strategy is used:

S-12 CLARIFYING IDEAS

Principle: Critical, independent thinking requires clarity of thought. A clear thinker understands ideas, and knows what kind of evidence is required to justify applying a word or phrase to a situation. The ability to supply a definition is not proof of understanding. One must be able to supply clear, obvious examples, and to use the idea appropriately. In contrast, for an unclear thinker, words float through the mind unattached to clear, specific, concrete cases. Different ideas are confused. Often the only criterion for the application of a term is that the case in question 'seems like' an example. Irrelevant associations are confused with what are necessary parts of the idea (e.g., "Love involves flowers and candle-light.") Unclear thinkers lack independence of thought because they lack the ability to analyze an idea, and so critique its application.

Application: The teacher can use a number of techniques for clarifying ideas. When introducing concepts, paraphrasing is often helpful for relating the new term (word or phrase) to ideas students already understand.

When introducing or discussing an idea that is not within students' experience, the teacher can use analogies which relate the idea to one with which students are familiar. For instance, when discussing 'mayor' (see "City Government in East Bend"), we recommend that the teacher have students think about leaders they have known, e.g., team captains.

When discussing ideas with which students are familiar, we suggest that teachers have students discuss clear examples of the idea, examples of the opposite idea (or examples which are clearly not instances of the idea), and examples for which neither the idea or its opposite are completely accurate ('border-line' cases). For instance, in "Places to Play," a lesson in which students categorize pictures as depicting city or country scenes, we suggest that the teacher supplement the pictures in the text with more examples, some of which are neither city nor country, e.g., a small town. For "Two Ways to Win," where the original lesson has students discuss what 'good sport' means, we suggest that students supply examples of 'good sports,' 'bad sports,' and 'good sports in some ways, bad in others.' In "At Work on the Earth," wherein students are introduced to the scientific concept 'work,' we suggest that students first analyze the concepts 'work,' and 'play' as they are used in ordinary language. We focus student attention on the related idea 'fun'.

36

For ideas that commonly have a lot of irrelevant associations, the teacher can have students distinguish those associations which are logically related to the idea, from those which are not. We recommend use of this technique in "Schools in India." First, the teacher can have students list everything 'school' makes them think of. Then the teacher asks, of each associated idea, whether it is a necessary aspect of the concept. Students are asked if they can describe a school without the feature; and name things other than schools which have the feature. Students see that many of their associations are not part of the concept. They are left with a clearer understanding of what is relevant to the concept, and will be less tempted to confuse mere association with the idea.

Lesson plans in which the strategy is used:

S-13 DISTINGUISHING IDEAS

Principle: Critical thinkers distinguish between different senses of the same word, recognizing the different implications of each. They understand that writers's or speakers's purposes determine the ways they use language. Critical thinkers recognize when two or more concepts have an important relationship to one another, yet have different meanings. They recognize the different implications of these words. They make clear distinctions, and do not confuse (literally, 'fuse together') distinct ideas.

Application: Whenever a text, or discussion, uses one term in more than one sense, the teacher can ask students to state how it is being used in each case, or have students paraphrase sentences in which they occur. Then the teacher can ask students to generate examples in which one, both, or neither meaning of the term applies. (See "At Work on the Earth") The teacher can encourage students to discuss what the user's purpose is, e.g. "Why would the scientist use the concept 'work' in this particular way?" (See "At Work on the Earth") And the class can discuss other differences between the ideas ("Why isn't 'play' related to the scientists' concept 'work'?")

The teacher can ask students to distinguish ideas by having them discuss the different implications of the concepts. Ask, "What does it imply if we say someone is hungry? What does it imply if we say they are undernourished? (see "How am I Like All Other Human Beings?")

Lesson plans in which the strategy is used:

S-14 MAKING ASSUMPTIONS EXPLICIT

Principle: We are in a better position to evaluate any reasoning or behavior when all of the elements of that reasoning or behavior are made explicit. We base both our reasoning and our behavior on beliefs we take for granted. We are often unaware of these assumptions. Although assumptions can be either true or false, it is only by recognizing them that we can evaluate them.

Application: Teachers should encourage students to make assumptions explicit as often as possible. Although it is valuable practice to have students make good assumptions explicit it is especially important when assumptions are questionable. The teacher can ask, "If this was the evidence, and this the conclusion, what was assumed?"

Lesson plans in which the strategy is used:

S-15 DEVELOPING CRITERIA FOR EVALUATION

Principle: Evaluation is fundamental to critical thinking. The critical thinker realizes that expressing mere preference does not substitute for evaluating. Awareness of the process of evaluating aids fairminded evaluation. This process involves the development and use of criteria. When developing criteria critical thinkers should understand the object and purpose of the evaluation, and what function the thing being evaluated is supposed to serve. Critical thinkers take into consideration different points of view when attempting to evaluate something. They ask themselves "What, if anything, is a necessary part of the criteria for evaluation?"

Application: Whenever students are evaluating something, the teacher can ask students what they are evaluating, the purpose of the evaluation, and the criteria they used. If, for example, a student says, "Oatmeal is a terrible breakfast," the teacher can ask for clarification (the student is evaluating oatmeal, taste may be one criterion.) Criteria usually presuppose a purpose of the object. With practice, students can see the importance of developing clear criteria, and applying them consistently. When developing criteria, rational discussion and reciprocity are more important than reaching consensus.

Lesson plans in which the strategy is used:

S-16 DISTINGUISHING RELEVANT FROM IRRELEVANT FACTS

Principle: Critical thinking requires sensitivity to the distinction between those facts that are relevant to an issue and those which are not. Critical thinkers focus their attention on relevant facts and do not let irrelevant considerations affect their conclusions. Furthermore, they recognize that a fact is only relevant or irrelevant in relation to an issue. Information relevant to one problem may not be relevant to another.

Application: When discussing an issue, solution to a problem, or when giving reasons for a conclusion, students can practice limiting their remarks to facts which are relevant to the issue, problem, or conclusion. Often students assume that all information given has to be used to solve a problem. Life does not sort relevant from irrelevant information for us. Teachers can encourage students to make a case for the relevance of their remarks, and help them see when their remarks are irrelevant (How would this fact affect our conclusion? If it were false would we have to change our conclusion? Why or why not?.)

Another technique for developing students' sensitivity to relevance, is to change an issue and compare what was relevant to the first issue to what is relevant to the second. (See "Sentences that Ask")

Lesson plans in which the strategy is used:

S-17 MAKING INFERENCES

Principle: Thinking critically involves the ability to reach sound conclusions based on observation and information. Critical thinkers distinguish their observations from their conclusions. They look beyond the facts, to see what those facts imply. They know what the concepts they use imply. They also distinguish cases in which they must guess from cases in which they can safely conclude. (See *S-26*) Critical thinkers recognize their tendency to make inferences that support their own egocentric world view and are therefore especially careful to evaluate inferences they make when their interests or desires are involved.

Application: Teachers can ask students to make inferences based on a wide variety of statements and actions. Students, for example, can make inferences from story titles and pictures, story characters' statements and actions, as well as their fellow students' statements and actions. Students should be encouraged to distinguish their observations from inferences. Teachers can have students give examples, from their experience, of inferring incorrectly, and encourage them to recognize situations in which they are most susceptible to uncritical thought. The class can discuss ways in which they can successfully minimize the effects of irrationality in their lives. Remember, every interpretation is based on inference, and we interpret every situation we are in.

Lesson plans in which the strategy is used:

S-18 SUPPLYING EVIDENCE FOR A CONCLUSION

Principle: Critical thinkers, interested in the free exchange of ideas, are comfortable being asked to describe the evidence on which their conclusions are based, rather than finding such questions intimidating, confusing, or insulting. They value reaching conclusions based on sound reasoning (rather than, say, convenience or whim). They realize that unstated, unknown reasons can be neither communicated nor critiqued. They are able to cite relevant and sufficient evidence to support their conclusions.

Application: When asking students to come to conclusions, the teacher should ask for their reasons: How do you know? Why do you think so? What evidence do you have?" etc. When the reasons students supply are incomplete, the teacher may want to ask a series of probing questions to elicit a fuller explanation of student reasoning: What other evidence do you have? How do you know your evidence is true? What assumptions are you making? Do you have reason to think your assumptions are true?" etc.

When introducing a term the teacher can speak in pairs of sentences: first, using the critical vocabulary; then, rephrasing the sentence without the new term, e.g., "What facts are relevant to this issue? What facts ought we to consider in deciding this issue? What information would we pay attention to?" The teacher can also rephrase students' statements to incorporate the vocabulary.

Lesson plans in which the strategy is used:

S-19 EVALUATING SOURCE CREDIBILITY

Principle: Critical thinkers recognize the importance of using reliable sources of information when formulating conclusions. They give less weight to sources which either lack a track record of honesty, contradict each other on key questions, are not in a position to know, or have a vested interest in selling a product or idea. Critical thinkers recognize when there is more than one reasonable position to be taken on an issue; they compare alternative sources of information, noting areas of agreement; they analyze questions to determine whether or not the source is in a position to know; and they gather information where sources disagree.

Application: When the class is discussing an issue about which people disagree, the teacher can encourage students to check a variety of sources stressing the importance of familiarizing themselves with opposing points of view.

The class can discuss the relevance of a source's past dependability, how to determine whether a source is in a position to know, and how the motivations of others should be taken into account when determining whether they are a credible source of information. The teacher can ask the following questions: Is this person in a position to know? What does he know about this issue? Where did he get his information? Has he been reliable in the past? Does he have anything to gain by convincing others to see the issue as he does? Is he selling a product or idea?

Finally, the teacher can use examples from the students personal experience (e.g. trying to determine who started a fight at home or on the playground) and encourage students to recognize the ways in which their own motivations affect many of the conclusions they reach.

Lesson plans in which the strategy is used:

S-20 RECOGNIZING CONTRADICTIONS

Principle: Consistency is a fundamental ideal of critical thinkers. Critical thinkers can recognize when two claims are contradictory. They strive to remove contradictions from their beliefs, and are wary of contradictions in others. Fairminded thinkers judge like cases in like manner. Perhaps the most difficult form of consistency to achieve is that between word and deed. Self-serving double standards are one of the most common problems in human life. Children are in some sense aware of the importance of consistency ("Why don't I get to do what she gets to do?") They are frustrated by double-standards, yet are given little help in getting insight into them and dealing with them.

Application: When discussing conflicting lines of reasoning, inconsistent versions of the same story, or egocentric reasoning or behavior, the teacher can encourage students to practice recognizing contradictions. ("What does x say? What does y say? Are they saying the same thing? The opposite thing? Could both claims be true? Why or why not?") The teacher may also want to have students discuss the value of consistency. The teacher may begin such a discussion with a simple example, such as "Can a light be on and off at the same time?" After students have discussed similar examples, they could talk about how those examples are like and unlike other contradictions (and apparent contradictions).

Lesson plans in which the strategy is used:

S-21 EXPLORING IMPLICATIONS

Principle: The critical thinker can take statements, recognize their implications (i.e. if x is true, then y must also be true), and develop a fuller, more complete understanding of their meaning. He realizes that to accept a statement he must also accept its implications. By following out the implications of subtle changes in a story, or instance of reasoning, critical thinkers see how such changes can affect meaning, often in significant ways.

Application: The teacher can ask students to state the implications of material in student texts, especially when the text materials lack clarity. The process can help students better understand the meaning of a passage or an idea (see "Looking to the Future" and "At the Television Studio,"respectively.) The teacher can suggest, or have students suggest, changes in stories, and then ask students to state the implications of these changes and comment on how they affect the meaning of the story.

Lesson plans in which the strategy is used:

S-22 EVALUATING ASSUMPTIONS

Principle: Critical thinkers have a passion for truth, and for accepting the strongest reasoning. Thus, they have a passion for seeking out and rejecting false assumptions. They realize that everyone makes some questionable assumptions. They are willing to question, and have others question, even their own most cherished assumptions. They consider alternative assumptions. They base their acceptance or rejection of assumptions on their rational scrutiny of them. They hold questionable assumptions with an appropriate degree of tentativeness.

Independent thinkers evaluate assumptions for themselves, and do not simply accept the assumptions of others, even those assumptions made by everyone they know.

Application: There are no rules for determining when to have students evaluate assumptions. Students should feel free to question and discuss any assumptions they suspect are questionable or false. Students should also evaluate good assumptions. Doing so gives them a contrast with poor assumptions. For instance, in "Measuring Air" we suggest that students discuss the assumption that a sponge can hold the same amount of air as water.

The following are some of the probing questions teachers can use when a class discusses the worth of an assumption: Why do people (did this person) make this assumption? Is this belief true? Sometimes true? Seldom true? Always

43

false? (Ask for examples.) Can you think of reasons for this belief? Against it? What, if anything, can we conclude about this assumption? What would we need to find out to be able to judge it?

Lesson plans in which the strategy is used:

S-23 EVALUATING ARGUMENTS

Principle: Rather than carelessly agreeing or disagreeing with arguments based on their preconceptions of what is true, critical thinkers use analytic tools to determine the relative strengths and weaknesses of arguments. When analyzing arguments, critical thinkers recognize the importance of asking, "What would someone who disagrees with this argument say?" They are especially sensitive to the strengths of arguments that they disagree with, recognizing the tendency of humans to ignore, oversimplify, distort, or otherwise dismiss them. The critical thinker analyzes questions and places conflicting arguments in opposition to one another, as a means of highlighting key ideas, assumptions, implications, etc.

Application: Often texts claim to have students analyze and evaluate arguments, when all they have them do is state preferences, and locate factual claims, with very limited discussion. They fail to teach most techniques for analyzing and evaluating arguments. Instead of asking students why they agree or disagree with an argument the teacher can ask, "Which argument do you think is strongest and why?" (see "An American City With a Problem.") Students should then be encouraged to place arguments in opposition to one another. Ask, "What would someone who disagreed with this argument say?" Students should be encouraged to argue back and forth, and modify their positions in light of the strengths of others' positions. Students can become better able to evaluate arguments by familiarizing themselves with, and practicing, specific analytic techniques such as making assumptions explicit and evaluating them; clarifying issues and ideas; developing criteria for evaluation; recognizing contradictions; distinguishing relevant from irrelevant facts; evaluating credibility; and exploring the implications of conclusions. (See these strategies.) After extended discussion, have students state their final positions. Encourage them to qualify their claims appropriately.

Lesson plans in which the strategy is used:

S-24 EVALUATING SOLUTIONS

Principle: Critical problem solvers want to find the best solution they can. They evaluate solutions, not independently of, but in relation to one another (since 'best' implies a comparison). They have reflected on such questions as "What makes some solutions better than others? What does the solution to this problem require?" Although they use all available information relevant to their problems, including the results of solutions others have used in similar situations, they are flexible and imaginative, willing to try any good idea whether it has been done before, or not.

Fairminded thinkers take into account the interests of everyone affected by the problem and proposed solutions. Their commitment is to finding the best solution, not to getting their way.

Application: We recommend, first, that the teacher have students state the problem, if it has not been done in, or called for by the text. Rather than simply asking students if a given solution is good, the teacher could encourage an extended discussion of such questions as: Does this solve the problem? How? What other solutions can you think of? What are their advantages and disadvantages? Are we missing any relevant facts? (Is there anything we need to find out before we can decide which solution is best?) What are the criteria for judging solutions in this case? (How will we know if a solution is a good one?) How do the solutions compare with each other? Why? What are some bad ways of trying to solve the problem? What is wrong with them? What if this fact about the situation were different? Would it change our choice of solutions? Why or why not?

Lesson plans in which the strategy is used:

S-25 EVALUATING ACTIONS

Principle: Critical thinking involves more than an analysis of clearly formulated instances of reasoning; it involves analysis of behavior and a recognition of the reasoning that behavior presupposes. When evaluating the behavior of themselves and others, critical thinkers are conscious of the standards they use, so that these, too, can become objects of evaluation. Critical thinkers are especially concerned with the consequences of actions, and recognize these as fundamental to the standards they use to evaluate.

Critical thinkers base their evaluations of behavior on assumptions to which they have rationally assented. They have reflected on such issues as: What makes some actions right, others wrong? What rights do people have? How can I know when someone's rights are being violated? Why respect people's rights? Why be good? Should I live according to rules? If so, what rules? If not, how should I decide what to do?

Application: The teacher can encourage students to raise ethical questions about the behavior of themselves, and others. Students can become more comfortable with the process of evaluating, if they are given a number of opportunities to consider the following kinds of questions: Do you think the action(s) of x were fair? Why or why not? What are the probable consequences of these actions? How would you feel if someone acted this way toward you? Why? What reasons were your evaluations based on? Might someone else use a different standard to evaluate? Why?

Lesson plans in which the strategy is used:

S-26 SUSPENDING JUDGMENT

Principle: Critical thinkers distinguish what they know from what they don't know. They are not afraid of saying "I don't know" when they are not in a position to be sure of the truth of a claim. They are able to make this distinction because they are in the habit of asking themselves "How could one know whether or not this is true?" To say "In this case I must suspend judgment until I know more" does not make them anxious or uncomfortable. Children have an especially hard time distinguishing what they know from what they do not.

Application: Teachers can take advantage of any situation in which students are not in a postion to know, to encourage the habit of saying "I don't know." When materials call on students to make claims for which they have insufficient evidence, we suggest the teacher encourage students to suspend judgment. In "Sue's Mistake," the text has teachers ask "Did Sue learn from her mistake?" All that the students know is that Sue apologized. They know nothing about her future behavior, the true test of having learned, attempts to avoid similar mistakes. We suggest a replacement: How could we tell whether Sue had learned from her mistake?

When students are asked to catagorize pictures in "How is My School Like My Home?" we suggest that the teachers add pictures from which the students can draw no justifiable conclusions.

Lesson plans in which the strategy is used:

S-27 USING PROBABILITY QUALIFIERS

Principle: One of the strongest tendencies of the egocentric, uncritical mind is to see things in terms of black and white, "all right" and "all wrong." Hence, beliefs which should be held with varying degrees of certainty are held as certain. Critical thinkers are sensitive to this problem. They understand the relationship of evidence to belief and so qualify their statements accordingly. The tentativeness of many of their beliefs is characterized by the appropriate use of such qualifiers as 'highly likely', 'probably', 'not very likely', 'highly unlikely', 'often', 'usually', 'seldom', 'I doubt', 'I suspect', 'most', 'many', and 'some.'

Application: The teacher can encourage students to qualify their statements when they have insufficient evidence to be certain. By asking for the evidence on which student claims are based, and encouraging students to recognize the possibility that alternative claims may be true, the teacher can help students develop the habits of saying "I'm not sure," and of using appropriate probability qualifiers.

Lesson plans in which the strategy is used:

S-28 CRITIQUING TEXTS

Principle: Critical thinkers realize that everyone is capable of making mistakes and being wrong, including authors of textbooks. They also realize that, since everyone has a point of view, everyone sometimes leaves out some relevant information. No two authors would write the same book, or write from exactly the same perspective. Furthermore, since a textbook is an introduction to the subject, it is not a complete description of it. Therefore, critical readers recognize that reading a book is reading one limited perspective on a subject, and that more can be learned by considering another perspective.

Application: Students should feel free to raise questions about materials they read. When a text is ambiguous, vague, or misleading, teachers can raise such questions as: What does this passage say? What does it imply? Assume? Is it clear? Does it contradict anything you know or suspect to be true? How do you know? How could you find out? What might someone who disagreed with it say? Does the text leave out relevant information? Why do you suppose it was written this way? How could we rewrite this passage to make it clearer or more accurate?

Lesson plans in which the strategy is used:

Introduction To Remodelling Language Arts
Lesson Plans

Language Arts are mainly concerned with skills of listening, speaking, reading, and writing. These basic skills are practiced through reading and discussing stories and pictures, and learning elements of grammer. Yet these basic skills are conceived superficially by textbook writers: I listen and read in order to be able to recall facts and follow directions; I speak and write in order to present facts, practice using proper formats (e.g. question marks,) and state my preferences. Texts do not seem to appreciate how all four activities are really practice in *thinking*. I may not have to think in order to remember what is said, or written, but I must think in order to understand, evaluate, and incorporate what I hear and read. Similarly with speaking and writing, I don't have to think (much) in order to speak or write facts, summaries, and describe preferences, but I must think when I evaluate, try to communicate an important idea or belief, answer questions I have not considered before, or explain why I hold my beliefs. In other words, speaking and writing are a chance for me to develop and clarify my ideas, and understanding. Numerous extended discussions are crucial to developing both listening and speaking skills.

Many stories presented in Language Arts curriculum provide material for fruitful, exploratory discussion about ethics, problem solving, emotions, serious and important issues and concepts. The suggested discussion questions, however, fall far short of taking advantage of the stories to provide students practice engaging in thoughtful discussion. Rather than focusing on and pursuing crucial ideas in depth, many lessons merely contain a jumble of questions, having little relation to one another. Rather than asking students to evaluate a character's behavior (and explain and defend their evaluations) texts tend to simply ask students which characters they liked best.

We recommend, then, that discussions about stories become occassions for students to practice developing and explaining their ideas, and listening and responding to the ideas of others, that students should be encouraged to probe beneath the surface of issues and ideas found in stories, to take their own ideas, and ideas of others, seriously. They should have a chance to think aloud when talking, consider what others say when listening, organize and expand on their ideas when writing, and analyze and evaluate when reading.

Generally, Language Arts materials fail to take advantage of opportunities to have students engage in reciprocity (except, occasionally, they have students take the 'points of view' of animals or in-animate objects). Especially when discussing issues important to children, e.g., common disputes between parents and children, students should be encouraged to seriously consider points of view in opposition to their own. Whenever possible, take advantage of discussion time to foster insight into egocentricity. Students should consider such questions as "Is it ever hard to listen carefully to ideas with which you disagree? Why?"

Text questions frequently ask students what an important concept or idea means. Yet they do not have students analyze the ideas in depth. They do not have them compare examples with examples of opposite ideas, discuss values implicit in using some concept (such as 'good sport',) or explore the implications of applying the concept.

When discussing feelings, texts rarely ask students to consider the relationship between what someone feels and what he thinks.

When text questions do not require students to state the issue or problem, the teacher should do so. Text questions fail to ask students to discuss at length the requirements for settling an issue or problem (i.e., "Do we have to clarify ideas? Do we need facts? Are we evaluating anything? etc.") They typically don't have students discuss the criteria for judging solutions, compare possible solutions, or describe what is wrong with bad solutions.

Texts discourage independent thought by presenting techniques and concepts as given. Students are not required to consider alternative techniques or concepts. Nor do texts have students discuss the purpose of using a technique or concept.

Texts fail to teach critical vocabulary (such as 'infer,' 'relevant') even when such ideas are under discussion. Furthermore, the inferences students are asked to make are not distinguished from what they can observe or must guess. Students are asked to provide answers to questions even when the most appropriate response would be "I don't know" or "I can't tell." Furthermore, the texts lack valuable discussions concerning the potential problems caused by unjustified inferences.

Listening Ears
(Language Arts - Kindergarten)

Objectives of the Remodelled Lesson

The student will:

- begin to develop insight into the importance and difficulty of listening to understand
- practice critical listening by restating other students' positions

ORIGINAL LESSON PLAN

PURPOSE: to stress how important it is to listen carefully.

PROCEDURE:

1. Introduce the lesson by asking children to sit very quietly and listen. After a short period of quiet, discuss the sounds they heard. Encourage informal talk about how we hear with our ears.

2. Bring attention back to the first picture. Ask: Is the mother rabbit listening carefully? Why do you think she is listening so very carefully? What do you suppose she hears? What will the mother rabbit do if she thinks there is reason to be afraid? Are the baby rabbits listening carefully, too? Does the mother rabbit want to teach them to listen carefully? Why?

3. Go on to the second picture, inviting similar interpretation of it. What do you think the boy is saying to the dog? Do you think the dog is listening carefully?

4. Similarly, take up each picture at the bottom of the page. Bring out how important it is to listen carefully to *directions* (the boys and girls listening to the crossing guard) and how important it is to listen carefully in the classroom (the introductory number lesson).

5. Extend the lesson by inviting pupils to tell of personal listening experiences (directions for games, doing errands, etc.).

6. To summarize the lesson, say: We have talked about why we should listen carefully. Think about it, then tell us why it is important to listen carefully.

SUPPLEMENTARY: Give directions to be followed, as: Open the door. Put this book on my desk, etc., then name a child to do as directed. Proceed to more extended directions, as: Go to the board, get an eraser, and put it under my desk.

from *Let's Talk and Listen.* Yellow Level
Language for Daily Use Mildred A. Dawson,
et al. Harcourt Brace Jovanovich. 1973. p. 4.
Used by permission.

Critique

Although the objective of "Listening Ears" is to learn the importance of listening carefully, discussion is limited to the importance of listening to authorities for instruction and safety. A critical education demands students also be encouraged to listen to new ideas, and other points of view. Unless we understand a position well enough to present it ourselves, we cannot agree or disagree with it. Since no one person can know everything, we should listen to others, distinguish what they know from what they don't know, and adjust our beliefs to accommodate what we have learned.

The original lesson doesn't distinguish listening as hearing from listening as understanding, and therefore ignores the difficulties of listening to understand. Children should begin to develop the insight that listening requires more than just hearing; it requires a sincere attempt to grasp what is said. The difficulties of listening arise from the complexity of the process of understanding, and our natural resistance to ideas different than our own. Listening is hardest when we have something to gain by getting our own point across. When we assume the correctness of our own position, we have difficulty in listening to whatever contradicts it. We either fail to give credit where credit is due by dismissing, ignoring, or forgetting evidence, oversimplifying, or other forms of distorting; or we misinterpret the position so that it agrees with our own.

Strategies Used to Remodel

S-3 fostering reciprocity
S-2 developing insight into egocentricity

REMODELLED LESSON PLAN

We believe that it is crucial to practice incorporating the aforementioned insights about listening into the solutions of genuine problems that arise at school. We encourage teachers to take advantage of as many problems, decisions, and disputes as possible. When students claim to disagree with each other, have them state each other's ideas fairly and accurately. **S-3** Ask questions of clarification to elicit points overlooked. Then facilitate a discussion in which students describe any problems they had in trying to listen, **S-2** and why it was important to listen.

51

Following is a list of questions the teacher can ask to further encourage students to think about the importance and difficulty of listening: "Why should we listen to other people? Has anything bad happened to you because you didn't listen? When? Why should we listen to friends? Family? Classmates? Teachers? etc. When is it hard to listen? *S-2* Why? Can you think of a time when you weren't listening to someone? Who was trying to talk to you? Why didn't you listen? Do you ever act as though you are listening when you aren't? How do you feel when people don't listen carefully to you? *S-3* Is it easy or hard to listen (a) when you are angry, scared, or excited? (b) to someone you like? (c) to someone you don't like? (d) when someone says something that sounds dumb or crazy to you? *S-2* (e) when you don't understand? How can you tell if someone is listening?"

To help teachers generalize from specific remodelling moves, and so facillitate their grasp of strong sense critical thinking and how it can be taught, we have devised a list of teaching strategies. Each strategy highlights an aspect of critical thought. Each use illustrates how that aspect can be encouraged in students.

Places to Play
(Language Arts - Kindergarten)

Objectives of the Remodelled Lesson

The student will:

- practice using clear, opposite and borderline examples to clarify ideas
- practice categorizing into given groups
- practice creating and naming new categories to supplement given groups
- practice focusing attention on an issue (i.e. when does 'city' apply?)

ORIGINAL LESSON PLAN

Abstract

The lesson shows pictures of children playing. The students are asked which are city pictures, which are country pictures, and how they know. Students describe personal experiences similar to those pictured. They discuss differences between features of city and country, and note similarities between games played in the city and the country.

from *Let's Talk and Listen.* Yellow Level
Language for Daily Use Mildred A. Dawson,
et al. Harcourt Brace Jovanovich. 1973.
pp. 2-3. Used by permission.

Critique

The original focuses on play in the city and country. We decided to use the lesson as an introduction to a technique for clarifying ideas, so we focus our remodel on the city/country distinction. Although this lesson requires students to supply evidence for their conclusions, it misses the opportunity to have them discuss and struggle with problematic cases, make new categories, and decide when to suspend judgment.

To think for yourself, you need command of ideas. This requires that you not only have concepts, but also that you are conscious of how you use them, and aware of their limitations. In this lesson plan we make some suggestions for developing the student's ability to clarify concepts and build on their emerging ideas through discussion of cases to which the concept (city) clearly applies, clearly does not apply, partially applies, and cases in which the evidence is insufficient to allow a reasonable judgment.

Strategies Used to Remodel

S-12 clarifying ideas

S-26 suspending judgment

S-16 distinguishing relevant from irrelevant facts

REMODELLED LESSON PLAN

Before class: Assemble 10-20 pictures. Some should be obviously city scenes, others country scenes, others that are neither (e.g. a small town). Others should be fairly hard to judge (e.g. a park with sky-scrapers in the distant background). Others should be impossible to judge **S-26** (e.g., a drawing of a house with no surroundings, the inside of a house). If possible, find pictures of the same scene, with some irrelevant difference **S-16** (e.g. one picture taken in summer; another in winter). These pictures will be sorted into piles by the class.

The activity: Begin with several easy pictures (i.e. pictures which are either obviously of a city, or obviously of a country setting); the rest should be mixed. Hold up the first picture and ask, "Is this in a city or in the country? **S-12** How do you know?" Let the students discuss the picture until the pertinent details have been covered. As you do the same with the rest of the pictures, sort them into piles as students decide into which category they fit. To avoid leading the students or limiting their answers, ask of each subsequent picture "And what about this picture; what does it show? Do I put this one here, there, or where? Why?" Or ask "What shall we call this one?" Allow discussion. Elicit as many reasons for student responses as possible.

If the students have problems, refer back to the sorted pictures. "Is this like that, or the others?" If they remain stumped or cannot agree, come back to it later, when the rest have been sorted, and compare it to pictures in each pile.

To sum-up use the following questions: What in the pictures was important in helping us decide where to put the pictures? What didn't matter? **S-16** For each pile ask, "What do these have in common? Were some easier to place than others?   Which? Why? Why were the hard ones hard? Using the pictures as guides, what can we say about each category (concept, idea)?"

Follow up by having students bring in their own city/country pictures, and discuss what groups they belong to.

Toby
(Language Arts - Kindergarten)

Objectives of the Remodelled Lesson

The student will:

- practice thinking up multiple explanations for an event
- see how conclusions about an event require supporting evidence
- learn when it is appropriate to suspend judgment
- practice using probability qualifiers

ORIGINAL LESSON PLAN

Toby heard a loud growl and saw the cat run up a tree. Why do you think the cat climbed the tree? (The cat was afraid; a dog was after it.) What do you think will happen next? (Answers will vary.)

from *Look, Listen, and Learn.* Level R, *HBJ Bookmark Reading Program* Margaret Early. Harcourt Brace Jovanovich. 1974. p. 143. Used by permission.

Critique

In order to promote a critical thinking atmosphere in the classroom, the appropriate suspension of judgment, the consideration of all reasonable alternatives, and sensitivity to the ways in which altering the evidence effects the conclusion, should be actively encouraged.

We believe that this lesson does not promote such an atmosphere insofar as it encourages students to jump to a conclusion, and to assume that the two events described are necessarily connected. Furthermore, it is a missed opportunity to give students practice in exploring the relationships between evidence and conclusion, and develop familiarity with, and the habit of using, probability qualifiers.

Strategies Used to Remodel

S-1   fostering independent thinking

S-27 using probability qualifiers

S-17 making inferences

S-26 suspending judgment

REMODELLED LESSON PLAN

In order to address the problems in the original lesson, we recommend a discussion that highlights alternatives to the conclusion that the lesson forces. *S-1* The teacher should try to elicit a variety of responses to "Why do you think the cat ran up the tree?" Then he could lead a discussion about the probability of, and the evidence required to eliminate, some of the alternatives. For instance, if one response was "The cat ran up the tree after a bird", the teacher could call for a description of the evidence that would support that conclusion (e.g., Toby would see the cat staring at the bird, Toby would not see a barking dog chasing the cat). Several of the responses should be followed up by relevant questions. The teacher could then ask, "Which of these responses are 'very likely,' 'possible,' 'unlikely' and why?" *S-27* Next, the teacher may want to reverse the process by supplying evidence and asking, "What can we conclude given this evidence?" (e.g., Toby's brother crawling around the corner growling.) *S-17*

Finally, the teacher should wind up the discussion by focusing on suspending judgment by asking, "do we know which was true in this case?" "Why not?" *S-26* Review the examples, pointing out how different conclusions require different evidence, and how our judgments of the different conclusions require the use of probability qualifiers.

Your first remodels should use those skills or insights clearest to you. Other principles can be integrated as they become clear.

Sandy
(Language Arts - Kindergarten)

Objectives of the Remodelled Lesson

The student will:

- practice making and evaluating assumptions
- recognize the relationship of "good reasons" to "safe assumptions"
- learn the concepts "safe assumption", "fairly safe assumption", "not very safe assumption", and "unsafe assumption"

ORIGINAL LESSON PLAN

Sandy said "Good morning" to the teacher. The other children were in their seats. Where do you think Sandy was? (at school, in the classroom, at the teacher's desk) How do you know? (the teacher was there, other children were in their seats, etc.)

from *Look, Listen, and Learn.* Level R, *HBJ Bookmark Reading Program* Margaret Early. Harcourt Brace Jovanovich. 1974. p. 143. Used by permission.

Critique

Critical thinking requires distinguishing assumptions that are safely made from those which are fairly safe, not very safe, and unsafe. The sample answers given the teacher confuse safe with unsafe assumptions. Sandy was probably in school, but there is no reason to assume that she was at the teacher's desk. By treating all answers equally, the lesson fails to encourage students to question their assumptions, and to exercise caution when coming to conclusions.

Strategies Used to Remodel

S-27 using probability qualifiers

S-22 evaluating assumptions

REMODELLED LESSON PLAN

We suggest that teachers using this lesson require students to distinquish justified from unjustified conclusions. First, for each response to the question "Where do you think Sandy was?" ask, "How safe is it to assume that Sandy is ...? Is it a safe assumption, a fairly safe assumption, or an unsafe assumption? *S-27* Why do you think so?" Whenever an assumption is questioned, the reasons for questioning it should be discussed *S-22*. In summing up, we suggest that the teacher review student responses and discuss with the class the degree of safety of the assumptions made.

All the various strategies explained in the handbook are couched in terms of behaviors. The principles express and describe a variety of behaviors of the 'ideal' critical thinker; they become applications to lessons when teachers canvass their lesson plans to find appropriate places where those behaviors can be fostered. The practice we recommend helps guard against teachers using these strategies as recipes or formulas, since in each case good judgment is required in the application process.

Listen and Think
(Language Arts - Kindergarten)

Objectives of the Remodelled Lesson

The student will:

- develop the habit of thinking about how to settle questions, rather than simply attempting to answer them
- describe the processes required to settle various questions
- distinguish questions which they are in a position to settle from those which they are not

ORIGINAL LESSON PLAN

> To stimulate the children to listen and think, make several general statements such as those given below and ask the children to tell whether each statement is true or false.
>
> - There are books in this room.
> - In the morning we go to sleep.
> - (name a child) is wearing (name a color) pants.
> - A clock tells us what time it is.
> - Cars can talk like people.
>
> from *Look, Listen, and Learn.* Level R, *HBJ Bookmark Reading Program* Margaret Early. Harcourt Brace Jovanovich. 1974. p. 143. Used by permission.

Critique

One obstacle to critical thought is the tendency to agree or disagree with statements immediately, without first reflecting on what we need to do to be in a position to judge their truth. Reformulating statements as questions is a first step toward developing reflective habits. Students need lots of practice considering what must be done to answer different kinds of questions.

By simply asking students to judge sentences as true or false, this lesson fails to encourage students to reflect on how they know. They should practice describing how to find out, that is, what facts would be relevant, how they could get those facts, what ideas they need to understand, whether something is being evaluated, and if so, what standards apply. By using only statements about which students can decide, the lesson fails to give students practice distinguishing what they are in a position to know, from what they are not.

59

Strategy Used to Remodel

S-11 clarifying issues

S-26 suspending judgment

REMODELLED LESSON PLAN

In order to encourage awareness of the process of settling questions, we recommend that teachers add to this lesson plan a discussion of how the students know the answer. Although statements can be used, we recommend questions. Furthermore, we recommend a larger variety of questions including some the students are not in a position to know.

To facilitate the discussion, the teacher could take a question such as, "Are there books in this room?" and ask, "Is this true? How do we know that this is true? Did we use our senses? Which senses? Did we do anything else?" (Such as counting, using memory, thinking, understanding the meaning of a word or expression, doing an experiment.) When using questions that students do not know the answer to, such as, "How many tigers are there in the zoo?", the teacher could ask, "Can we answer this question now? Why not? **S-26** How could we find out? What could we do? Do we need to use our senses?" etc.

Below is a list of different kinds of questions that could be added to the lesson.

- How many blue-eyed people are in this room?
- Can Sarah jump two feet high?
- Is John taller than Tim?
- Is it raining today?
- How many people live in our town?
- What color is my car?
- What did Julie have for breakfast?
- Are the book shelves made of wood?
- Do Mary and Gloria disagree?

The rest of the questions are more difficult. Students may need exposure to them over several lessons. You may want to use a question such as "Is a spinster a married woman?" to illustrate that knowing the meanings of words settles some questions. The teacher could read the dictionary definition to the class, and ask, "How did we learn the answer to this question?" By learning what the word 'spinster' means.

- Are babies young?
- Are trees a kind of fish?

60

• Is July in the summer?

• Are pajamas clothes that you wear to bed?

• Do men make natural objects?

• Are cities places with no people in them?

The following are evaluative questions. See **S-15** for some background on how to settle this kind of question.

• Is this a good book?

• Which toy is better?

• Is "Inspector Gadget" a funny show?

• Are these good rain boots?

• Is a lot of candy good for you?

• Did Billy play fairly this morning?

• Are cats as smart as people?

• What is the best breakfast?

• Is Tom a good friend of Sam's?

• Should all children play fairly?

• Should Sally have gotten mad?

To sum up, the teacher may have students group a number of questions by similarities in how they are settled. E.g. "Were there any other questions that you would settle in the same way as 'How many books are there in this room?' Which questions? How did you settle them? Were there any differences in the ways you settled these questions?"

In teaching for critical thinking in the strong sense, we are committed to teaching in such a way that children learn as soon and as completely as possible how to become responsible for their own thinking.

Evaluative Thinking

(Language Arts - Kindergarten)

Objectives of the Remodelled Lesson

The student will:

- practice evaluating behavior
- give reasons for evaluative conclusions
- discuss standards of evaluation

ORIGINAL LESSON PLAN

Assign role-playing situations to several groups of two or three children. Ask each group to act out its assigned situation, and then have the remaining children discuss what took place. Ask the children to volunteer any suggestions as to how the situation might have been different if any one of the role-play group had done something different from what he or she did. For example, a role-play situation for three children might be the following:

A teacher asks a child to write an answer on the chalkboard. The child is shy and forgets what the answer is. Another child laughs at the first child.

Encourage the children to discuss the role play by asking questions such as:

1. Sometimes we get shy or embarrassed, and we can easily forget what we are supposed to do next; has that ever happened to any of you? Can you tell us about it?

2. Sometimes we get nervous and feel as though we have to laugh, even though we don't really think something is funny. Can anyone tell us about a time that happened to you?

3. Have any of you ever felt sorry for someone who was nervous or timid, and if so, what did you do?

4. Has anyone ever been in a situation where you felt sad because people laughed at someone? Can you tell us about it?

After the role-play has been discussed, ask the children what they think might have happened if instead of laughing, the second child had looked encouragingly at the first.

Other role-play situations include:

A child who has several toys is playing with only one; a second child has no toys and asks to share the toys. The first child agrees. For comparison study of this role play, suggest that the first child refuses to share the toys.

A school's crossing guard has halted children at the crosswalk, and is facing traffic. One child is standing and waiting at the crossing; a second child comes running toward the crossing, looking behind over his or her shoulder, not paying atention. The first child shouts, alerting the school crossing guard to possible danger. For comparison study, suggest the child does not shout a warning.

In developing role-play situations for the children, you may wish to assign placid or passive roles to the aggressive children and vice versa. In this way you will encourage them and the rest of the class to see themselves and each other in a new light.

from *About Me,* Bernard J. Weiss, et al.
Copyright © 1980. Holt Rinehart and
Winston, Publishers. pp. 175-176.
Reprinted by permission of the publisher.
All rights reserved.

Critique

This lesson is a confusing introduction to evaluative thinking because none of the questions asked call upon the students to evaluate anything. To evaluate accurately and fairly, students should understand what they are evaluating, and why. Critical thinkers are conscious of the standards they use when evaluating so that these, too, become objects of evaluation. Although reasonable people can disagree, making standards themselves objects of evaluation increases the liklihood of rational discussion and agreement.

Although the stories in the original lesson clearly suggest evaluative conclusions, neither the process of evaluation, standards of evaluation, or evaluative conclusions are elicited by the questions. Furthermore, this lesson encourages absolutistic (i.e., "all or nothing") thinking, by using stories which describe cases of "all right" or "all wrong" whereas most real-life cases involve at least some degree of shared blame. Also, some of the questions lead students to make questionable inferences, e.g., when suggesting that the second child in the first role-play laughed from nervousness. The value of these exercises, as they stand, lies in showing how our behavior has consequences, and that changing our behavior can change the situation we are in.

Strategies Used to Remodel

S-4 exploring thoughts underlying feelings

S-21 exploring implications

S-25 evaluating actions

S-6 exploring underlying purposes

S-10 integrating critical vocabulary

REMODELLED LESSON PLAN

The questions used in the original lesson can be used to elicit situations that the children are familiar with. However, since they don't require students to evaluate, we suggest that they be followed by questions which first call for an evaluation, then clarify the object of the evaluation, the purpose of the evaluation, and the standards used to evaluate. Whenever variations on the original story are introduced by the students or the teacher, the teacher should ask "Does changing the story this way affect any of our conclusions? Why or why not?" **S-21**

Begin discussion of each situation by having students discuss what the characters felt and thought and why. **S-4** To elicit and probe evaluations in the first situation, the teacher could ask, "Was it better for the second child to have laughed, or to have looked encouragingly? Why? **S-25** Who are we evaluating in this situation? Why is this important?" **S-6** The teacher should point out any standards of evaluation the students use. For example, if a student states "It was mean because it hurt his feelings," the teacher could say, "You used the standard of not hurting other people's feelings to conclude that this was wrong." **S-10** When a variation is introduced, such as, "the child wrote a funny answer on purpose when he forgot the right answer," the teacher should say, "Now we have a different story. How is this story different, and what do we want to say about it?" We encourage teachers to use any critical thinking vocabulary (such as: assume, standard, conclude, infer, imply) during the course of the discussion.

> **The critique should inform the remodel; the remodel should arise out of the critique.**

Susan, Tom, & Betty
(Language Arts - 1st Grade)

Objectives of the Remodelled Lesson

The student will:

- practice making good inferences
- distinguish safe inferences from cases in which there is more than one reasonable possibility
- distinguish cases in which they can make good inferences from cases in which they must guess at an answer
- practice critiquing assumptions

ORIGINAL LESSON PLAN

Abstract

Students discuss three rows of pictures in which children are portrayed doing different things. They are asked to describe events preceding and following the scenes pictured, and to make judgments about the characters' personalities.

from Teachers' Edition of Book I-1 *Ginn Elementary English,*, series, © Copyright, 1968, by Silver, Burdett & Ginn Inc. Used with permission. pp 33-34.

Critique

The section of the original lesson entitled "Interpreting the Pictures" provides four different kinds of questions without distinguishing them. Such lack of discrimination may lead students to believe that they are making equally good inferences in all cases. Some of the questions, such as, "Where is Tom in this picture?" and, "Is father just leaving or returning?" call upon students to make good inferences from pictures; others, such as, "What do you think the dog will do with Susan's clothes?" and, "What do you think will happen after Susan gets in the house?" have more than one reasonable answer. (The dog might chew the clothes or bury them; Susan might clean her arm, or her mother or a babysitter might clean it.) Some questions, such as, "What makes you think Betty may not have many new dresses?" and, "How can Tom get the paint off the floor?" contain questionable assumptions. Still others can be answered only by guessing "Where do you suppose Tom's father has been? Do you think someone suggested that Betty bring the flowers to her teacher or that she thought of it herself?".

The next section, entitled "Drawing Inferences," contains a number of leading questions such as, "Do you think Susan is thoughtful, careless, or careful?" and "In what ways might she have helped herself in these pictures?" Such questions discourage suspending judgment, and encourage questionable assumptions.

Strategies Used to Remodel

S-26 suspending judgment

S-22 evaluating assumptions

S-10 integrating critical vocabulary

REMODELLED LESSON PLAN

First, **S-26** using the questions provided in the lesson, ask of each one, "Can we be sure?" and "How?" "Is one answer more likely than others? Why? Can we say anything about this question? How do you know?"

Next, **S-22** for questions containing questionable assumptions (such as "What makes you think Betty may not have many new dresses?" and "How can Tom get the paint off the floor?") ask students to critique these assumptions. For example, ask the following questions: Do we have reason to believe that Betty doesn't have many new dresses? Was this a good or bad assumption? Do we have reason to believe that Tom is painting the wagon on a floor? (vs. a driveway or the ground) Was this a good or bad assumption?"

Finally, **S-10** have students review the pictures. Ask: "What were some of the things we could infer from these pictures? What were some of the things we could not infer from these pictures?"

A Toy for Mike

(Language Arts - 1st Grade)

Objectives of the Remodelled Lesson

The student will:

- practice suppositional thinking
- practice stating the problem under discussion
- practice comparing different solutions
- practice explaining why some proposed solutions are not good

ORIGINAL LESSON PLAN

Abstract

Students read a story about Pat and Ann. Pat and Ann have a problem. While they are trying to wrap a present for their friend Mike, the string breaks. They are in a hurry to go. Pat finds a solution to the problem. Students are asked if they think Pat's plan was a good idea.

In the second section, entitled "Think About It", children read very short stories in which problems are presented (e.g., Dad gets a flat when he is leaving for work), and choose two of the three solutions presented. Then they discuss their choices and suggest other solutions.

from *Tag In And Out All Around*
Theodore L. Harris et al. The Economy
Company, © 1973. pp. T204-205. Used by
permission.

Critique

Although students are asked if they think Pat's solution is a good idea, they are not asked to discuss the criteria of a good solution, or to compare the solution to other solutions. The students should reflect on solutions, and how to evaluate them, and begin to develop well thought-out, practical ideas about choosing good solutions. In the section entitled "Think About It", they do not discuss what is wrong with the bad solutions, nor do they describe the relevant facts required to make a good decision. In neither the story nor the "Think About It" section are the students called on to state the problem, whereas defining the problem should be the first step in solving it.

Strategies Used to Remodel

S-11 clarifying issues

S-24 evaluating solutions

S-15 developing criteria for evaluation

S-16 distinguishing relevant from irrelevant facts

REMODELLED LESSON PLAN

First, **S-11** after the students read the story, ask, "What was Pat and Ann's problem?" Next, **S-24** when discussing alternatives, ask "How can we decide which solution is best? What would a good solution involve?" **S-15** Keep a list of student responses so, if needed, you can aid them in the sum-up when they are asked to apply the criteria they develop to different solutions. Last, ask "What facts are relevant? Why?" **S-16**

Then, **S-11** for each problem in the "Think About It" section, ask "What is the problem?" Next, ask, "What would you need to know to decide on a good solution? What facts are relevant?" **S-16** (Distance from work, availability of other transportation, existence of a spare tire.) Encourage the use of "if, then" statements when describing the desirability of the solution ("If work is near home, then it's best to walk.") Have the students explain why they didn't choose the other solution.

To sum-up, ask "What is the best solution to Pat and Ann's problem, and why?" Have the students compare different solutions, and use the criteria for a good solution as the means of evaluation. **S-24**

Every trivial lesson you abandon leaves more time to stimulate critical thinking.

Moving Day
(Language Arts - 1st Grade)

Objective of the Remodelled Lesson

Students will discuss the relationship between thoughts and feelings.

ORIGINAL LESSON PLAN

Abstract

Students discuss their feelings about moving and read a story about Jud. Jud is unhappy about moving away from his friends and home, into an apartment. But when he moves, he discovers that he likes the elevator in his building, makes a new friend, and his feelings change.

Students are asked to describe characters' feelings and explain behavior; order story events; and find sentences in the story which answer a number of questions.

from *Sun and Shadow, Reading Skills 4.*
Margaret Early, et al., Harcourt Brace
Jovanovich. 1970. pp.169-175.

Critique

Although students discuss how Jud first felt about moving to his new home, and that he felt differently after he was there, they are not encouraged to recognize how the change in Jud's feelings arose from the change in his understanding of his new situation.

This lesson is a missed opportunity to have students practice seeing the relationship between thoughts and feelings and thereby confront the common misconception that our feelings exist independently of how we think about situations. With practice they can begin to see how changing the way they think about a situation can affect the way they feel about it.

Strategies Used to Remodel

S-4 exploring thoughts underlying feelings

S-14 making assumptions explicit

S-3 fostering reciprocity

REMODELLED LESSON PLAN

After reading the first half of the story entitled "Moving Day", ask the following questions **S-4** : How did Jud feel about moving? What did Jud think that made him feel sad? Angry? etc. (He would miss his friends, he would miss his house, it wasn't his decision.) What did he assume about his new home? **S-14** (He wouldn't have any friends.) Could he have thought of something that would have made him feel less sad? What? (He will make new friends; it will be fun to live in a new place.)

After completing the last half of the story, entitled "The Apartment", ask, "What changed toward the end of the story? What did Jud learn that made him feel better? What makes you think so?"

As an extension, the class could discuss questions like the following: How can one person have so many different feelings about one event? Is moving an important event? Do people often have different, even conflicting feelings about an important event? Does everyone feel the same about moving as Jud did? Why might someone else feel excited about moving? Afraid? etc. How do you feel about moving? Why might someone feel differently than you? **S-3**

> Macro-practice is almost always more important than micro-drill. We need to be continually vigilant against the misguided tendency to fragment, atomize, mechanize, and proceduralize thinking.

Splash! Splash!

(Language Arts - 1st Grade)

Objective of the Remodelled Lesson

Students will practice finding the main idea of the story, and illustrating it through appropriate story titles.

ORIGINAL LESSON PLAN

Abstract

Students discuss the title of the story, "Splash! Splash!" Then they read and discuss the story about Kevin, Jan, and a dog named Sandy. In this story, Sandy jumps in a pond, splashing the children. Then Sandy chases a duck and a turtle but cannot catch them. Most of the questions ask for story details. Others merely serve to create interest. One asks students to make and justify an inference. After the story, they ask students why the title is a good one have them describe characters' feelings and make and justify simple inferences. Finally, students are asked to locate ideas in the story that mean essentially the same as sentences they are given on a list.

from *A Happy Morning HBJ Bookmark Reading Program* Level 2 Grade 1 Margaret Early, et al. Harcourt Brace Jovanovich, Inc. 1973. pp. 52-54. Used by permission. All rights reserved.

Strategies Used to Remodel

S-1 fostering independent thinking

S-15 developing criteria for evaluation

REMODELLED LESSON PLAN

In the original lesson they ask "Why is 'Splash! Splash!' a good title for this story?" We suggest changing this to "Is 'Splash! Splash!' a good title for this story?" **S-1** and adding "Why? What makes a title a good title?" **S-15** Probe responses with questions like the following: What is the main idea of the story? Can you think of any other titles for the story? Do they express the main idea? Why or why not?" Have students suggest bad titles, and compare them to good titles.

Two Ways to Win

(Language Arts - 2nd Grade)

Objectives of the Remodelled Lesson

The student will:

- use analytic terms such as: assume, infer, imply
- make inferences from story clues
- discuss and evaluate an assumption about making friends
- clarify 'good sport' by contrasting it with its opposite, 'bad sport'

ORIGINAL LESSON PLAN

Abstract

Students read a story about a brother and sister named Cleo and Toby. Cleo and Toby are new in town and worried about making new friends. They ice skate at the park every day after school, believing that winning an upcoming race can help them make new friends (and that they won't make friends if they don't win). Neither of them win; Cleo, because she falls, Toby, because he forfeits his chance to win by stopping to help a boy who falls. Some children come over after the race to compliment Toby on his good sportsmanship and Cleo on her skating.

Most of the questions about the story probe the factual components. Some require students to infer. Questions ask what 'good sport' means and if Cleo's belief about meeting people is correct.

from *Mustard Seed Magic,* Theodore L. Harris
et al. Economy Company. © 1972. pp. 42-46.
Used by permission. All rights reserved.

Critique

There are a number of good questions in the original lesson which require students to make inferences, e.g., "Have Toby and Cleo lived on the block all their lives?" The text also asks students if they know who won the race. Since they do not, this question encourages students to suspend judgment. Although 'good sportsmanship' is a good idea for students to discuss, the text fails to have students practice techniques for clarifying ideas. Instead, they ask students to list the characteristics of a good sport (a central idea in the story) with no discussion of what it means to be a bad sport. The use of opposite cases to clarify ideas helps students develop fuller and more accurate ideas. With such practice a student can begin to recognize borderline cases as well; e.g., where someone was a good sport in some respects, bad in others.

Strategies Used to Remodel

S-12 clarifying ideas

S-18 supplying evidence for a conclusion

S-10 integrating critical vocabulary

S-14 making assumptions exlicit

S-22 evaluating assumptions

REMODELLED LESSON PLAN

Where the original lesson asks, "What does 'a good sport' mean?", we suggest an extension, **S-12** . The teacher should make two lists on the board of the students' responses to the question "How do good sports and bad sports behave?" Students could go back to the story and apply the ideas on the list to the characters in the story, giving reasons to support any claims they make regarding the characters' sportsmanship **S-18** . In some cases there might not be enough information to determine whether a particular character is a good or bad sport. Or they might find a character who is borderline, having some characteristics of both good and bad sports. Again, students should cite evidence from the story to support their claims. The students could also change details of the story to make further points about the nature of good and bad sportsmanship. (If the girl had pushed Cleo down in order to win the race, that would have been very bad sportsmanship.) To further probe the idea of good sportsmanship, ask questions like the following: How did Toby impress the other children? Why did they think he did a good thing? If you had seen the race, what would you have thought of Toby? Why do we value the kind of behavior we call good 'sportsmanship'? Why don't we like bad sportsmanship? Why are people ever bad sports?

There are a number of places in the lesson where the teacher could introduce, or give students further practice using, critical thinking vocabulary **S-10** . Here are a few examples "What can you infer from the story title and picture? What parts of the story imply that Toby and Cleo will have some competition in the race? What do Toby and Cleo assume about meeting new people and making new friends? **S-14** Is this a good or a bad assumption? **S-22** Why? Why do you think they made this assumption? Have you ever made similar assumptions? Why? What can you infer that Cleo felt at the end of the story? How can you tell?"

Messages Without Words

(Language Arts - 2nd Grade)

Objectives of the Remodelled Lesson

The student will:

- practice using critical thinking vocabulary
- discuss problems involved in inferring incorrectly

ORIGINAL LESSON PLAN

Abstract

Students read and discuss a passage about how we receive messages from people through facial expressions and body movements. The discussion questions ask students to find main ideas of paragraphs, make and justify inferences from pictures, discuss their own examples of non-verbal communication, and summarize the passage in one sentence.

from *Mustard Seed Magic*, Theodore L. Harris et al. Economy Company. © 1972. pp. T62-63. Used by permission. All rights reserved.

Critique

The strength of this lesson lies in its subject matter, making inferences from body language. It encourages students to think about the many subtle clues that they take into account when drawing conclusions.

Its weaknesses include a lack of use of critical vocabulary (infer, conclude) and a missed opportunity to discuss the potential problems involved in inferring incorrectly. Students should discuss a variety of ways people misinterpret evidence to support misconceptions. By discussing only examples of inferring correctly, this lesson fails to develop this insight.

Strategies Used to Remodel

S-10 integrating critical vocabulary

S-2 developing insight into egocentricity

REMODELLED LESSON PLAN

Use the critical vocabulary whenever possible **S-10** . For example, when the original lesson asks, "What message is discussed on this page and shown in the illustration?" substitute "What can you infer this person wants to say? What can you conclude about this picture? Why?"

We suggest that the teacher facilitate a discussion about why people make inaccurate inferences, and what the consequences of doing so might be. The teacher might begin by suggesting an example of making a faulty inference (e.g., ask students if they ever inferred that someone didn't like them because they wouldn't play with them at recess, but later discovered that the person was shy).

Then, discuss the consequences of the bad inference, and why it was made. Encourage students to look at the egocentric motivations for making bad inferences, by discussing examples like the following: A child's mother won't let him go to the park. He concludes that she is mean, without considering the reasons she gives for not letting him go. **S-2** When the students understand what is meant by faulty inferences, ask them to give examples from their personal experience. For each example ask "Why was that not a good inference? What else, if anything, might you have inferred? Why did you make the inference? Did making a faulty inference in this situation hurt you or someone else?"

Critical thinking requires sensitivity to the distinction between those facts that are relevant to an issue and those which are not. Critical thinkers focus their attention on relevant facts and do not let irrelevant considerations affect their conclusions.

Marvin's Manhole
(Language Arts - 2nd Grade)

Objectives of the Remodelled Lesson

The student will:

- select story details to support a conclusion
- discuss different interpretations of a character's behavior

ORIGINAL LESSON PLAN

Abstract

The students read "Marvin's Manhole" a story about a boy who, rejecting his mother's explanation of the purpose of a manhole, decides that there is a 'scary thing' living below his street. Marvin tries to make contact with the thing, but fails. One day he finds the manhole open. After looking for the thing, Marvin climbs into the manhole, has a scare, and meets a workman who confirms his mother's explanation.

Students are asked to recall details, discuss Marvin's personality, discuss parts of Marvin's reasoning, read an emphasized word as Marvin would have said it, discuss some of the pictures, discuss Marvin's feelings, and describe what may have happened after the end of the story.

from *People Need People,* Eldonna L. Evertts.
Holt Publishing. 1977. pp. T222-231.

Critique

This lesson fails to take advantage of the ambiguous nature of Marvin's story. It is not clear whether Marvin really believes in the existence of the 'scary thing,' or is merely pretending to believe in it. Most of Marvin's behavior can be interpreted either way. This lesson misses the opportunity to have students argue for one interpretation over another, or see how each interpretation affects the readers' understanding of the details in the story.

Early in the story, when Marvin hits the manhole cover with his baseball bat and runs away, the reader could interpret his actions as bravely trying to get the scary thing to come out, or as part of a game. The faultiness of Marvin's reasoning (as when he concludes that the scary thing eats the bread he leaves on the street overnight) suggests that he's joking. Yet, when he discovers that the manhole cover is open, he behaves as though he believes in the thing.

The sugggested questions do nothing to explore the possible different points of view. Only one raises the issue of Marvin's belief ("How strongly do you think Marvin believed in the scary thing by this point in the story?") Another assumes his belief in the thing ("Do you think Marvin finally believed what his mother had told him about the manhole?")

The different interpretations, then, should be the main focus of the questions.

Strategies Used to Remodel

S-23 evaluating arguments

S-10 integrating critical vocabulary

S-17 making inferences

S-3 fostering reciprocity

S-18 supplying evidence for a conclusion

REMODELLED LESSON PLAN

The process of sorting out the different interpretations of the story should begin with Marvin's claim that he thinks there is a scary thing in the manhole. The teacher should ask the students "Why do you think Marvin said that there was a thing in the manhole?" Encourage a discussion of multiple points of view on the question. Then focus attention on the issue "Does Marvin really believe in the scary thing?" Raise this issue again, throughout the rest of the story, and allow discussion. Ask "Does this part of the story support, or weaken your conclusion? **S-23** How? If you think he does believe in the thing, why do you think he did this? **S-17** What did you infer from his actions? **S-10** If you think he doesn't believe in the thing, why do you think he did this? What did you infer from his actions?"

Accept any position a student may maintain. The possibilities include: Marvin believed in the thing the whole time; Marvin believed part of the time; Marvin was pretending to believe in the thing; Marvin believed in the thing, but didn't really think it was scary. Encourage the students to use 'if, then' statements when discussing the implications of their ideas, e.g., "If Marvin believed in the thing, he didn't make a good inference when he concluded that the thing ate the bread." Have students state each other's positions **S-3** . Finally, after the story has been read and discussed, review the different positions taken, and assign an essay writing exercise. Have the students state the issue, and defend their positions with details from the story. **S-18**

Sentences That Ask

(Language Arts - 2nd Grade)

Objectives of the Remodelled Lesson

The student will:

- practice formulating appropriate questions
- practice inferring facts about other students from their choice of questions
- practice reciprocity
- discuss how changing an issue can change which facts are relevant

ORIGINAL LESSON PLAN

Lesson: Think of your pet or of a pet you would like to have.   Talk about your pets. This sentence asks a question: "What is your pet?" 1.Think of three other questions you could ask about a pet. Your teacher will write your questions on the board. 2.Write your questions in your best writing. What mark is at the end of each of your questions? Put a question mark at the end of a sentence that asks.

Purposes: To teach the sentence that asks and to teach the use of the question mark.

Procedure: Have the first two introductory sentences read.   Encourage discussion about various pets. Have the children ask one another questions about their pets. After several questions have been asked, proceed with the idea in lines 3 and 4; that is, *the sentence that asks a question.*

Continue by having the pupils read silently, and then discuss Exercise 1. Call attention to the question mark each time you write the children's questions on the board. Show how it is made. Call attention to the capital letter which begins each sentence and to the fact that all sentences, whether they tell or ask, begin with a capital letter.

Next, after reading and discussing the directions for Exercise 2, have the children copy three or four of the board questions. Read and stress the rule before work begins.

from *Language for Daily Use,* Level 2 Red.
Dorothy S. Strickland et al. copyright © 1973
by Harcourt Brace Jovanovich,Inc. Reprinted
by permission of the publisher. p.19.

Critique

This lesson does not introduce children to the importance of questioning. It emphasizes the mechanics of writing questions (begin with a capital letter; end with a question mark) at the expense of exploring the function of questioning. Children should begin, as early as possible, to learn to formulate appropriate questions, and to see the ways in which these questions can elicit useful responses.

In the lesson, students are asked to think of any three questions they could ask about a pet, but they are given no guiding purpose for formulating them. This approach misses the opportunity to show students the ways in which their needs and purposes determine their questions, and is therefore an incomplete introduction to questions.

We have added activities which give students practice making inferences and using reciprocity.

Strategies Used to Remodel

S-5 fostering insight into mechanical skills

S-16 distinguishing relevant from irrelevant facts

S-17 making inferences

S-3 fostering reciprocity

REMODELLED LESSON PLAN

First, instead of having students ask any three questions about pets, the teacher can ask students to think of at least three questions they might ask a pet seller to determine if a particular pet is a good pet for them. This will give students a guiding purpose, though any reasonable purpose will do, for formulating appropriate questions *S-5* . Ask, "What would you need to know? What facts about the animal seem relevant to you?" *S-16*

After the students have listed their questions, and have corrected any mechanical errors, such as forgetting a question mark, the teacher should write one student's questions on the board, so the class can discuss what that student wants in a pet *S-17* . Then, when a number of students' responses have been covered, have the students imagine that they are going home to ask their parents if they can have the pet they want. Have them list their parent's questions *S-3* . Ask, "What facts would your parents think are relevant?" *S-16*   Then discuss the things that most concern the parents. This activity gives the students practice in reciprocity, seeing an issue as someone else would see it, as well as more practice formulating and writing questions properly.

Next, *S-16* in order to give students practice seeing how changing a problem slightly can change the nature of the relevant questions, ask students to imagine that they have moved (from a house with a yard to an apartment, or vice versa). Have them list questions that they would now ask when deciding on a pet. Finally, ask the following questions: "How did your questions change when you learned you were moving to a small apartment? Did you have to change your mind about the pet that was best for you? Why or why not?"

A teacher who is unable to learn how to use basic critical thinking principles so as to critique and remodel some of his own lesson plans probably won't be able to implement someone else's effectively. Providing teachers with the scaffolding for carrying out the process for themselves, and examples of its application, opens the door for continuing development of critical thinking skills and insights.

Words That Go Together
(Language Arts - 2nd Grade)

Objective of the Remodelled Lesson

The students will practice recognizing the reasons underlying the associations they make among ideas.

ORIGINAL LESSON PLAN

Abstract

Students are asked to list words they associate with words the teacher mentions, such as 'playground.' The answers are discussed.

Students then use their texts. They are informed that words can be grouped, and given an example of a word and associated words. They are then asked to complete the first exercise in which there are lists of words. The first word from each list is underlined. They are to underline related words from the rest of the list. In each case, there are three 'associated' words, and one word which has no similarity or relationship to the original word.

from *Our Language Today,* David A. Conlin
and A. Renee LeRoy. American Book Co.
1970. pp. G38, 113.

Critique

This lesson requires students to practice word association without asking them to distinguish the different relationships between the main ideas and associated words. In some of the activities in exercise A, the related words have the same relationship to the main word, whereas in others, the related words have different relationships to the main idea. To encourage precise thinking, students should practice distinguishing different relationships between ideas. In our remodel we will show how the introductory Procedure and Exercise A can be used to give students such practice.

Strategy Used to Remodel

S-7 recognizing reaons underlying categories

REMODELLED LESSON PLAN

In the opening procedure of the original lesson, students are asked to name words that they associate with "playground." We suggest students group these words based on their different relationships to the main idea. Imagine that students have named the following words:

Fun	Games	Hopscotch	Jump	Play
Slide	School	Run	Park	
Recess	Swingset	P.E.	Jumprope	

The teacher should choose a word from the list, such as "swingset", and ask "Why do you associate this word with 'playground?' **S-7** Are there any other words on the list that you associate with 'playground' for the same reason?" Begin to group these words on the board and ask students to supply labels for the groups. For example, the group containing "swingset" and "slide" might be called "things found on playgrounds." Then ask "Can anyone think of an example that is not on the list that fits in this category?" Continue this process for the entire list.

Then, when using exercise A, after students copy words that go with the main idea, we suggest that the teacher ask, "Do all of these words have the same relationship to the main idea?" Discuss. If children experience difficulty generalizing, you can ask of each copied word "What is the reason that this word is associated with the main idea?"

> **The reader should keep in mind the connection between the principles and applications, on the one hand, and the character traits of a fairminded critical thinker, on the other. Our aim, once again, is not a set of disjointed skills, but an integrated, committed, thinking person.**

Any Old Junk Today?

(Language Arts - 3rd Grade)

Objectives of the Remodelled Lesson

The student will:

• practice clarifying key concepts in a story

• practice critical reading

• discuss assumptions about why some objects are more valuable than others

• discuss two sides of a dispute

• practice using such critical vocabulary as: issue, point of view, imply, relevant, contradiction, assume, criteria

ORIGINAL LESSON PLAN

Abstract

Students read a story about Eddie Wilson and his father. Eddie collects things that he calls 'valuable property,' but his father calls 'junk.' One day, when the family goes to an antique store, Eddie buys two things. At first his father is angry and wants to throw them away. But then he decides he wants one of the objects, and buys it from Eddie. Eddie's mother buys the other. Eddie's father is proud of the profit Eddie has made, and suggests that they go into business together "selling junk."

In the discussion questions, students are asked to do the following things: recall story details; guess Eddie's mother's attitude; list objects found in antique stores; make and justify inferences; describe the difference between junk and antiques; calculate Eddie's profit; and select a sentence which expresses the main idea of the story.

from *Air Pudding and Wind Sauce.*
Theodore L. Harris, et. al. © The Economy Co.
1972 pp. T37-41. Used by permission. All
rights reserved.

Critique

This story describes a clash of two perspectives. The disagreement between Eddie and his father provides an excellent model for many conflicts. It includes a specific issue (i.e. "Does Eddie collect junk or valuable property?"); two sets of incompatible concepts applied to the same phenomena; and two lines of reasoning based on contradictory evaluative assumptions (i.e.: objects which look interesting or appealing are valuable; only those objects which can be used or sold for profit are valuable.) Yet the suggested questions fail to take advantage of the story.

Students are not required to engage in careful critical reading of the story, analysis of the reasoning, or evaluation of the assumptions or arguments implied by numerous details. Although students are asked "What is the difference between junk and antiques?" they do no detailed clarification of concepts, nor apply their insights to the issue.

Most of the inferences required by the lesson only ask students to make calculations about the financial exchanges. The text identifies the key concepts for the students, thereby discouraging independent thought. Students should practice identifying key concepts. The authors assume Mr. Wilson's point of view by referring to Eddie's collection as junk, thereby discouraging open-mindedness.

Strategies Used to Remodel

S-3	fostering reciprocity
S-1	fostering independent thinking
S-10	integrating critical vocabulary
S-12	clarifying ideas
S-21	exploring implications
S-16	distinguishing relevant from irrelevant facts
S-17	making inferences
S-20	recognizing contradictions
S-14	making assumptions explicit
S-15	developing criteria for evaluation

REMODELLED LESSON PLAN

Rather than using the questions in the original lesson, we suggest that the teacher make the disagreement between Eddie and his father the focus of discussion. After students have read the story once, ask, "How would you describe the dispute between Eddie and Mr. Wilson through most of the story? What is the issue?" (Is Eddie's collection junk or valuable property? Should Eddie keep collecting things? etc.) If students give a one-sided formulation (e.g., "Why does Eddie collect all that junk?") ask how the other side sees the issue *S-3* . Insist on a fair formulation; one that doesn't favor either side.

Then ask, "What are the key terms? *S-1* How does Eddie describe his collection? What is it from his father's point of view?" *S-10* Have the students clarify the terms ('junk', 'valuable property', 'rubbish', 'antique', etc.). They should analyze at least one term from each point of view. Ask them for clear examples of each concept. *S-12* Have them discuss disputed and unclear cases. (Keep lists.) Ask them what calling an object 'x' implies about it *S-21* . (For example, junk or rubbish should be thrown away.)

Next, have the students read the story a second time. Tell them to note every detail relevant to the issue *S-16* ; anything that sheds light on the points of view of the main characters.

Relevant details:

• Eddie collects what he calls 'valuable property.'

• Eddie says "I had a very enjoyable day today" whenever he collects something.

• Eddie disagrees with his father's characterization of his collection of 'junk'.

• When his father tries to explain 'antique,' Eddie asks, "You mean junk?"
  Regarding antiques, Eddie says, "Looks like junk to me."

• Eddie thinks he can find valuable property in the antique store.

• Eddie thinks the carriage lamp looks like valuable property.

• Eddie buys a grinder with "Swell wheels."

• Eddie looks at a "swell old" rusty lock.

• Eddie defends his purchases by saying, "Please, Dad. That isn't junk. It's
  valuable antique property."

• Eddie says, "When I grow up, I'm going to sell junk. I can make a lot of money
  selling junk."

• Mr. Wilson calls Eddie's collection 'junk.'

• Mr. Wilson says, "This junk collecting has to stop. Every week the neighbors
  put out all their rubbish, and every Saturday you bring most of that rubbish to
  our house."

• Mr. Wilson says that the telephone pole was "different. I could use that pole."
  And that the pole was the "only thing we were ever able to use."

• Mr. Wilson explains to Eddie that "antiques are old things." And "antique things
  are very valuable. They sell for a lot of money."

• Mr. Wilson calls the rusty lock 'junk.'

• Mr. Wilson starts to dump Eddie's purchases in the rubbish can.

• Mr. Wilson says, "Say! This could be a good carriage lamp!" and pays Eddie for
  it.

• Mr. Wilson says, "How about us selling junk together?"

When they have finished, let them share the details and discuss their significance *S-17* . Have them point out contradictions between Eddie's beliefs and his father's; and inconsistencies and changes of mind within each perspective

S-20 . Ask, "What does Eddie assume? *S-14* His father?" Also ask what criteria each character used when evaluating objects. Regarding changes of mind, ask "What, exactly, changed? Assumptions? Use of terms? Values? etc."

Then have the students review the lists of objects made when clarifying terms. Have them discuss and compare the criteria they used with those of the characters *S-15* . Ask, "What is your point of view on the assumptions we found? What do you think gives objects value?" *S-1* Discuss at length. The teacher may want to split the class into pairs or small groups for discussion. Have students argue each other's positions. *S-3*

Finally, assign an essay or dialogue in which students present arguments about the issues and ideas covered in the discussion.

This is not a "good-boy/bad-boy" approach to thinking, for everyone must think his own way to the ethical insights that underlie becoming a fairminded thinker. We are careful not to judge the content of the student's thinking. Rather, we facilitate a process whereby the student's own insights can be developed.

Listening Game

(Language Arts - 3rd Grade)

Objectives of the Remodelled Lesson

The student will:

- recognize contradictions
- discuss how to judge the accuracy of conflicting versions of a story
- recognize when to suspend judgment
- see how point of view shapes interpretation of events

ORIGINAL LESSON PLAN

OBJECTIVES: Understanding and evaluating sounds in order to remember information, make judgments, and follow directions.

Ask for five volunteers to participate in the game, and have them leave the room. Then read the following story to the class. Read it only once, reminding students to listen very carefully.

The Dizzy King

A king was once very dizzy. He decided that things with wheels made him dizzy, so he told everyone in the kingdom to throw away anything that had wheels. So they threw away cars, bikes, toys, Scotch tape, clocks, watches, and telephones. Everything with wheels went to the dump.

But the king was still dizzy. So he went to see the royal doctor. It was a long walk, because there were no cars. He got hot and even dizzier. He didn't know what time it was because he had no watch.

The royal doctor wasn't home. The king had not been able to telephone to say he was coming, because there were no telephones. So the king had to wait. When the royal doctor finally arrived, he asked the king, "Where are your royal glasses?"

"They are in my pocket, broken," said the king.

"You should be wearing them," said the royal doctor. "If you don't wear them, you will be dizzy all the time."

"Oh, dear," said the king. "I think I have made a mistake."

Ask one student from the class to call in Person 1 and retell the story. Then Person 1 tells Person 2. After all five students have been recalled and retold the story, discuss how it changed. Were details left out? added?

from *Using Our Language.* Dr. Anne D. Ross.
Bowmar Noble Publishing Inc. © Economy Co.
1977. p. 55. Used by permission. All rights
reserved.

Critique

      This lesson addresses only the problem of remembering a number of details from a story. Since the story doesn't involve, or appeal to, anyone's self interest, the lesson overlooks the motives people have for changing stories. Although listening to remember details is an important skill, the more profound problems that children, as well as adults, face in listening carefully involve understanding the story as a whole (of which details are parts,) distinguishing credible from uncredible sources of information, recognizing contradictions, determining the effect of point of view, and suspending judgment when they don't have enough information to know.

Strategies Used to Remodel

S-21 exploring implications

S-2 developing insight into egocentricity

S-20 recognizing contradictions

S-26 suspending judgment

S-19 evaluating source credibility

REMODELLED LESSON PLAN

      First, use the original lesson. Then, when discussing how the story changed, add the following questions: Did any of the changes effect the meaning of the story? **S-21** Which changes? How did they change the meaning? Why did some changes not effect the meaning of the story?

      We then suggest adding a detailed discussion of the motivations people have for changing or distorting stories. **S-2** Ask "Did you ever hear two or more different versions of the same story?" If you need examples to get the students on track, mention how people might describe a fight on the playground differently, siblings might explain a quarrel differently to their parents, etc. (If the students can't come up with personal examples, perhaps they can think of an example from a movie or TV show.)

      After getting a number of examples, have students discuss them. Ask the following questions: Why do you think people told different stories? (To avoid blame; make self or friend look good; make someone else look bad; saw different parts; made different inferences.) Could all of the versions of the story be true? Why or why not? **S-20** (Have students distinguish consistent from contradictory claims. Point out, if necessary, that two contradictory statements

88

cannot both be true.) Could you tell if any particular version of the event was true? Were parts of the story true but not other parts? Can you ever not decide what is true, and therefore suspend judgment? *S-26* Tell us about a time you had to suspend judgment, and why. What could you do to find out what really happened? *S-19* (Find out if the source of information is credible, neutral, in a position to know, usually tells the truth; decide which version of the story is most plausible; find points at which different versions agree.) When is it hardest to find out what happened? (When we lack credible sources, and are not witnesses ourselves.) Point out that being sure is a matter of degree.

Finally, encourage students to think about how their own points of view affect the stories they tell, just as the stories told by others reflect their points of view. Discuss at length. Ask "When is it hardest for you to tell the truth?" Discuss at length. *S-2*

> **Lesson plan remodelling is well done when the person doing the remodel understands the strategies and principles used, when the strategies and principles are well thought-out, when the remodel clearly follows from the critique, and when the remodel teaches critical thinking better than the original.**

The Horse Was In the Parlor

(Language Arts - 3rd Grade)

Objective of the Remodelled Lesson

The student will:

- practice making implied beliefs explicit
- discuss story characters' evaluative assumptions

ORIGINAL LESSON PLAN

Abstract

The students read a story about Pat and Nora, who move into a new, nicer house. They decide to use their old house as a barn for their animals. Nora's aunt, a snobbish woman who had angered the couple by "looking down her nose" at them, writes to say that she will visit again. Nora works hard to make everything ready.

When the aunt arrives, not knowing they have moved, she enters the old house. She thinks that Pat and Nora are living with their animals and says that she will never visit again. After she learns of her mistake and sees the new house, she becomes friendlier toward the young couple.

After reading the story the students are asked to recall details; describe the characters' personalities; say who they liked the most, and reread the funniest parts of the story.

from *Fun All Around,* Nila Banton Smith et al. The Bobbs-Merrill Company, Inc. © International Reading Association.1964. pp. T25,114-120. Used by permission. All rights reserved.

Strategies Used to Remodel

- **S-14** making assumptions explicit
- **S-18** supplying evidence for conclusions
- **S-20** recognizing contradictions
- **S-22** evaluating assumptions
- **S-3** fostering reciprocity

REMODELLED LESSON PLAN

The teacher can take advantage of the ethical nature of the story by having students explore the beliefs and underlying assumptions of the main characters. The class should discuss the following questions: What does it mean to "look down your nose" at someone? What did Aunt Bridget think of Nora and Pat? (She is more important than they are.) What was she assuming? *S-14* (You're a more important person if you have a nicer house.) What did Nora think of Aunt Bridget's attitude? Did she agree with her Aunt's reasoning, or the assumption that your house shows how important you are? How do you know? *S-18* How did Nora try to change her Aunt's opinion of her? What did Aunt Bridget assume when she went into the old house? How did she feel when she learned of her mistake? How do you know?

The teacher should ask students to discuss whether Nora's beliefs are consistent *S-20* . (Although Nora criticizes her Aunt for her pride, she seems to accept the assumption that a person's house shows how important they are.)

The class could also discuss Aunt Bridget's assumption. Ask the students if they agree with the assumption *S-22*. Have them give and discuss their reasons. Ask them to explain why they think Aunt Bridget has that belief, and what reasons she might use to justify it *S-3* .

The class could relate the ideas in the story to their own experiences. Ask: Have you ever worried about what other people thought of you? What assumptions were the people making? Do you agree with those assumptions? Do you use those assumptions when you form opinions of others? When is it important to worry about what other people think of you? When is it not important? Discuss at length.

Socratic questioning should be available to the teacher at all times. Questions, not answers, stimulate the mind.

Kate and the Big Cat

(Language Arts - 3rd Grade)

Objectives of the Remodelled Lesson

The student will:

- infer from pictures, story titles, and unit titles
- practice reciprocity
- distinguish relevant from irrelevant facts for two questions

ORIGINAL LESSON PLAN

Abstract

Students read a story about Kate, who has just moved to a new apartment. Kate has two problems. First, she feels that her parents treat her like a baby. She is discouraged when they hesitate to leave her alone in the new apartment. Her second problem arises while she is alone. As a circus caravan passes by her apartment, a cage door swings open and a tiger jumps out. Kate, after being frustrated by a disbelieving police officer on the phone, develops an ingenious plan for trapping the tiger.

Before reading the story, students are asked to imagine a story that they would write to go with the unit and story titles. Then students read part of the story and state Kate's problem and how they would solve it. Later students are asked to distinguish important from unimportant details concerning what the police would need to know to capture the tiger; predict what Kate will do after the policeman doesn't believe her; and distinguish true from false statements.

from *Air Pudding and Wind Sauce,* Theodore L. Harris et al. The Economy Company. © 1972. pp. T26-34. Used by permission. All rights reserved.

Critique

Two exercises in this lesson give students valuable critical thinking practice: one, (Exercise 3) has students distinguish relevant from irrelevant facts; another, (Rereading Section), requires students to make inferences, rather than simply finding facts in the story.

This lesson, however, misses the opportunity to have students make a number of inferences from story pictures and titles. It fails to have students probe the idea of 'being treated like a baby', or practice reciprocity by taking Kate's parents' point of view. Furthermore, in some cases, this lesson leads students to confuse their pure imaginings with good inferences.

Strategies Used to Remodel

S-17 making inferences

S-12 clarifying ideas

S-3 fostering reciprocity

S-10 integrating critical vocabulary

REMODELLED LESSON PLAN

In the "Story Motivation" section (p.27, of the original lesson), rather than asking students to pretend that they are the author who will write the story to go along with the titles, we suggest asking them "What can we infer that this story is about?" **S-17** Have them distinguish what they are sure of from what is merely possible. (They can infer that there is a big cat; a tiger; someone named Kate; and that the tiger and Kate will have an interaction involving a trick, a trap or a deal. It is fairly safe to assume that the cat is on the loose.)

In the "Guided Reading and Comprehension" section (p.28) we suggest that after the students have described Kate's problem, they discuss what it is like to be treated like a baby. **S-12** Ask, "What does it mean? Why is it a problem? How would Kate rather be treated? Give examples." Then have students consider Kate's parents' point of view. **S-3** Ask "How would her parents describe their treatment of Kate? Why were they reluctant to let Kate stay at home?" Discuss at length.

In Exercise 3 (p.29 of the original lesson), where students are asked to mark the important things Kate should have said to the police when calling for help, we suggest asking of each detail cited, "Is this relevant or irrelevant to the police knowing how to catch the tiger? Why?" **S-10** Then change the problem, and repeat the process for the new problem so that students can see how different problems require different facts. For instance, the teacher may point out that the policeman probably didn't believe Kate because it seemed unlikely that a tiger would be wandering near an apartment. Ask, "If this is true, which of these facts are relevant to Kate when convincing the policeman that she was serious? Why?" (The tiger escaped from the circus truck.)

In the "Story Motivation" section (p.32 of the original lesson), students are asked to say what they think Kate will do about the tiger. In order to discourage students from confusing guesses about the story from inferences, we suggest asking "Do we have any way of knowing what Kate might do?" **S-17** (The students have good reason to conclude that Kate will trap the tiger, but no reason to conclude that she will use any particular method.)

The "Rereading" section (p.34), asks students which statements in a list are true. We suggest asking "Did the story say this or did you have to infer it?" **S-10** Have students either tell where they found the answer or explain how they figured it out. **S-21**

Finally, have students discuss the following questions: Did Kate solve both of her problems? How?

School time is too precious to spend any sizeable portion of it on random facts. The world, after all, is filled with an infinite number of facts. No one can learn more than an infinitesimal portion of them. Though we need facts and information, there is no reason why we cannot gain facts as part of the process of learning how to think.

Poor Little Puppy

(Language Arts - 3rd Grade)

Objectives of the Remodelled Lesson

The student will:

- explore the nature of pride and shame
- recognize and evaluate story characters' assumptions

ORIGINAL LESSON PLAN

Abstract

Students read a story about Sam and Sally who have a new puppy, Lady, of which they are very proud. One day a big boy comes by and makes fun of Lady. Sam and Sally begin to compare Lady to other people's dogs, and realize that there are many things she cannot do. They try to teach her several new tricks to no avail. The children feel ashamed of their puppy. Sam and Sally have given up in dismay when a little boy comes by and loses his ball down a deep hole. Lady saves the day by digging the ball out. Sam and Sally are again proud of Lady.

Students are asked to answer factual questions about the story, and discuss the following questions: What kind of boy was the big boy who made fun of Lady? What would you have said if someone had made fun of your dog? Why did Lady not learn to do the tricks that Sam and Sally tried to teach her? Why was digging for a ball a trick she did not have to learn?

from *Fun All Around,* Nila Banton Smith et al. The Bobbs-Merrill Company, Inc. © International Reading Association.1964. pp. T12-13, 24-33. Used by permission. All rights reserved.

Strategies Used To Remodel

S-14	making assumptions explicit
S-22	evaluating assumptions
S-12	clarifying ideas
S-4	exploring thoughts underlying feelings

REMODELLED LESSON PLAN

In order to probe the central ideas of pride and shame, when the story has been read, the teacher should supplement the original questions with the following: "How did Sam and Sally feel about Lady at first? Why? What happened to make them ashamed of Lady? What did they assume? **S-14** (Dogs aren't good unless they can do tricks.) Is it a good assumption? **S-22** Why or why not? Why do you think they made that assumption? (Discuss at length.) How did they act toward Lady when they felt ashamed? How else could they have reacted to the boy? Why did they become proud again? What about the situation changed? (They learned about something Lady could do well. Their assumption didn't change.) What reasons should people have for being proud of their puppies? Ashamed? **S-12** (Compile lists and compare.) Would everything on the 'proud' list have to be true of your puppy for you to be proud of it?"

As an extension, the class could discuss and evaluate other reasons for feeling proud and ashamed. Encourage students to make the reasoning underlying the feelings explicit **S-4** . Ask, "If you felt ashamed of your family, what might you be thinking? What else could you think that would make you feel differently?"

To think critically about issues we must be able to consider the strengths and weaknesses of opposing points of view. Since critical thinkers value fair-mindedness, they feel that it is especially important that they entertain positions with which they disagree.

The Camel and the Jackal
(Language Arts - 3rd Grade)

Objective of the Remodelled Lesson

The student will practice giving reasons for moral judgments.

ORIGINAL LESSON PLAN

Abstract

Students read a story about two animals. The jackal wants to cross the river to get crab to eat, but he can't swim. So he tells the camel that there is sugar cane, which the camel loves, across the river. After they cross the river, and the jackal has eaten his fill, he runs to the sugar cane field, and laughs and sings, catching the attention of people nearby. He hides while the people attack the camel and chase him away. The jackal explains to the camel "I always laugh and sing after dinner." The camel takes him back across the river. Halfway across, the camel says "I always roll over after dinner." He does so, and the jackal falls into the water.

The students are asked to recall story details, decide which animal is smarter, and which they like the most.

from *Fun All Around,* Nila Banton Smith et al. The Bobbs-Merrill Company, Inc. © International Reading Association.1964. pp. 200-3, T35. Used by permission. All rights reserved.

Strategy Used to Remodel

S-25 evaluating actions

REMODELLED LESSON PLAN

In order to take advantage of the moral nature of the story, the class should discuss and evaluate the actions of the animals *S-25* . Interrupt the story after each deception or trick and ask "Was this fair? Why or why not? Could he have done something better? What? What makes you think that would be better?" At the end of the story, ask "Is this the best way for the camel to have taught the jackal a lesson? Why or why not?" Discuss at length.

Introduction to Remodelling Social Studies Lesson Plans

People respond to social issues from one of a variety of mutually inconsistent points of view. Each point of view rests on assumptions about human nature. The unreflective adoption of one point of view as the truth limits our understanding of issues. Therefore, practice entering into and coming to understand divergent points of view is crucial to Social Studies. Children already face the kinds of issues studied in Social Studies and are in the process of developing a set of assumptions about human nature. The assumptions they make concern issues like the following:

> What does it mean to belong to a group? What rights and responsibilities do I have? Does it matter if others do not approve of me? Is it worthwhile to be good? What is most important to me? How am I like and unlike others? Whom should I trust? Who are my friends and enemies?

Adults, as well as children, tend to assume their own unexamined points of view. People often discredit or misinterpret ideas based on assumptions different than their own. In order to address social issues critically, it is essential that students continually evaluate their assumptions by contrasting them with opposing assumptions. From the beginning, Social Studies instruction should encourage the fair-minded discussion of a variety of points of view and their underlying beliefs.

Traditional lessons cover several important subjects within Social Studies: politics, economics, history, and psychology. They stress the importance of good citizenship, emphasizing pride in country and the importance of people working together. They compare and contrast our culture with other cultures and encourage students not to criticize them. They stress that it is important to accept a diversity of points of view in the student's peer group, community, nation, and world. Some lessons are designed to increase a student's self-awareness and empathy by discussing feelings, beliefs, and the consequences of actions. The materials, however, typically fall short of teaching the subject matter in a way that best fosters critical thought.

Traditional lessons do not usually discuss the difficulty of being a good citizen (e.g., getting information before voting;) nor do they discuss the positive aspects of dissent, i.e., the benefits of considering different ideas. Texts consistently confuse facts with ideals (especially about the U.S.) and genuine patriotism with show of patriotism or false patriotism. The first confusion discourages us from seeing ourselves, others, and the world accurately; we often don't see the gap between how we want to be and how we are. The second encourages us to reject constructive criticism.

Although the texts treat diversity of opinion as necessary, opinions are not presented as subject to examination or critique. Students are encouraged to accept that others have different beliefs, but are not encouraged to understand why; yet it is by understanding how others have reached their conclusions that students can learn what other points of view have to offer, and can strengthen their own views accordingly. The text writers's emphasis on simple tolerance serves to end discussion, whereas students should learn to consider all beliefs as subjects of rational discussion.

When contrasting our nation with others, students are not encouraged to recognize and combat their own natural ethnocentricity. Texts encourage ethnocentricity in two ways. First, the text writers often present American ideals as uniquely American when, in fact, everyone shares at least some of them. Second, although beliefs about the state of the world, and about how to achieve ideals vary greatly, the American version of these is often treated as universal or self-evident. Students should learn not to confuse their limited perspective with universal belief; they should practice entertaining points of view of people who see the world differently than most Americans. They should see that others see themselves and the United States differently than we do, and critique their own point of view, making it increasingly more accurate, in light of the strengths of these different points of view.

The lessons designed to foster self-awareness and empathy overlook the intimate relationship between feelings and thoughts. Too often people experience their feelings as "just happening" to them, or as the direct and necessary result of situations, rather than seeing feelings as logically connected to the way they think about situations. Lessons about feelings could be used to foster insight into the relationship between thoughts and feelings and to show how each illuminates the other.

TOOLS
(Social Studies - Kindergarten)

Objective of the Remodelled Lesson

To emphasize the defining characteristics of tools.

ORIGINAL LESSON PLAN

Abstract

Students are asked to comment on what tools can be used to make specific tasks easier; to review pictures of tools and tell what jobs they help people do; to state which of the pictured tools are in their classroom; to draw pictures of tools which are in the classroom but not already pictured on their activity sheets; to divide pictures into two categories -- "tools in the classroom" and "tools not in the classroom"; to discuss what kinds of jobs tools help people do and whether more than one job can be done by certain tools; and to classify tools as cleaning, cutting, or lifting tools. In all cases the tools are ones that students are probably familiar with.

from *Me*, Harlan S. Hansen et al. Houghton Mifflin Company. © 1976. pp. 140-143 Used by permission. All rights reserved.

Strategies Used To Remodel

S-1   fostering independent thinking

S-12 clarifying ideas

REMODELLED LESSON PLAN

Rather than giving students a set of categories, students should list tools they've seen used, and develop their own ways to categorize them. *S-1* Encourage students to accept multiple sets of categories as appropriate.

Then, in order for children to develop a clear concept of tools and the value of tools the teacher should add examples of objects not ordinarily thought of as tools, *S-12* e.g., some Latin women use scarves, that we think of as decorative clothing, for carrying groceries and babies. People who lived a long, long time ago used rocks as tools. People pass the hat to collect and carry money. We can use sticks to draw or write in the dirt. We can use a piece of paper as a megaphone. The students should be asked to think of examples of things they use as tools. They could then be asked whether that use is typical or usual (what the thing was designed to do) or unusual (using something in a way not designed.)

Seeing a variety of ways in which the various component strategies can be used in classroom settings: What do critical thinkers do? Why? What do they avoid doing? Why? When can this aspect of critical thought be fostered? What questions or activities foster it?

How Is My School Like My Home?

(Social Studies - Kindergarten)

Objectives of the Remodelled Lesson

The student will:

- practice suspending judgment
- practice using probability qualifiers
- practice using critical thinking vocabulary

ORIGINAL LESSON PLAN

Abstract

Students discuss some of their basic needs, e.g. love, food, shelter and clothing, and how they meet those needs. Then they are given twelve pictures of children at home or school having these needs met. Students are asked what need is being met in each. Finally, they sort the pictures into two groups: needs met at home; needs met at school.

from *Me*, Harlan S. Hansen et al. Houghton Mifflin Company. © 1976. pp. 106-7 Used by permission. All rights reserved.

Critique

Young children have an especially hard time saying they don't know. They need practice distinguishing cases in which they do have enough information to know, from cases in which they don't. This lesson misses the opportunity to have them do so. This lesson can also be used to have students practice using analytic vocabulary Furthermore, this lesson is a missed opportunity to have students recognize that many of their beliefs should be held with varying degrees of tentativeness.

Strategies Used to Remodel

S-26 suspending judgment

S-10 integrating critical vocabulary

S-27 using probability qualifiers

REMODELLED LESSON PLAN

We suggest that the teacher encourage suspension of judgment by adding pictures that aren't clearly home or school, e.g., two children playing in a sandbox **S-26** . Also **S-10** , have students practice using the terms "infer" and "suspended judgment." The teacher should ask of each picture "Can you infer if this is at school or at home?" and have the students give reasons to support their conclusions. If the cases aren't clear cases, but there are some clues that point to the probability of it being a school or a home, have students practice using probability qualifiers **S-27** , e.g., "This is probably a school, because there are five children working on a project, and that happens more often at school than at home."

A teacher committed to teaching for critical thinking must think beyond subject matter teaching to ends and objectives that transcend subject matter classification. To teach for critical thinking is, first of all, to create an environment that is conducive to critical thinking.

Do Communities Change?

(Social Studies - Kindergarten)

Objectives of the Remodelled Lesson

The student will:

- practice evaluating community changes
- practice reciprocity

ORIGINAL LESSON PLAN

Abstract

First, students review changes that have occurred in their personal lives (e.g., height, weight). Then they discuss a number of common community changes and how they feel about them.

from *Me*, Harlan S. Hansen et al. Houghton Mifflin Company. © 1976. pp. 126-7 Used by permission. All rights reserved.

Strategies Used to Remodel

S-12 clarifying ideas

S-3 fostering reciprocity

REMODELLED LESSON PLAN

In order to allow students to evaluate changes, the question from the original lesson "How do you feel about this kind of change in your community?" should be followed by "Is this a good change or a bad change? Why?" *S-12* Take note of the children's responses and discuss each one afterwards. When referring to their responses, point out the features that good changes have in common, and then do the same for bad changes.

In addition, the students could use this lesson to practice reciprocity. *S-3* After encouraging them to give as many responses, and reasons for their responses, as possible, ask "Do you think someone else might like a change that you didn't? Why?" If students cannot think of any reason someone would disagree with them, the teacher should provide examples. Discuss at length.

Why Did the Girl Say "No"?

(Social Studies - 1st Grade)

Objective of the Remodelled Lesson

To introduce critical vocabulary to students.

ORIGINAL LESSON PLAN

Abstract

Students are asked to examine decisions, and figure out what was important to the person who made the decision. Among the decisions they examine is the following: A teacher chooses between a pair of worn, comfortable looking shoes and a pair of fashionable, less comfortable looking shoes. Students are expected to infer whether the teacher most values comfort or fashion.

from *Things We Do*, Frank L. Ryan, et al.
Houghton Mifflin Co. © 1976. pp. T116-117.
Used by permission. All rights reserved.

Strategy Used to Remodel

S-10 integrating critical vocabulary

REMODELLED LESSON PLAN

The teacher should rephrase questions and comments to include critical thinking vocabulary *S-10* . For concepts that you are introducing, ask each question twice; first with the new term, and then with words the students are familiar with. For example, ask "What did the girl's response imply about what she thinks is most important? What did the girl's response tell us about what is most important to her?" The teacher should also rephrase student responses to include the vocabulary. For example, if a student says "I think comfort is most important to you," say "You inferred from my action that comfort is most important to me." Continue this process throughout the lesson.

Emotions: Anger
(Social Studies - 1st Grade)

Objective of the Remodelled Lesson

The student will discuss the relationship between thoughts and feelings.

ORIGINAL LESSON PLAN

Abstract

We have selected two lessons on anger from a series of lessons on children and emotions.

In the first lesson, students are asked to interpret what a boy in a picture is feeling, and to cite specific context clues to support their interpretation. They then discuss what makes them feel angry. Following this, students review two sets of pictures in which someone is allegedly portrayed as being angry. Students are asked "Why are they angry? When do you feel this way?" In summary, students are asked to mention things that make people angry, and to discuss whether they think everyone is angry sometimes.

In the second lesson, students are asked to describe a picture (of three children working together, shooing away a girl who wants to join them) and infer that the girl is angry. They discuss two ways she could keep from being angry (by playing by herself, by bringing materials to the group and thereby gain admittance).

from *Things We Do*, Frank L. Ryan, et al.
Houghton Mifflin Co. © 1976. pp. T66-9.
Used by permission. All rights reserved.

Critique

Critical thinking requires understanding oneself. When feelings are discussed in terms of the thoughts associated with them, they can be more fully explored. We can probe the bases of our feelings by understanding the thoughts behind them. Thinking about our thoughts helps us better understand our feelings. The reverse is also true. Using the insight that our thoughts and feelings are connected, we can use our feelings to better understand our thinking.

This lesson misses the opportunity to develop this crucial insight. Students should practice discussing their feelings and thoughts in relation to one another, and finding the assumptions behind their feelings.

Strategies Used to Remodel

S-4 exploring thoughts underlying feelings

S-10 integrating critical vocabulary

S-14 making assumptions explicit

REMODELLED LESSON PLAN

This remodel will stress the relationship between thoughts and feelings, and how changing the way one thinks about a situation can change the way one feels.

In the first lesson, follow the question "Why do you think the people in these pictures are angry?" with "What kinds of things are they probably thinking?" *S-4* . If the students don't mention that being angry involves thinking that something isn't right or fair, point this out. Use critical thinking vocabulary whenever possible *S-10* . We suggest the use of the following format:

What happened?

What was assumed?

What was concluded?

How did the person feel?

In the second lesson, after asking "How do you think the girl who is being told to stay away feels?" and "Why?" encourage different responses, rather than forcing the conclusion that the girl is angry. Some students, for example, may recognize that the girl may feel hurt. For each response ask, "If she feels ... , then what is she probably thinking?" *S-4* (again, use format above). In the original lesson, they ask "What could the girl do to keep from being angry?" We suggest stressing to students the important relationship between thoughts and feelings. If the students don't mention them, point out that there are two ways to change how you feel: you can change the situation, or change how you think about the situation.

When doing a unit on emotions, we believe that the class should discuss as great a variety of emotions as the student can name. For each emotion, have students give examples of when someone may feel it. Put the examples into the above format. Then have the students discuss the kinds of assumptions operating behind different emotions *S-14* .

Examples (using format)

A. Student states, "I got mad at Sally because she pushed me down." Use questions to elicit explanations.

1. You felt Sally push you down and it hurt.

2. You assume that people should not hurt each other.

3. You concluded that Sally was wrong to push you down.

4. That's why you felt mad.

B. Student states, "I was excited because my birthday was the next day."

1. You knew your birthday was the next day.

2. You assumed that birthdays are fun.

3. You concluded that you would have fun.

4. That's why you felt excited.

The highest development of intelligence and conscience creates a natural marriage between the two. Each is distinctly limited without the other. Each requires special attention in the light of the other.

How Would You End the Conflict?

(Social Studies - 1st Grade)

Objective of the Remodelled Lesson

Students will practice evaluating solutions to conflicts.

ORIGINAL LESSON PLAN

Abstract

Students discuss pictures of three conflicts. They are asked to state the causes of the disagreements; draw pictures which show how they would resolve the disagreements; and explain the reasons for their choices. The "Summary and Evaluation" section asks students to consider why other students prefer solutions different from their own.

from *Things We Do*, Frank L. Ryan, et al.
Houghton Mifflin Co. © 1976. pp. T132-3.
Used by permission. All rights reserved.

Critique

This lesson gives students valuable practice in reciprocity when asking them to consider why other students might choose solutions to conflicts which are different from their own. Overall, however, this lesson discourages the evaluation of solutions by stating that "there are no right or wrong solutions" when, in fact, some solutions are clearly better than others.

By focusing on preference as the sole criterion for judging resolutions, the lesson suggests that there can be no objectivity, shared standards, or rational discussion.

Strategy Used to Remodel

S-24 evaluating solutions

REMODELLED LESSON PLAN

For each conflict discussed, the teacher should ask students for examples of good and bad solutions to the conflicts presented. Keep a list of these under headings of "good" and "bad". Ask the students for reasons why each solution is good or bad, focusing their attention on the consequences **S-24** . Begin a separate category for solutions provided by students which are not clearly good or bad. Ask students what the good solutions have in common and what the bad solutions have in common. The class can also discuss why some solutions were hard to judge. To summarize the lesson, have students compare solutions, focusing on comparing reasons and consequences. For more detailed information about evaluating solutions refer to the 3rd grade Social Studies lesson remodel entitled "Problem Solving" p. 138.

Getting experience in lesson plan remodelling: How can I take full advantage of the strengths of this lesson? How can this material best be used to foster critical insights? Which questions or activities should I drop, use, alter or expand upon? What should I add to it?

Rules
(Social Studies - 1st Grade)

Objective of the Remodelled Lesson

The student will probe deeper into the nature of rules.

ORIGINAL LESSON PLAN

Abstract

Half of the lessons in this unit focus on a class planning a field trip, and discussing rules they need to make. The rest discuss laws, police, and rules in the home. The unit covers the following points: We need rules to keep us safe, and give everyone a fair chance. Bad consequences would arise if we had no rules. Laws are necessary. Police help us. Families have rules. Rules help families. Everyone is responsible for following rules.

from *At School*. Virginia Finley, et al. of TIEGS-ADAMS; PEOPLE AND THEIR HERITAGE, © Copyright, 1983. by Silver, Burdett & Ginn Inc. pp.34-39. Used with permission.

Critique

This lesson is a missed opportunity to encourage students to recognize how rules are based on human purposes and therefore can and should change according to those purposes. Students should practice evaluating rules, and explaining how to change them, and why. They should also discuss how human needs, and sense of right and wrong, often require suspending or making exceptions to rules. The class should also discuss how individual and group interests affect how we use rules. And students should think about their impulses to apply rules inconsistently or break them. Students should learn to recognize that rules should be changed if they do not meet the alleged purpose, or when the purpose itself should be rejected.

Strategies Used to Remodel

S-12 clarifying ideas

S-6 exploring underlying purposes

S-2 developing insight into egocentricity

S-13 distinguishing ideas

REMODELLED LESSON PLAN

The teacher should facilitate discussion of the following questions:

1. What is a rule? *S-12*

2. Do you ever make rules? Why do you make them? *S-6*

3. Are there good rules and bad rules? What's the difference between good rules and bad ones? (Have students give examples of each and compare.) *S-12*

4. Why is it sometimes OK to ignore rules? (If the teacher has recently made an exception to a rule in class, students may discuss its justification. Encourage students to give their own examples of exceptions to rules.) *S-6*

5. Why do we sometimes break rules when we shouldn't? *S-2* (Students can discuss when they wanted to break or did break a rule.) Why did you feel that way? What were the consequences? Did you think the rule was a good rule? Do you feel differently when you break a rule than when someone else does, e.g., borrowing without permission?

6. What different kinds of rules are there? *S-13* How and why are they different? Does breaking them have different consequences? Does it follow that it is worse to break one kind of rule than another? (Compare games to safety rules, for example.)

To sum up, have students give examples of rules they would like to change, and have them discuss why they think they should be changed. The teacher should point out to the students when their reasons fall into the aforementioned categories, i.e. the rule doesn't meet the purpose, the purpose should be rejected. Encourage further class discussion of examples given.

When discussing rules, keep in mind the points below.

A. All rules have a purpose.

B. Analyzing the purpose helps us evaluate rules.

C. All rules have advantages and disadvantages.

D. To change a rule you must show that either: (1) the rule doesn't meet the purpose, or (2) the purpose should be rejected.

One does not learn about critical thinking by memorizing a definition or set of distinctions.

Our Country's Birthday and Martin Luther King, Jr.'s Birthday
(Social Studies - 1st Grade)

Objectives of the Remodelled Lesson

The student will:

• develop the idea of personal freedom in America

• practice making the distinction between facts and ideals

• distinguish the idea of "free from England" from "freedoms of individuals"

• practice recognizing assumptions

ORIGINAL LESSON PLAN

Abstract

We have put these two lessons together because of the important relationship between their subjects. In the first lesson, students read and discuss a passage about the 4th of July. Students are informed that, on July 4, 1776, Americans said they wanted to be free from England. We celebrate the day because we are proud to be free. In the discussion they are told that with freedom comes responsibilty, and that freedom can be lost if tyrants take over.

In the second lesson, students are told that: January 15 is Martin Luther King's birthday; he was an important leader of Black people; he believed in peace; he was given the Nobel Peace Prize. The teachers' text mentions some discriminatory social policies King opposed.

from *At School*. Virginia Finley, et al. of TIEGS-ADAMS; PEOPLE AND THEIR HERITAGE, © Copyright, 1983. by Silver, Burdett & Ginn Inc. pp.81,91. Used with permission.

Critique

The first lesson confuses two different senses of 'freedom': 'freedom (of the country) from England', and 'freedom of individual Americans'. The first we achieved after the Revolutionary War. The second, we must continually strive to achieve and perfect. The text, by neglecting this distinction, implies that the struggle to achieve individual freedom ended with our separation from England. Therefore, it confuses facts with ideals. Furthermore, by suggesting that the primary danger to freedom is the possibility of a tyrant taking over, the text neglects the more

113

constant problem of some people not having freedoms. Some groups, such as Blacks, women, and Native Americans, have only recently had freedoms equal to or approaching those of other Americans. During the McCarthy era, many Americans lost freedoms. Students need to see how the ideal of individual freedom has been violated in the past, in order to understand what safeguarding these freedoms really involves.

The second lesson is vague because it does not explain the variety of problems that black people faced and therefore why King was an important leader. It also confuses facts with ideals by neglecting to discuss the conditions of many black Americans today, and therefore may suggest that the race problems have been solved. Furthermore, King was a leader in the Civil Rights Movement; not only Blacks followed him. The text, however, refers to him merely as a leader of Blacks.

Strategies Used to Remodel

S-13   distinguishing ideas
S-12   clarifying ideas
S-9   distinguishing facts from ideals
S-14   making assumptions explicit
S-8   discouraging stereotyping

REMODELLED LESSON PLAN
First Lesson

In the following lesson remodel there may be a number of times when the students may not be able to supply the information called for. It is important, however, that they be given the opportunity to struggle with each question before the teacher provides the material.

After the students have read the first lesson, the teacher should draw the students' attention to the two uses of 'freedom' in the passage. *S-13* Ask "What does 'free from England' mean?" If they cannot answer, point out that when Americans were under English rule they weren't allowed to make many important decisions for themselves because the people in America weren't fully represented in the English government. Then have the students reread the last sentence on the page. Ask "What does the text mean by 'we are proud to be free'? Does the text mean merely that we are proud to be free from England?" Allow time for students to respond. If the students haven't recognized the different meaning of 'freedom', mention our individual freedoms. Then discuss some of the freedoms we have. *S-12* Tell the students about one of our freedoms (such as freedom of religion) and explain what it means (no one can force us to believe in or practice a particular religion). Then ask the students if they know of any other freedoms that we have. Have them label and explain them. Use questions to help the students clarify them when needed. Supply important freedoms the students miss such as, freedom of speech, freedom to travel and live where we want, freedom of assembly, freedom to choose our occupation, freedom of peaceful protest, freedom to vote however we want, freedom to run for public office, etc.

Mention that having these freedoms is an important American ideal. Ask the students if they know what an ideal is. If not, explain that an ideal is something that we value highly, and try to achieve. Point out that success is a matter of degree (like cold and hot), rather than simply a matter of all or nothing (like a light switch), **S-12**   Ask the students if they have any ideals that they have trouble living up to. The teacher may use an example from his personal experience here, such as "Being kind and pleasant to my friends is an ideal, but sometimes I lose my temper and snap at them. This makes me feel bad because I haven't lived up to my ideals. I know I have to try harder."

Return the discussion to American ideals. Say "Since we achieved freedom from England we have had these ideals, though many of them have not been facts for all Americans since then." Use examples here such as treatment of Native Americans, mention that women couldn't vote until 1919, or that in the 1950's many people got into trouble because of friends they had, or groups they joined.

Finally, have students review the distinction between individual freedom, and freedom from England.

Second Lesson

When students have read the second lesson, ask "What does this text mean by 'his people? What does 'his dream was about a better life for his people' assume about their lives? (that their lives were not good enough). **S-14**   Do you know about any of the problems that Blacks faced that King was struggling against?" **S-12**

Then refer back to the discussion of individual freedom from the previous lesson. The teacher should mention that among the problems that blacks faced was the lack of some of these freedoms. Discuss a few of these such as: many blacks weren't allowed to vote, they couldn't get jobs they wanted because of prejudice and inferior education, they often couldn't live where they wanted because white people wouldn't sell or rent houses to them, etc. Stress that these examples show the difference between the ideals of the country, and facts about the country. **S-9** Point out that good citizens work to change the facts that are opposed to our ideals. You may also want to point out some of the other examples of discriminatory

115

treatment of blacks, if the students are unfamiliar with them (separate bathrooms, water fountains, restaurants, schools, 'back of the bus', etc.).

Next, ask students if they know why King was an important American leader. (He worked, sacrificed, even spent time in jail, in order to bring the country closer to its ideals.) Ask, "For whom was King a leader?" (He was a leader for most people who supported the Civil Rights movement, whatever their color.)

S-8

To summarize these two lessons, ask "Are Americans more free today than they were in 1776 when we gained independence from England?" Allow discussion. Have them give examples of ways in which we may or may not be freer. Elicit ideas about why our freedoms are important.

If we simply present the teacher with pre-packaged finished lesson plans, ones designed by the ciritcal thinking of someone else, someone who used a process that is not clearly understood by the teacher, then a major opportunity for the teacher to develop her own critical thinking skills, insights, and motivations will have been lost.

Schools in India
(Social Studies 2nd Grade)

Objectives of the Remodelled Lesson

The student will:

 • practice clarifying the concept 'school'

 • distinguish relevant from irrelevant facts

ORIGINAL LESSON PLAN

Abstract

The students read and discuss their text, which covers the following points: since India is poor, not all children can go to school; not all schools have school buildings; sometimes villagers build school buildings; many adults go to school at night; children in India learn reading, writing, health, and practical skills.

from *Families and Social Needs,* Frederick M. King et al. By permission of Laidlaw Brothers, A Division of Doubleday & Company, Inc.. 1968. pp. 119-121, T107-109.

Critique

In order to think clearly and accurately about ideas, it is necessary to distinguish features which are necessarly related to an idea from those which we simply associate with the idea. Although the original lesson discusses some of the similarities and differences among schools, it does not emphasize what is fundamental to all schools. The students miss a chance to practice struggling to clarify a concept. Furthermore, the material about schools in India encourages stereotyping by giving the impression that all schools are small village schools with no electricity or other modern conveniences.

Strategies Used to Remodel

S-12 clarifying ideas

S-8 discouraging stereotyping

S-16 distinguishing relevant from irrelevant facts

S-10 integrating critical vocabulary

REMODELLED LESSON PLAN

As an introduction, ask the children, "What do you think of when you think of school?" **S-12** Make a permanent list of the children's responses; it can later be compared to material discussed in the lesson.

Then review the original text materials about schools in India. Ask "Are all Indian schools like these? **S-8** Are there cities in India? Are there schools in the cities? Are those schools like the schools in the text? Like ours?"

In order to distinguish relevant from irrelevant criteria concerning what makes a school a school **S-16** , the teacher should take each association listed earlier, and ask if there are any counter-examples. (Responses will fall into two types: too limiting, and not limiting enough.) For instance, if a student says "Schools have lots of books," the teacher could ask, "Is there a place that has a lot of books but isn't a school?" or "Are there schools that don't have a lot of books?" Continue this process for as many responses as possible. The students should not be expected to arrive at an accurate definition, but rather practice struggling with the concept. As the list is discussed, the teacher should write each item on the board under the headings "Relevant to being a school" and "Irrelevant to being a   school." This will give students practice using critical vocabulary **S-10** as well as clarifying ideas **S-12** .

Finally, give a short writing assignment in which the students describe what 'school' means.

The analytical vocabulary in the English language, with such terms as 'assume', 'infer', 'conclude', 'criteria', 'point of view', 'relevance', 'issue', 'contradiction', 'credibility', 'evidence', 'distinguish', enables us to think more precisely about our thinking.

At the Television Studio

(Social Studies - 2nd Grade)

Objectives of the Remodelled Lesson

The student will:

- develop an understanding of the purpose and nature of ads
- learn to recognize common tricks of the trade in children's commercials
- discuss ways of being a smart consumer
- practice analyzing ads

ORIGINAL LESSON PLAN

Student text: At the televison studio.

Bob's mother works at a television studio. She is taking pictures for a program. The program is about pets. A dog food company pays for the program. Part of the program tells about dog food. The company wants people to buy its dog food. Bob's dog is a television star. Her name is Dusty. She helps sell the dog food.

STUDENT OBJECTIVES: The student should understand that: (1) the costs of commercial television are met by selling program time to sponsors. (2) A company that buys program time uses part of that time to sell the product the company makes. (3) Some television studios move around on trucks.

STUDENT ATTITUDES: Recognizing that the purpose of advertising is to convince the consumer to buy a product. Appreciating the importance of using good judgment in choosing television programs. Practicing courtesy and thoughtfulness in use of the television at home.

CREATING INTEREST: Discuss with students why companies sponsor entertainment or informational programs that have no direct bearing on the products that they make and sell. Help children realize that in sponsoring a program on a regular basis a sponsor's name and product are automatically connected with the show. Discuss with children why thousands of dollars are spent to produce a television commercial.

GUIDING READING AND LEARNING: Have students read the text silently. Afterward, ask why Bob's mother is taking pictures of Dusty eating dog food. Ask students why they think people buy things they see advertised on television. Have students name some of the things they have wanted after viewing a television commercial.

Discuss with the class the differences between commercial television and public television. You may need to point out that public stations rely on public, government, and business contributions to pay for their operating costs.

Write on the chalkboard Plan and Work Together. Ask pupils why they think planning is important in making television programs. Also ask what would happen if the many different people on a program did not work well together.

from *In Neighborhoods,* Virginia Finley, et al. of TIEGS-ADAMS; PEOPLE AND THEIR HERITAGE, © Copyright, 1982. by Silver, Burdett & Ginn Inc. p.9 Used with permission.

Critique

This was one of a very few lessons that discussed advertising, so we decided to focus our critique and remodel on that aspect of the lesson. Since most school-age children have been exposed to and influenced by commercials, a lesson on evaluating advertising could be an opportunity to help students recognize manipulative techniques, and so be in a better position to decide which products to choose.

The most serious problem with this lesson is that it doesn't explicitly have students follow out the implications of the statement "the purpose of advertising is to convince the consumer to buy." Therefore it does not cover the ways in which ads are often designed to mislead the audience. When they ask students why people buy products they've seen advertised, they should also have students reflect on the adequacy of those reasons. Although it asks the students to name things they have wanted after seeing commercials, it misses the opportunity to have students examine the ways ads influence them. They should ask the students why they wanted those products and discuss whether those products met their expectations. Furthermore, rather than using a dog food commercial as its example, it should have used a commercial aimed at children. And finally, by not discussing how a smart consumer would decide which product to buy, the lesson doesn't help the student overcome the influence of commericals.

Strategies Used to Remodel

S-21 exploring implications

S-12 clarifying ideas

S-19 evaluating source credibility

S-16 distinguishing relevant from irrelevant facts

REMODELLED LESSON PLAN

Before doing this lesson, the teacher should spend as much time as possible watching children's commercials. Rather than using the original, begin this lesson with the following questions *S-21* : "What are commercials and other advertisements? Why are they made? What does this purpose imply about ads? (Advertisers try to make the product look good and don't tell you what's wrong with it.) Have any of you ever wanted something after seeing a commercial for it? Why did you want it? Have you ever gotten something you wanted after seeing an ad? Were the products what you expected them to be like? Have you ever not loved a product when an ad had convinced you that you would?" Point out that although advertisers cannot lie, they can mislead. If students have trouble understanding this, use an example of a child defending herself as an analogy. *S-12* For example, a child may truthfully say, "I didn't touch the lamp" when she knocked the table the lamp was on, causing it to fall and break. In a case like this, we would not praise the child for telling the truth.

Next, have the students brainstorm different ways in which commercials try to convince the audience to buy. Write these on the board. (E.g., Commercials show children playing with toys and acting as though they are having a great time. They claim that everyone wants their product, and suggest that you will be the only one left out if you don't get it. Announcers use an excited tone of voice. Cereal companies advertise toys and contests that they put in or on boxes. Showing food and showing people eating food make you hungry for the food.) Then have the students discuss the items they listed. For each, ask, "Is this misleading?" *S-19* If the students miss the following points, bring them up: children in commercials are actors paid to look like they are having fun; there may be no difference between an advertised, more expensive product, and an unadvertised, cheaper product; some aspects of commercials have nothing to do with the product (e.g., cartoon characters, designed as advertising gimmicks.)

Then discuss what being a smart consumer entails. *S-16* Ask students how they should decide which product is the best to buy. Make sure that the following points are covered: comparing the product to similar products, past experience with similar products, distinguishing facts about products from irrelevant or misleading information *S-16* , talking to people who have tried the product.

Finally, teachers with access to VCR's should videotape commercials for children's products, show them in class, and discuss them. If the teacher doesn't have access to a VCR, bring in other forms of advertising for children's products.

Sue's Mistake
(Social Studies - 2nd Grade)

Objective of the Remodelled Lesson

The student will probe deeper into the idea of "learning from a careless mistake."

ORIGINAL LESSON PLAN

Abstract

The student's text tells about a student, Sue, who forgot her field-trip permission slip. Her father brings it to her, and she apologizes. The discussion includes the following ideas: Sue's mistake inconvenienced her father. Everyone makes mistakes. When we make mistakes we should apologize and thank anyone who helps us. We should learn from our mistakes.

The reinforcement activities suggest the following situations for role play: a child breaks a window; a child scatters raked leaves; a child leaves his jacket outside; a child forgets to give water to his pet dog.

> from *At School*. Virginia Finley, et al. of TIEGS-ADAMS; PEOPLE AND THEIR HERITAGE, © Copyright, 1983. by Silver, Burdett & Ginn Inc. pp.42-3. Used with permission.

Strategies Used to Remodel

S-26 suspending judgment
S-12 clarifying ideas

REMODELLED LESSON PLAN

First, since the question "Did Sue learn from her mistake?" encourages students to come to a conclusion when the evidence provided is inadequate, replace it with "How could we tell if Sue had learned from her mistake? *S-26* If Sue had learned, how would she behave in the future?" *S-12* These questions will give students practice distinguishing learning from a mistake in a practical sense, from substituting verbal rituals for a change in behavior.

122

Then, after the roleplaying exercises in the original lesson (which encourage students to accept responsibility and say "I'm sorry,") have a general discussion of how learning from a mistake involves more than just saying you are sorry.

The class should discuss the following questions: Does saying that you're sorry mean that you've learned from your mistake? What if you repeat the mistake and the apology again and again? When can someone tell that you have learned from a mistake? (When you make things right -- as in the text, by raking up the leaves -- and when you make an effort to not repeat the mistake.) Have students give other examples, from their experience, and ask if the case is one of learning from a mistake.

Evaluation is fundamental to critical thinking. The critical thinker realizes that expressing mere preference does not substitute for evaluating. Awareness of the process of evaluating aids fairminded evaluation.

Does Earth Move?
(Social Studies - 3rd Grade)

Objective of the Remodelled Lesson

The student will discuss the importance of open-mindedness.

ORIGINAL LESSON PLAN

Abstract

This lesson covers the following points: Copernicus disagreed with others, and said that the Sun, not the Earth, is the center of the solar system; later Galileo began to agree with Copernicus; some people got mad and had Galileo arrested. Students discuss the differences between the old and new ideas about the solar system, and perform an experiment which shows why it is hard to say which idea is correct. Students play-act 'Galileo's Trial' and discuss whether or not people forgot about Galileo's ideas after he had been put under house arrest.

from *Who Are We?* Sara S. Beattie, et al. ©
The Houghton Mifflin Co. 1976. pp. T68-71.
Used with permission. All rights reserved.

Critique

This lesson misses the opportunity to discuss the importance of open-mindedness. Galileo's life presents an excellent example of someone who was punished for having a good idea, because the people around him were closed-minded and refused to listen. Yet the lesson, because it doesn't relate the material to the student's lives, fails to foster insight into the importance of listening to someone with a new idea. Nor does it foster insight into the student's egocentricity by having students reflect on times when they have closed-mindedly rejected a new idea.

Strategies Used to Remodel

S-2 developing insight into egocentricity

S-4 exploring thoughts underlying feelings

S-25 evaluating actions

S-1 fostering independent thought

S-20 recognizing contradictions

REMODELLED LESSON PLAN

When discussing Galileo's trial, encourage students to reflect on the importance of listening carefully, especially to those with whom they disagree, by having the class discuss the following questions: "Why did people get mad at Galileo? *S-2* What were they assuming? *S-4* (That is, what might they have been thinking that made them angry?) Who was in a better position to know if he was right, Galileo or his critics? Why? Did the people who didn't want to listen to Galileo miss out on anything? Should Galileo have changed his mind because everyone disagreed with him?" *S-25* Relate the material to the students' experience by asking, "Have you ever gotten mad when someone questioned a belief of yours? *S-1* Is that a good thing to do? Why or why not? *S-25* Did you ever miss out on learning a new idea because you were angry and wouldn't listen? What can you do about this problem? Have you ever said something that everyone disagreed with? *S-1* How did the other people react? How did you feel? Why? *S-4* Did you change your mind? Why or why not? Is there something wrong with believing that other people should listen carefully to you, and take your ideas seriously, but you don't have to listen to them?" *S-20*

The teacher should emphasize that we should not dismiss an idea, even if everyone we know disagrees with it, before we consider it.

> **Though everyone is both egocentric and critical (or fairminded) to some extent, the purpose of education in Critical Thinking is to help students move away from egocentricity, toward increasingly critical thought.**

The Health Department

(Social Studies - 3rd Grade)

Objectives of the Remodelled Lesson

The student will:

• develop insight into egocentricity

• probe deeper into the need for regulatory agencies

ORIGINAL LESSON PLAN

Abstract

The student text describes a number of functions of the Health Department, such as: testing for germs; checking the quality of food, and the cleanliness of workers and machines; working in clinics.

> from *At School.* Virginia Finley, et al. of TIEGS-ADAMS; PEOPLE AND THEIR HERITAGE, © Copyright, 1979. by Silver, Burdett & Ginn Inc. pp.66-67. Used with permission.

Critique

This lesson is a missed opportunity to have students discuss one of the most profound problems in human nature. The need for regulatory agencies is a symptom of a greater problem than poor food quality and lack of cleanliness; it is a symptom of our tendency to ignore the rights and needs of others when our own interest is involved. Using a specific example, like the need for the Health Department, can highlight for students the ideal of Government as a protector of peoples' rights from people with more narrow interests.

Strategies Used to Remodel

S-2 developing insight into egocentricity

S-3 fostering reciprocity

S-6 exploring underlying purposes

REMODELLED LESSON PLAN

Before introducing the original lesson on the Health Department, encourage students to reflect on the problem of egocentricity *S-2* by saying, "We know that we have some rules to keep us from hurting other people (i.e., ignoring their rights and needs)." Ask students to name a few of these. If they need help thinking of any, mention that we have rules saying that we shouldn't use other peoples' possessions without their permission. Say "Has anyone ever broken this kind of rule? Why? Did you ever break a rule because you wanted something that you didn't have a right to have? Give examples." Then *S-3* , ask, "Did you think about the other people involved when you broke this rule? Would you have broken it if you knew you would be caught? Why or why not?" Discuss at length.

Next have students read the original lesson on the Health Department. In order to probe deeper into the need for regulatory agencies, the teacher should supplement the original lesson with the following questions: Why do we need the Health Department? *S-6* In what ways do they help all citizens? In what ways do they help consumers? In what ways do they help businessmen? Why do Health Department workers have to check places where food is stored, processed, sold, and served? Why don't workers at those places check health conditions? *S-2* Could the Health Department people simply ask the people who work with food? Or their bosses? Would some people ever ignore the rules? Why? (Discuss at length.)

Sum up the lesson by facilitating a discussion relating the Health Department to other ways in which Government tries to protect the rights of citizens. If students have trouble mentioning examples, mention some of the following: Police Department, the Food and Drug Administration, Environmental Protection Agency.

Clarifying the global concept: What is it to think critically? How is the fairminded critical thinker unlike the self-serving critical thinker and the uncritical thinker?

City Government in East Bend

(Social Studies - 3rd Grade)

Objectives of the Remodelled Lesson

The student will:

- clarify concepts by contrasting opposites
- discuss the difficulty of voting intelligently
- distinguish relevant from irrelevant evidence
- discuss what sources a voter should rely on
- practice analyzing texts

ORIGINAL LESSON PLAN

Abstract

The students read about the mayor of East Bend. They read that she went on TV to try to convince citizens that some new plans will be good for the people of the city. The students read that she talks and listens to many different people, and has the help of city workers who are paid with tax money. The class discusses the importance of citizens and city workers working together. Students learn that mayors are elected, and are asked whether or not the mayor is good at her job.

from *In Communities*. of TIEGS-ADAMS;
PEOPLE AND THEIR HERITAGE, © Copyright,
1979. by Silver, Burdett & Ginn Inc.
pp.61-2. Used with permission.

Critique

Although a number of important concepts are introduced in this lesson, none of them are made sufficiently clear. Since the lesson neglects to contrast good citizen with bad citizen, many of the important details of citizenship are overlooked. Among these is intelligent voting as the basis of a free and democratic society. As early as possible, students should consider the difficulty of being good citizens.

Students are asked if the mayor of East Bend is a good mayor without any discussion of the criteria for judging mayors. The lesson lists some of the mayors duties, but nowhere suggests that the list is incomplete. This lesson also confuses facts with ideals by saying that city planners listen for ideas from citizens, rather than saying that good city planners listen to citizens and take their concerns into account.

Strategies Used to Remodel

S-12 clarifying ideas

S-16 distinguishing relevant from irrelevant facts

S-19 evaluating source credibility

S-28 critiquing text

S-9 distinguishing facts from ideals

REMODELED LESSON PLAN

To highlight the fundamental characteristics of good citizenship, the teacher should help students contrast 'good citizen' with 'bad citizen'. **S-12** Say "Since a good citizen of a country helps the country to be better, a bad citizen either doesn't help the city, or does things that hurt it." Then ask the students: "What can people do to help or hurt their city?" Possible contrasting examples include the following:

Show concern for their city.	Don't care about their city.
Work for change whenever necessary.	Don't work for needed changes. Hinder needed changes.
Have a high regard for the function that good laws serve.	Have no regard for the laws of the city.
Work to change laws that don't meet the peoples' interests.	Break laws with no attempt to change them.
Keep the city clean.	Make the city messy.
Help the city government make good decisions.	Try to get city government to make bad decisions (usually for self interest).
Try to vote for the best people for each elected position.	Don't vote, or vote without knowing or caring what is best for the city.
When voting, know what the elected position requires.	Don't understand the nature of elected offices.
Know about the candidate.	Don't know enough about the candidates.

Next, tell the students that they will be focusing on elections, and how to decide who to vote for for mayor. Ask them what a good citizen must know to choose a mayor. The teacher should help the students contrast good with bad mayors. **S-12** For each item mentioned discuss its opposite. For example, if a student says that a good mayor is honest, ask "What would a bad mayor be? What forms could the dishonesty take?" Use analogies of leaders that the students will be familiar with, such as team captains, scout leaders, or teachers. After the students have given as many examples as they can of characteristics of good and bad mayors, mention important duties that they have overlooked, e.g., mayors appoint other city officials, help decide how the city money is spent, etc.

Below are some ideas that could be contrasted in the discussion. We have distinguished those which were mentioned in the text (but not contrasted) from those which were not mentioned. Point out that how good a mayor is, is a matter of degree.

IN BOOK:

tells citizens plans	inaccessible, secretive
works hard	is lazy, takes long breaks, inefficient
talks to lots of different citizens, is a good listener, cares	doesn't listen or care, or cares only about friends
works with city planners and other skilled people	doesn't get help from relevant people

NOT IN BOOK:

makes wise appointments	gives jobs to friends, appoints wrong people
is fair and honest	is unfair, dishonest, takes bribes
uses funds efficiently	misuses or wastes funds
has authority	can't get people to listen or obey
shares the citizen's goals	doesn't share citizens' goals

After this discussion, the teacher should say to the students "Now we are going to talk about voting for a mayor." Ask, "What do we need to know about the candidates, to be able to decide who would make the best mayor? *S-16* What facts are relevant? How can we find out what the candidates are like? *S-19* What facts are irrelevant to our decision? (nice smile, good looking, kisses babies, funny.) Why do you think so? What do candidates say they will do if elected? What kinds of things will candidates not mention? What sources can we trust to give us accurate information about candidates?" The teacher should emphasize the importance of looking at the candidates' past performances, especially evidence regarding their honesty, fairness, and efficiency.

To sum up the lesson, ask the following questions: Is voting wisely easy or hard? What is hard about trying to be a good citizen? Have the students review the text and write an evaluation of it. **S-28** "What does the text include? Leave out? Do we know enough about this mayor to judge whether she is a good mayor or not? Do all city planners listen to citizens? Is the claim that they do, a fact or an ideal? **S-9** Rewrite the sentence so that it states a fact."

One cannot develop one's fairmindedness, for example, without actually thinking fairmindedly. One cannot develop one's intellectual independence, without actually thinking independently. This is true of all the essential critical thinking traits, values, or dispositions. They are developmentally embedded in thinking itself.

The Pledge of Allegiance

(Social Studies 1st-3rd Grades)

Objectives of the Remodelled Lesson

The student will:

- discuss the meaning of the pledge of allegiance
- develop a concept of 'good citizen'
- develop an appreciation for 'our republic', 'liberty', and 'justice'
- practice distinguishing ideals from facts
- practice reciprocity (by discussing how other people feel about their nations)

ORIGINAL LESSON PLAN

> We have not used a specific lesson for this remodel. Since each of the lessons on the Pledge of Allegiance we reviewed had different faults and shortcomings, a critique and remodel of any one would have been incomplete.

Critique

The lessons we reviewed on the subject overemphasized the flag, while de-emphasizing allegiance to the country. They confused ideals of the country with facts about the country, thereby failing to suggest that it takes work to improve our country. The common belief that loving your country means finding no fault with it is a major obstacle to critical thought. Fairminded thinking requires us to consider criticisms.

The lessons we reviewed do not fully explain the ideas in the pledge; therefore, students are making a promise they don't understand. Ideas as important and complex as 'good citizenship' aren't covered sufficiently.

Furthermore, many lessons lead students to believe that our ideals are uniquely American, rather than discussing how many others have similar ideals. This practice encourages socio-centric stereotyping of non-Americans. Therefore, we suggest that students think about how others feel about their countries, and discuss ideals that others share with us.

The remodel can be substituted for any lesson on the pledge. Some teachers may also want to have students critique the pledge lesson in their text.

Strategies Used to Remodel

S-12   clarifying ideas

S-17   making inferences

S-9   distinguishing facts from ideals

S-3   fostering reciprocity

S-8   discouraging stereotyping

REMODELLED LESSON PLAN

We have designed this lesson as a complete third grade level discussion. We believe, however, that the pledge should be discussed as early as the children recite it. For first and second grades, use as much of this lesson as your students can understand.

Teachers of second and third grades may have a pre-activity. Have the students look up the words in the pledge in the dictionary. Then ask them to rewrite the pledge in their own words. We then recommend a thorough discussion of the pledge, as described below.

A pledge is a promise. *S-12* What is a promise? Why keep promises? How do you feel when someone breaks a promise to you? Is something a promise if you can't choose whether or not to make it?

Allegiance is loyalty. (Use 'allegiance to a friend' as an analogy to enhance discussion.) So we are making a promise to be loyal. Loyal to what? (Flag and country.) The flag is a symbol of our country. (If necessary, discuss the meaning of 'symbol.') To be loyal to the flag is to show respect for it. We do this as a way of showing respect for our nation. (Discuss our country's name.)

"And to the republic for which it (the flag) stands." Our country is a republic. That means that we have the right to pick our representatives and leaders. (Compare this to other forms of government, including direct democracy if possible. Discuss the difficulties and benefits of direct democracies versus representational democracies.) Do people in every country get to pick their leaders? If we select our leaders, then who is responsible for our government? *S-17* Why? (Discuss how the country is made up of land, people, and government, and so we have to care for all three.)

Our country has ideals. *S-12* (Discuss 'ideals.' See the remodel of "Our Country's Birthday" for ideas.) 'Indivisible' means something that stays whole, and is not split into parts. (Use households as an analogy to generate a discussion of why unity is important.) (Define 'liberty' and 'justice.') We say "with liberty

133

and justice for all." Why are these things important? How do you feel when you are treated unfairly? How would you feel if you couldn't decide anything for yourself? (Then discuss that last phrase, and ask who is meant by 'all'?) Is the idea that everyone is free and is always treated fairly a fact or an ideal? *S-9* What is the difference between a fact and an ideal? (Discuss) Are freedom and fairness easy or hard for a country to achieve? (Discuss)

Therefore, when we say the pledge, we promise to respect the flag and be good citizens. Since we live in a republic, the citizens are responsible for the government. So we promise to take care of the land, keep our country whole, and strive to make our government treat everyone fairly and let people be free.

The teacher should point out that the students are not required to say the pledge, that they have a choice to decide whether it is a promise they want to make.

Understanding Points of View in Other Countries

The inability to see the world from any frame of reference other than one's own is a major obstacle to critical thought. As early as possible students should develop the habit of appreciating how non-Americans feel about their countries. In the following extension we suggest a number of questions the teacher can use to encourage students to practice seeing the world as people from other countries see it.

First, have children look at pictures or models of flags from other countries. Ask, "Which do you like best? Which do you think is best because of the nation it represents?" Mention that most Americans like our flag the best because it represents our nation, and that most Americans share the point of view that our country is best.

Ask, "Which flag is the best from the French point of view? *S-3* According to the French point of view, which country is best? Which point of view is right? Which point of view do the French think is right? Are French people loyal to their country?" Tell the students that the French people hold the ideals of liberty, brotherhood, and equality. Have the students compare these to our ideals, then ask, "What do French and American points of view have in common?"

Ask, "If you could choose any country in which to live, which would you choose? Would you choose your own home? What nation would a French child choose? Why? Would French children want their own home? Do you think the French are proud of their country?"

134

Ask similar questions about the Soviet point of view. *S-8* Stress that equality is an important Soviet ideal. Similar questions can be asked of any nation with which the students are familiar. Try to get the students to generalize about other countries, and how people like and are proud of their countries. Discuss different degrees of variance between facts and ideals.

The next section is an introduction to the idea of a symbol, and helps the students distinguish between symbols and that which they represent.

Symbols

Use our flag, the skull-and-crossbones sign, and traffic lights as examples of symbols. Ask the students for more examples. *S-12* Then ask "Is there a symbol for you?" Use the analogy of the students' names as symbols of them in the following discussion: Is a symbol the same as the thing it symbolizes? Is the symbol as important as what it symbolizes? Why might people get upset when a symbol is mistreated? Is it right to treat or react to the symbol the way you treat or react to the thing it symbolizes? Why or why not?

To sum up for all lessons ask, "What did you learn from this lesson? What was the most important part of this lesson? Is there anything you don't understand?" For the flag lesson, ask, "What do you think is the most important part of being a good citizen? (Have students discuss at length.) For the point of view lesson, ask, "Do you think everybody loves their own country best? Why or why not?"

It should not be assumed that there is a universal standard for how fast teachers should proceed with the task of remodelling their lesson plans. A slow but steady evolutionary process is much more desirable than a rush job across the board.

Looking to the Future
(Social Studies - 3rd Grade)

Objectives of the Remodelled Lesson

The student will:

- discuss the implications of a passage
- critique a student text
- evaluate sources of information

ORIGINAL LESSON PLAN

> In one part of Washington, houses were very old. Repairs were needed to make them safe. Too many people lived in these houses. This part of Washington was a slum. So better houses were found for the people who lived in this slum. Bulldozers were brought in. They knocked down thousands of houses. Then builders put up new apartments and houses.
>
> Lafayette Square is near the White House. Old buildings have been torn down. New houses have been built. But these new houses don't look new. They look like ones that were built long ago on this square.
>
> from *At School*. Eleanor Thomas, et al. of TIEGS-ADAMS; PEOPLE AND THEIR HERITAGE, © Copyright, 1983. by Silver, Burdett & Ginn Inc. pp.180-1. Used with permission.

Critique

This student text may lead students to believe that slums no longer exist in Washington, D.C. By mentioning only one case, a case in which improvements were made, they overlook the majority of cases, in which improvements were not made. They do not mention or allude to the work that remains to be done.

Since the student text is misleading, the student should be given a chance to critique it. Students need practice critiquing written material. They need to practice discussing the implications of claims, and comparing the credibility of various sources of information.

Strategies Used to Remodel

S-12 clarifying ideas

S-21 exploring implications

S-28 critiquing text

S-19 evaluating source credibility

REMODELLED LESSON PLAN

First, have students read the original passage. The teacher can use the following questions as a pre-activity: **S-12** What is a slum? Why are there slums? Why do people live in slums? What would it be like to live in a slum? Must there be slums? How can people get rid of slums?

Then, have the students read the passage again, and use the following questions to facilitate a discussion of the text. "What does the text say about Washington, D.C.? When the text says 'In one part of Washington, houses were very old ...' does that imply that the city had only one slum? **S-21** Does the passage imply that there are no more slums in Washington?" Discuss at length. (The teacher may use a similar example, such as, "One girl in this room has a red dress." Ask, "Does that mean that no other girl in the room has a red dress? Would people usually think that that's what it means?" Though a logician would say 'no', most people would say 'yes'.)

Next, the teacher should ask, "How could we find out about the slums? Why do you think the text was written this way?" **S-28** The teacher should mention that there are a variety of points of view on the causes of, and solutions to, the slum problem.

For further discussion of slums, or for reinforcement, use the following questions: "Is getting rid of slums a difficult or easy problem? Why? Do we understand the causes of slums? What do we agree about? Disagree? How is this problem different from one like who should get to watch their choice on TV? How can we find out what a city is like if we can't go there? What different sources of information might we find? Which of these would most likely leave out problems like slums? Which of these would be most likely to include such problems? Why do you think so?"

Stress to students the importance of determining how credible a source is by asking, **S-19** "When can you assume that what you read is true? Under what conditions should you be skeptical and check other sources? (When someone is 'selling' products or ideas.) What kinds of materials can you trust? Why? Have you ever not believed what you heard or read? Have you ever tried to mislead someone? Why?"

For additional practice in critical reading, the students could compare tourist information about Washington with other factual material (when available.) Or they could read and discuss Chamber of Commerce material for their town.

Problem Solving
(Social Studies - 3rd Grade)

Objectives of the Remodelled Lesson

The student will:

- practice applying a three step problem solving technique
- practice seeing a problem from more than one point of view
- practice suspending judgment when they have insufficient information
- use information to help solve problems
- evaluate proposed solutions

ORIGINAL LESSON PLAN

Abstract

Students read about some of the problems caused by unplanned growth in the city of East Bend. They review five steps for solving problems, and mention possible solutions. Then they read different citizens' ideas about city problems, and see how some ideas conflict. They discuss the importance of people planning together.

The steps for problem solving are:

1. state the problem clearly

2. make a list of possible solutions

3. gather and examine information

4. choose the solution that seems best

5. test the chosen solution to find out it if really solves the problem

from *In Communities*. Eleanor Thomas of TIEGS-ADAMS; PEOPLE AND THEIR HERITAGE, © Copyright, 1979. by Silver, Burdett & Ginn Inc. pp.61-2. Used with permission.

Critique

This lesson is typical of the several lessons on problem solving we reviewed. The lesson provides a technique for problem solving, yet the text never applies it, or has the students apply it to problems. At most, in any given problem solving lesson, the text or student apply two of the five steps. Students never see the whole technique used. Students can't be expected to learn how to use a technique which they never practice. Although students would find learning to apply the technique to a city problem difficult, they could use it first on problems within their experience.

Furthermore, the technique they suggest has significant problems. Step 1 of this technique calls on students to state the problem. Yet the first statement of a problem is seldom best. A problem cannot be stated accurately until information has been reviewed. In the above technique information gathering is left until step 3. Stating the problem is not as simple as writing a sentence; it requires a process in which the problem becomes increasingly clearer in the light of accumulating information. The more completely, clearly, and accurately the problem is formulated, the easier and more helpful the discussion of its solutions. Information gathering should include finding out the results of others' attempts to solve similar problems. No problem solving lesson we reviewed so much as alluded to this idea. Discussion of possible solutions should not precede information gathering.

Also, the technique fails to mention the criteria by which solutions are to be judged, except that of "seeming to be the best." As vague and arbitrary a criterion as this leads students to believe that they have evaluated solutions when they have not. Calling a solution 'best' implies a comparison to other solutions, a comparison that presupposes criteria. Furthermore, students are asked to judge which solution is best without first considering best for whom. Therefore their method encourages students to assume one perspective, at the expense of having them consider others. Therefore, the technique in this lesson misses the opportunity to have students practice reciprocity, dialogical reasoning, and the analysis of issues.

Strategies Used to Remodel

S-11	clarifying issues
S-3	fostering reciprocity
S-26	suspending judgement
S-24	evaluating solutions

REMODELLED LESSON PLAN

We developed an alternative set of problem solving steps, to substitute for the five-step technique outlined in the original lesson.

1. Define the Problem: Make a provisional statement of the problem. Raise questions about the details of the problem. Are any concepts unclear? What kinds of facts do we need? How can we find these facts? Is anything being evaluated? If so, what are the standards we will use to evaluate? Gather and examine the information needed to settle those questions. Restate the problem more clearly in light of that information. Continue this process until you can answer questions like the following: What, exactly, is wrong? What happens in the situation?

Why is this bad? What causes this to happen? Who and what are involved? How do the others involved see the problem? What other problems are related to this and how?

2. *Analyze the Problem:* Reflect on the final formulation of the problem, and answer the following questions: What would each person involved consider necessary to solve the problem? How will we know when we've solved the problem? What further facts do we need to know to formulate solutions?

3. *Decide on a Solution:* Find out how others have tried to solve similar problems. Think of other possible solutions. Compare your situation with that of others. In what relevant ways are their situations like and unlike yours? What were the effects of their solutions? Would any of these solutions satisfy everyone involved in the problem?

If not, have students argue with each other for different solutions. They should listen and respond to arguments for incompatible solutions. In the discussion, students should point out and evaluate their own, and others' assumptions, use of concepts, and the implications and consequences of the proposed solutions. The students should listen carefully to others and modify their ideas in light of the strengths of opposing arguments. Stress the idea that this is not a contest among solutions; rather students should look for a solution, or combination of solutions, that minimizes bad consequences, and maximizes relief from the problem.

Before students attempt to apply this problem solving technique to adult problems they should practice applying it to some of their own problems. After students have discussed a number of problems which they typically encounter, the class should decide on one for problem solving practice. Below is an example of how the problem solving technique might be applied to a student problem.

PROVISIONAL STATEMENT OF THE PROBLEM: My brother and I fight over T.V.

Step 1 QUESTIONS TO DEFINE THE PROBLEM *S-11* : (A) When do you fight? When do you not fight, i.e., what shows do you both like? (B) What happens when a fight occurs; what do you say? What do you do? What does he say? What does he do? (C) What is the result of the fighting? How do the fights end? (D) Why don't you like the situation? (E) How do you think your brother sees the problem? *S-3* Reformulations will vary, depending on the answers given to these questions. Here is an example of one possible clearer formulation of the problem.

140

REFORMULATION: It makes my brother and I unhappy when, on Saturday mornings and Tuesday nights, we argue, wrestle, and push each other around, hurt one another, and miss parts, or all, of our favorite shows.

Step 2 QUESTIONS TO ANALYZE THE PROBLEM: What do you and your brother agree is necessary to solve the problem? What do you both see a fair solution involving? Is there anything else we need to know about the situation? Which shows are most important to each of you? Least important? What might one brother do while the other is watching his favorite show? (This lesson will require a homework assignment at this point, in order for the student to gather information. The teacher should say, "We can't solve this problem until we have the answers to our questions.") *S-26*

Step 3 DECIDING ON A SOLUTION *S-24* : Ask the class, "Does anyone know of a problem similar to this one? Was it solved? How?" Then have the class brainstorm other possible solutions. (These may include, for instance, giving up less favorite shows to watch the most favorite, alternating each week, or getting another special privilege for giving up a favorite show.) Have the class discuss the most likely consequences of the solutions provided. The teacher may have students role-play the parts of the two brothers discussing the suggested solutions, or allow two or more students to argue for their favorite solutions.

Then, the child involved should decide which solution to try first. If it works, the lesson is finished with his report to the class. If not, another solution should be tried.

Finally, sum up using the following questions: What did we do? (First, next, last?) What was important for us to keep in mind? Which parts were easy? Hard? Why? Did we solve the problem? Would this solution work for everyone?

After the class has used the problem solving steps on problems the students have had, introduce the idea that cities also have problems. Have the students read the text. Ask them to describe the problem. Ask how it is like and unlike the child's problem. Point out important similarities and differences which they missed. Then attempt to apply the problem solving technique to this problem. Summarize this lesson by using the same questions as the sum-up above. Again, compare the analysis of the two problems.

Or, have students write an essay in which they argue for a solution to the city problem, or in which they compare the personal problem to the city problem.

An American City with a Problem

(Social Studies - 3rd Grade)

Objectives of the Remodelled Lesson

The student will:

- evaluate various arguments about a low income housing project
- consider what must be done to settle an issue
- consider ideas from opposing points of view
- practice recognizing their own prejudices
- show empathy for the ghetto dweller's situation

ORIGINAL LESSON PLAN

Abstract

This unit focuses on a low-income housing project, built in Forest Hills to move some poor people out of a New York ghetto. First, the students discuss the problem of over-crowding, learn what ghettos are, and discuss why people would want to leave them. Then the students learn about the Forest Hills plan, and discuss why Forest Hills was probably the chosen site for new housing. They discuss various forms of aid, and choose which kind of aid they would prefer receiving.

Next, the students read what some residents of Forest Hills said about why they didn't want the project there. The students are asked to decide which statements are 'facts,' and which 'opinions,' and are asked if they agree that it was unfair that Forest Hills residents weren't consulted about the project.

The students read what some people outside Forest Hills said about the project. Students are asked if people outside Forest Hills have a right to an opinion about the project. The class discusses the needs and wants of ghetto and Forest Hills dwellers, points out conflicts, and discuss possible compromises. Students are encouraged to come to their own conclusions about the worth of the project. Then the class discusses other big city problems.

In an activity on prejudice, the teacher explains how the two parts of the word, 'pre' and 'judge' together mean "judging something or someone before you know much about him, her or it." A student is asked to read aloud the following passage: "Many people in the ghetto are black. Almost everyone in Forest Hills is white. Those people in Forest Hills are just prejudiced against black people."

Then they are asked to rewrite the last sentence without using the word 'prejudice.' In an alternative activity on prejudice, students are asked to read the same quote then make lists of two or three kinds of people or foods they are prejudiced against. The teacher encourages an open discussion of the list, in which students try to convince others that their prejudices are in error.

from *Towns and Cities*. Ronald Reed Boyce, et al. © Addison-Wesley Publishing Co. pp. 102-113,115. Used with permission. All rights reserved.

Critique

We chose this lesson because it provides students with practice discussing a real social issue that involves arguments from more than one point of view. The empathy building exercises help students appreciate the seriousness of the problem by seeing it as those most affected might see it. The lesson provides an excellent introduction to the idea of prejudice. The exercise, which has students paraphrase a sentence containing the word 'prejudice' is a good concept building technique which we recommend. The alternative activity on prejudice forces students to recognize their own prejudices. Despite these strengths, however, this lesson creates obstacles to the development of critical thought.

Although the activities have such headings and objectives as 'analyzing and evaluating arguments', the activities do not require students to rationally consider and judge the arguments. Instead students are asked only to distinguish 'facts' from 'opinions,' to guess who said what, and to agree or disagree with one idea.

This lesson discourages critical evaluation when asking students to classify all statements as fact or opinion, rather than utilizing the three way distinction between 'matters of fact,' 'matters of mere opinion,' and 'matters of reasoned judgment.' Anyone who calls a statement a 'fact' implies that it is true. Anyone who calls a statement a 'matter of fact' implies that it is subject to possible verification, i.e., that to accurately judge it as true or false requires evidence. By putting everything but facts into the category of 'opinions,' the text fails to distinguish claims it makes no sense to argue about (matters of mere opinion, e.g., "Chocolate ice cream tastes best") from what can be reasonably argued about (matters of reasoned judgment, e.g., "People shouldn't eat red meat.") These categories are not exclusive, since reasoned judgments nearly always require some facts to support them. The distinction used in the original lesson discourages discussion and evaluation, because facts are true (and therefore there is no room for discussion) and everything else is opinion, and discussion is pointless.

The text requires students to state "who said what?" with no discussion of the possible relevance of this question. For instance, if we know that the person who said, "The government won't let criminals into the apartments" was a government official, the statement could be taken as an expression of policy. Whereas a ghetto dweller would probably not be in a position to know government intentions on this matter. Furthermore, the question misleads students into believing that they can tell who said what, when, in most cases, they can only guess.

Although the text includes a number of arguments, students discuss only one. Therefore, they are not in a strong position to evaluate the project when asked to do so. Of that argument, students are simply asked whether they agree or disagree with it, with no discussion of its worth.

Students are not given any useful tools of analysis or evaluation. They do not discuss how to determine the truth or reasonableness of the various ideas presented. Nor do they discuss the relevance of the arguments to the main issue. In no case are students asked, "What would someone who disagreed with these ideas say?", and therefore they get no practice in seeing the value of evaluating pairs of opposing arguments in relation to one another.

The text requires students to come to a conclusion regarding the housing project when, given the students lack of knowledge of the relevant facts, they should be encouraging the students to hold their conclusions tentatively.

Strategies Used to Remodel

S-11	clarifying issues
S-10	integrating critical vocabulary
S-3	fostering reciprocity
S-27	using probability qualifiers
S-14	making assumptions explicit
S-22	evaluating assumptions
S-16	distinguishing relevant from irrelevant facts
S-26	suspending judgment
S-20	recognizing contradictions
S-23	evaluating arguments

REMODELLED LESSON PLAN

The issue should be introduced, and discussed before students begin to evaluate arguments given in the text. It is a useful critical technique to determine what the requirements of solving a problem are (i.e., relevant facts, clarification of ideas, standards of evaluation, etc.) before attempting to evaluate arguments. We suggest that the teacher begin by defining the issue. Say, "For the next few days we will consider the question, 'Is the Forest Hills project a good idea?'" Next, have the students discuss the following questions (write their answers on the board) *S-11* : "Is this question clear? How could we rephrase it? What is the purpose of the project? Is the purpose worthwhile? What facts are relevant? *S-10* What kinds of facts do we need to know, to decide if the project would achieve its purpose? How could someone get these facts? Can you think of any problems this project might cause? Can you think of a better project than this?"

Then, have the students read and discuss the arguments from both inside and outside Forest Hills. Each argument from the original lesson will be followed by our suggested questions. During the discussion of each argument, the teacher should ask, "How could someone on the other side of the issue respond to this argument?" *S-3* Encourage the students to qualify their claims appropriately. *S-27*

Ideas from Forest Hills:

Argument 1: "Why did they decide to build those apartment buildings here? No one asked us if we wanted them. That's not fair!"

Questions: Is it fair to move a lot of people into a neighborhood without asking the people who already live there? How is this situation like and unlike other times people move to a new neighborhood? What does this person assume? *S-14* How do you feel when someone makes a decision that affects you, without asking what you think? *S-3* If you lived in a nice area like Forest Hills, and learned about the project, what would you think about it? Why? How is this argument related to the main issue?

Argument 2: "Think of all those people moving into those big buildings! Our subways and schools will be even more crowded than they are now!"

Questions: Given this objection, should the project be abandoned? Is there a way to deal with this problem besides abandoning the project?

Argument 3: "Most crime in New York is in the ghettos. If those people move here, there will be more crime here. I think we should help poor people, but I'm afraid of them."

Questions: Is there more crime in the ghetto? Why? What does this argument assume? *S-14* Are these good assumptions? *S-22* How could we find out whether crime is likely to go up? *S-11* (Here, if the students do not think of it themselves, the teacher should point out that we could find out what has happened in similar cases.) If the claim is true, does that mean that the project should be dropped? Who is this person afraid of and why? Is this person's fear a good reason to drop the project? Why or why not?

Argument 4: "I don't believe in moving people out of the ghettos. We should spend that money to fix up the old buildings in the ghettos."

Questions: What reasons might this person give for his idea that money is better spent on other ways of helping the ghetto people? (Note that this issue is related to the questions students were earlier asked (see abstract) about what form of assistance they would prefer. Point out the relationship between the answer given to that question, and agreement or disagreement about this point.) How would you feel if you lived in the ghetto, thought you were moving to Forest Hills, then found out you weren't moving, but your home would be replaced by a better building? *S-3* Is this question relevant to the main issue? *S-16*

Ideas From Outside Forest Hills

Before introducing the fifth argument we suggest doing the activities from the original lesson on prejudice. All of the necessary information is in the abstract.

Argument 5: "Many people in the ghetto are black. Almost everyone in Forest Hills is white. Those people in Forest Hills are just prejudiced against black people."

Questions: What does this person assume? *S-14* Is it a good assumption? *S-22* How could we find out if this idea is true? *S-26* Suppose we learned that the claims in arguments 1-4 were false. How would we find out whether prejudice was the reason for the Forest Hills people's response? (If they were prejudiced, they wouldn't change their conclusions in light of new evidence.) Does this argument refute 1-4? Is this argument important? How does it relate to the issue?

Argument 6: "People in other parts of New York will feel just the same way as the people in Forest Hills. Everyone thinks the apartment buildings are a good idea. But nobody wants them in his or her neighborhood."

Questions: Is this true? Probably true? Unlikely? *S-27* What follows from this argument? (This person may think that since no one wants the project in their area, the complaints of the Forest Hills people should be ignored.) If the claims are true, what do they mean for the project? Should it be abandoned, or should Forest Hills people's wishes be ignored? Why? (Discuss this argument in relation to arguments 1-4.)

Argument 7: "People in Forest Hills are afraid of black people and poor people. But most of them don't know any black people or poor people. After the apartment buildings are built, the black people and the white people will get to know each other. Then they will like each other."

Questions: What is the difference between this argument and argument 5? (The prediction that Forest Hills people will change.) What does this person assume? *S-14* How can we find out if this person is probably right? *S-11* (Related cases, and studies on people of different races living near each other.) Is this argument relevant to the issue? How? (If this belief is true, then the project is even better than people thought.) Do we have any evidence of the truth of this claim? Suppose these claims were true, why would the Forest Hills people be afraid? What assumption would they have to be making that would lead to fear, as opposed to some other emotion? *S-14*

Argument 8: "They won't let criminals into the apartment buildings. They will check everyone who wants to live there. People in Forest Hills won't have to worry about more crime because of those buildings."

Questions: Is this true? How could we know? *S-26* What argument does this contradict? (Argument 3) *S-20* How could the government know which people are criminals? What does this argument assume? *S-14* How does this argument relate to the main issue?

Argument 9: "I live in a ghetto now, but I would like to live in a place like Forest Hills. That part of New York is much prettier and safer than here. But I would be afraid to go there. Those Forest Hills people act dangerous. I'm afraid they would throw a rock through my window if I lived there."

Questions: Does this person have good reason to be afraid? Why or why not? What does this person assume? *S-14* Is it a good assumption? *S-22* How does this argument relate to argument 7? To argument 4? Does either side have good reason to be afraid? Who, if anyone, has more reason to fear? Why? How does this point relate to the main issue? What does it imply for the issue?

When all of the arguments have been discussed, ask students if there are any important ideas overlooked. Have the students discuss the relevance and relative importance of the different arguments. Ask, "Which arguments do you think are strongest? Why? *S-23* Then ask, "Is this project worthwhile?" Discuss at length. Remind them of what they said about the issue before they read the arguments. If a student doesn't listen to another, have that student restate the other's argument. *S-3* Encourage students to reach a compromise, or come up with a better plan.

Finally, have the students write an essay stating and defending their positions on the question: Is the Forest Hills project a good idea? Point out that assuming that you know more than you do weakens your argument. *S-27* Students should also write about what they don't yet know, and how they could find out.

How Am I Like All Other Human Beings?

(Social Studies - 3rd Grade)

Objectives of the Remodelled Lesson:

The student will:

- look at more than one point of view on the problem of hunger
- develop an understanding of the relationship between the causes of a problem and its solution
- develop empathy for the poor, and for multiple points of view on poverty
- develop an appreciation for good nutrition

ORIGINAL LESSON PLAN

Abstract

Students look at three pictures (of a child snorkeling, a child sleeping, and a child eating.) The students are supposed to infer that eating, sleeping, and breathing satisfy basic human needs. They discuss foods they eat and which foods they do or don't like. They reflect on their experiences of hunger, and read and discuss a poem written from the perspective of a hungry child. They discuss why some people go hungry (drought, poverty, overpopulation.) They write about being cold and tired. To conclude the lesson, the students either draw pictures or write about what they like most about needing food (e.g. helping to prepare or shop for food). If appropriate, the class might contribute food or money to feed the hungry.

from *Who Are We?* Sara S. Beattie, et al. ©
The Houghton Mifflin Co. 1976. pp. T252-4.

Critique

This lesson has several strengths. It encourages students to empathize with the world's hungry, and makes the problem of hunger concrete and real to students by having them reflect on their personal experiences with hunger. The last activity in the 'concluding' section confronts the common problem of divorcing thought from action by having students who have reflected on a problem act on their understanding of it. Activities like this give students a chance to experience their power to help. However, there are also a number of problems with the lesson.

Although no worldwide agreement has been reached regarding the causes of, and solutions to, the problem of hunger, the text assumes one limited perspective on the matter. No other points of view are suggested, nor it is stated that the causes of poverty may vary. Without an understanding of other people's points of view, the students will be unable to understand and evaluate other beliefs, claims, or arguments.

Also, the lesson lacks unity. It contains activities about these four subjects: The students' eating habits and preferences; nutrition; the students experiences of being tired, cold, and hungry; and the problem of widespread hunger. The lesson doesn't explore the important connections between some of these subjects.

The objective of inferring basic human needs from pictures is a misuse of the concept 'infer' (a common problem in texts in general.) Students cannot infer from the pictures given what humans need. The pictures of three children, eating, sleeping, and swimming cannot possibly justify the conclusion that, "All humans need to eat, breathe, and sleep." Since, by third grade, students should be familiar with the generalization that all people need food, air, and sleep, review of this idea doesn't warrant the space it is given.

The section on students' eating habits and preferences doesn't teach the students anything new, or add to their understanding of the other subjects covered.

The 'concluding the lesson' section makes no attempt to summarize or relate the previous activities. The first half is merely an extension of the student eating preferences activity and is therefore equally unhelpful. The second half would be more appropriate if students were encouraged to decide on a means of assisting people in their own community. The project they suggest does not involve the students in making the decision of who to help and how. Moreover, in asking students to help people they can barely imagine, it makes their power to help seem less real.

Strategies Used to Remodel

S-13	distinguishing ideas
S-1	fostering independent thinking
S-21	exploring implications
S-3	fostering reciprocity

REMODELLED LESSON PLAN

Since the two biggest problems, in the original lesson, are lack of unity between activities and one-sidedness, our suggestions focus on addressing them.

In order to bring unity to the subjects of nutrition, hunger, and the experiences of being cold, and tired, we recommend that the teacher change the focus of the lesson from hunger to poverty. Hunger, then, becomes one aspect of poverty. So, the class should discuss what it is like to be very poor.

After the children have discussed their experiences of being hungry, and have read and discussed the poem on hunger, the teacher can introduce the subject of nutrition and malnutrition. The teacher should ask, "Do you know what happens to people if they don't get the proper nourishment?" Emphasize the long term negative effects of malnourishment on physical and mental well-being and development. Then ask, "Is hunger the same as poor nutrition? *S-13* How could someone have enough food to not be hungry often, yet still be malnourished? What kinds of things would that person be eating?" Mention that although everyone who is malnourished is not hungry, most hungry people are malnourished.

In order to integrate the activity on the experiences of being cold and tired, ask, "Besides hunger and malnutrition, what other problems do very poor people have?" *S-1* Discuss as many responses as possible, making the casual connection between the problem and poverty explicit. Then have students do the cold and tired assignment, or allow them to choose their own subject, from those mentioned in the above discussion. Facilitate a discussion to relate poverty to these experiences.

To summarize this part of the lesson, ask students what they think is the worst part of poverty. Have them discuss their reasons.

To solve a problem, we must understand its causes. To understand the causes of a problem as difficult and complex as widespread poverty, we must consider different points of view. The text, however, encourages the students to assume one point of view. Instead, the teacher should mention that there are at least two commonly believed sets of ideas about the nature of the problem. Although there may be a tendency to simplify problems as complex as this, it is important that students get practice grappling with such complexities. Students are not expected to come to firm conclusions about the issue, but, rather, begin to develop their own point of view. Though confusion and uncertainty are unpleasant and frustrating, experiencing them is a fruitful, necessary part of education.

The teacher can begin by asking the children to give their ideas about the causes of poverty and hunger. *S-1* Then the teacher should mention that there are two major points of view on the subject and begin to categorize the children's ideas as belonging to these points of view. The teacher can refer to the section below for a summary of these perspectives. (The class could also discuss China, as an example of a country that has gone far toward eliminating its hunger problems.)

Why Do Hunger and Poverty Exist?
General Points

Point of View 1

Overpopulation, improper use of soil, drought, and increased cost of farming, are the main causes of poverty and hunger.

Point of View 2

Injustice, involving an unfair distribution of money, land, and power, is the main cause of poverty and hunger.

Specific Points

Many people lack access to, and information about, birth control.

Soil lays barren when crops are not rotated properly and land is not given sufficient rest.

There are long periods of time with little or no rain in many parts of the world.

The prices received for farm goods fluctuate dramatically.

A few large landowners own the vast majority of the good land.

Land owners force farmers to grow cash crops for export, rather than food for themselves.

Cattle is one major export commodity. Yet it takes a lot more grain to feed people beef than it takes to feed them grain.

There is a lot of unused land.

Big land owners bring in machines and fire many workers.

After the students' ideas have been discussed, the class should discuss, through examples, how accepting an idea as the cause determines the range of possible solutions to the problem. *S-21* Encourage the students to use hypotheticals: If this is the cause, then this is what we can do.

To sum up, have the students write a short essay on what causes poverty. Stress to the students the importance of supporting their ideas with reasons. Have them conclude the essay by saying what someone who disagreed with their ideas might say. *S-3*

Introduction to Remodelling Science Lesson Plans

Although there are well-developed, defensible methods for settling many scientific questions, it is essential that educators recognize that students have developed their own ideas about the physical world. Merely presenting established methods to the student does not usually affect those beliefs; they continue to exist in an unarticulated and therefore unchallenged form. Jack Easley, who has written a series of penetrating articles on mathematics and science education, says "cognitive research shows that young children develop and test alternative rational explanations which authoritative exposition can't displace."[1] Rather than transfering the knowledge they learn in school to new settings, they continue to use their pre-existing framework of knowledge. The child's own emerging egocentric conceptions about events in their immediate experience "are much more activated and real than any alternative conceptions fostered by classroom instruction or textbooks."[2] In the *Proceedings of the International Seminar on Misconceptions in Science and Mathematics* there is an example of a child who is presented with evidence about current flow that was incompatible with the child's articulated beliefs. In response to the instructor's demonstration the child replied, "Maybe that's the case here, but if you come home with me you'll see it's different there."[3] This child's response graphically illustrates the ways in which students can retain their own beliefs while simply juxtaposing them with the belief of an authority. Unless students practice expressing and defending their own beliefs, and listening critically to those of others, they will not critique their own beliefs and modify them in light of what they learn, a process essential for genuine understanding. "As children discover they have different solutions, different methods, different frameworks, and they try to convince each other, or at least to understand each other, they revise their understanding in many small but important ways."[4]

A critical approach to teaching science is concerned less with students accumulating undigested facts, than with students learning to think scientifically. As students learn to think scientifically they inevitably do organize and internalize "facts." But they learn them deeply, tied into ideas they have thought through, and hence do not have to "re-learn" them again and again.

Scientists are not given experiments; they begin with a problem or question, and have to figure out, through trial and error, how to solve it. Typical science texts, however, present the student with the finished products of science. These texts present information, and tell the students how to conduct experiments. They have students force things into given categories, rather than stimulating students to discover and assess their own categories. Texts require students to practice the skills of measuring and counting, in some cases simply for practice and no other reason. Texts also introduce scientific concepts. But students must understand scientific concepts through ordinary language and ordinary concepts. A problem is created when science concepts that have another meaning in ordinary language (e.g. 'work') are not distinguised in a way that highlights how purpose effects use of language. Furthermore, those texts which emphasize the distinction between observation and conclusion often fail to make the link between the two explicit. These faults can be overcome by a critical approach.

For a science activity to be meaningful to students, they should always understand its purpose. A critical approach to science education would allow students to ponder questions, propose solutions, and develop and conduct their own experiments. Although many of their experiments would not succeed, the attempt and failure provides a valuable learning experience. When an experiment designed by a student fails, that student should be stimulated to amend his beliefs.

Whenever possible, students should be encouraged to express their ideas and try to convince each other to adopt them. Having to listen to their fellow students' objections will facilitate the process of self-critique. Such discussion will also serve to make reasoning from observation to conclusion explicit. Students will be forced to state their assumptions, thereby making them available for critique.

[1] Jack Easley, "A Teacher Educator's Perspective on Students' and Teachers' Schemes: Or Teaching by Listening," Presented at the Conference on Thinking, Harvard Graduate School of Education, August, 1984, p. 1

[2] Richard Paul, "Dialogical Thinking: Critical Thought Essential to the Acquisition of Rational Knowledge and Passions," *Teaching Thinking Skills: Theory and Practice,* by W. H. Freeman & Company, Publisher, Joan Baron and Robert Steinberg, editors, 1987.

[3] Hugh Helm & Joseph D. Novak, "A Framework for Conceptual Change with Special Reference to Misconceptions," presented at the International Seminar on Misconceptions in Science and Mathematics, Cornell University, Ithaca, NY, June 20-22, 1983, p.3.

[4] Easley, op. cit. p.8.

Linear Measurement
(Science - Kindergarten)

Objectives of the Remodelled Lesson

The student will:

• discuss reasons for measuring

• discover the usefulness of standards of measurement

ORIGINAL LESSON PLAN

Abstract

The students use their hands to measure one side of a piece of paper. They then discuss why they arrived at different answers. Next, they use pencils to measure two sides of the paper. Then they use a meter-stick to measure different classroom objects, and determine which of four objects is longest and which shortest.

from *The Elementary School Science Program.*
Biological Sciences Curriculum Study.
Colorado © J.B. Lippincott Co. pp. 72-74.
Used with permission.

Critique

This lesson introduces students to the practice of measuring length without any discussion of the purposes which measuring serves. Although it gives students an experience which suggests the importance of standards of measurement, it has no explicit discussion of this idea. Students should discuss the potential problems arising from not using a standard.

Strategies Used to Remodel

S-5 fostering insight in to mechanical skills

S-1 fostering independent thinking

REMODELLED LESSON PLAN

As an introduction, the class should discuss the question "Why do people measure things?" **S-5** The teacher may begin by asking students to recall when they have seen people use rulers, tape measures, etc. The class should brainstorm reasons for measuring. Write these down.

Then, after the students have measured with their hands and discussed the differences in their answers, they should be given a chance to suggest the usefulness of everybody using the same length. **S-1** Remind students of the reasons for measuring that they gave earlier. Ask them if the 'hand method' would work well in each case. Focus their attention on cases in which lack of standards would cause problems. Ask students what problems could arise, and how they might be solved. If they don't mention that everyone could use one agreed upon length to measure, distribute pencils (or other objects which are of equal length). Have the students measure and discuss whether or this would solve the problems.

Before introducing the meter-sticks, ask the class what problems could arise from using pencils to measure ("Would everybody know exactly what 'six pencils long' means?") When distributing the meter-sticks mention that people all over the world use sticks that are exactly this length. Have the students compare the different meter-sticks.

Before the students measure, give them a reason to want to know the lengths of objects or spaces. **S-5** For example, you might say "Suppose we wanted to move these shelves over here? How could we tell if they would fit?" Or, to reinforce the importance of standards, have one student measure a space in the classroom, while others measure some outside object.

Finally, when the students have used their meter-sticks, the class should review reasons for measuring, and the importance of a standard.

Getting experience in lesson plan critique: What are the strengths and weaknesses of this lesson? What critical principles, concepts, or strategies apply to it?

Studying Animals That Are Pets
(Science - Kindergarten)

Objectives of the Remodelled Lesson

The student will:

• practice clarifing an idea, 'good pet,' by contrasting it with 'bad pet'

• be introduced to the word 'infer'

ORIGINAL LESSON PLAN

Abstract

Students describe pets they have, or animals that they think would make good pets. They describe other details about these pets, such as what they eat and what their favorite activities are. They categorize pictures of pets in different ways. Among the extension activities is an exercise in which students imitate a pet, while other students identify it.

from *Heath Science.* James P. Barufaldi, et al. Reprinted by permission of D. C. Heath and Company. © 1965. pp. 78-79.

Critique

Students are asked to tell what kind of pet they think is a good pet, without contrasting those characteristics with those of bad pets. This lesson misses the opportunity to have students discuss their different ideas of "good pets", and to practice using critical thinking vocabulary.

Strategies Used to Remodel

S-12	clarifying ideas
S-3	fostering reciprocity
S-10	integrating critical vocabulary

REMODELLED LESSON PLAN

Have students discuss the characteristics of animals that they believe make them good pets and characteristics of bad pets. *S-12*   Allow lots of room for exchange of ideas and disagreement. Ask, "What is a good pet? What is a bad pet? Why do you think so? Might someone else choose another pet? *S-3*   Why might they think this pet is a good pet but choose another? What are the differences between good and bad pets?"

Under "extending activities" #2, when students imitate a pet, ask of each response "Why did you say that?" Encourage them to use the vocabulary word "infer" by repeating back what they say using 'infer.' *S-10*   (E.g., if a student says "It's a bird, because you flapped your arms." The teacher should say "You saw John flap his arms. You inferred that John was pretending to be a bird.")

To sum up, ask students to summarize the different ideas they had about the characteristics of good and bad pets. Have them recall what they thought the imitated animals were, and why. Encourage them to use the word 'infer.'

Do not to spend too much time on the general formulations of what critical thinking is, before moving to the level of particular strategies, since people tend to have trouble assimilating general concepts unless they are made accessible by concrete examples.

Ways in Which Things Move
(Science - Kindergarten)

Objectives of the Remodelled Lesson

The student will:

- practice limiting his responses to those relevant to movement
- discuss the reasons for forming categories
- discuss relevant differences between objects in a category

ORIGINAL LESSON PLAN

Abstract

Students make various objects (bell, yo-yo, book, crayon, top) move. They describe the way each object moves (slides, rolls, bounces, swings, spins). Then students pair up pictures of things that move the same way.

from *Science*. George G. Mallinson. Silver
Burdett Company. © 1978. pp. 72-73. Used
with permission. All rights reserved.

Critique

The lesson has students put objects into previously formed groups. It does not allow them to create their own categories, and make the categories they form explicit (e.g., these things go together because they roll.) This lesson is a missed opportunity to have children practice distinguishing what is relevant from what is irrelevant to the question "How do things move?"

Strategies Used to Remodel

S-7	recognizing reasons underlying categories
S-1	fostering independent thinking
S-16	distinguishing relevant from irrelevant facts

REMODELLED LESSON PLAN

In the original lesson it is not clear how the teacher is supposed to elicit the idea that different objects move in similar ways. We suggest asking students, of each object, "What else moves like this?" *S-7* (Keep a list of responses.) Students should then discuss how items within categories are different regarding how they move. *S-1* Ask, "These items are all alike in one way. What way is that? (They all roll.) Can you think of any differences in how they move?" (Students may recognize that some objects could fit into more than one category, e.g., a crayon and ball both roll but a ball also bounces.)

If students come up with similarities or differences irrelevant to the question of motion, the teacher should say, "Yes, that's true, but now we are discussing only those similarities and differences relevant to how objects move." *S-16*

Everyone learning to deepen her critical thinking skills and dispositions comes to insights over time. We certainly can enrich and enhance this process, even help it to move at a faster pace, but only in a qualified way. Time to assimilate and grow is essential.

Finding the Light
(Science - 1ˢᵗ Grade)

Objective of the Remodelled Lesson

The student will practice using analytical vocabulary.

ORIGINAL LESSON PLAN

FINDING THE LIGHT

Main concept of the lesson (pages 82-85): A person can tell which direction the light is coming from by studying the shadows which have been cast.

PERFORMANCE OBJECTIVE: After studying the information provided in this lesson, the children should be able to identify the direction from which light is coming by looking at the shadows cast by the light and noticing the direction of the shadows which are formed.

IMPORTANT WORD: light

SAMPLE ANSWER: In the top picture, the light is coming from the left; in the bottom picture, it is coming from the right. (If the children have not yet mastered "left" and "right," they will most likely say "from here" and point to the direction from which the light is coming.)

SHADOWS IN THE MORNING

Main concepts of the lesson (pages 86-87): The sun is in the east in the early morning. When a shadow is behind you in the morning, you are facing east.

PERFORMANCE OBJECTIVE: After studying the information provided in this lesson, the children should be able to find east by looking at their shadow in the early morning and find east by finding the sun in the early morning.

IMPORTANT WORDS: sun, east, morning, shadows

SAMPLE ANSWER: When their shadow is behind them in the early morning, the girls are facing east.

from *Exploring Science.* Milo K. Blecha, et al. By permission of Laidlaw Educational Publishers, A Division of Doubleday & Company, Inc. © 1979. pp. 82, 86.

Strategy Used for Remodel

S-10 integrating critical vocabulary

REMODELLED LESSON PLAN

The teacher should model and have students practice using, the terms 'see,' 'infer,' conclude,' and 'assume.' In the first lesson, when students have given their answers, say "We see the shadow on the right, and infer (or conclude) that the light comes from the left." *S-10* In the second lesson, say "The girls see their shadows behind them. They assume that the sun is in the east. They conclude that they are facing east."

Lesson plan remodelling as a strategy for staff and curriculum development is not a simple one-shot approach. It requires patience and commitment. But it genuinely develops the critical thinking of teachers and puts them in a position to understand and help structure the inner workings of the curriculum.

Water from the Air

(Science - 1st Grade)

Objectives of the Remodelled Lesson

The student will:

- develop and conduct an experiment to answer a question.
- practice distinguishing what they see from what they conclude.

ORIGINAL LESSON PLAN

Abstract

Students experiment to discover that the water which appears on the outside of containers of cold water comes from the air. They put food coloring in cold water, and notice that the water appearing on the outside of the container is clear, not colored.

from *Discovering Science 1*. Albert Piltz, et al. Charles E. Merrill Publishing Co. © 1973. pp. 82-83, T101-T102. Used with permission. All rights reserved.

Critique

By presenting the experiment to the students, this lesson misses the opportunity to allow students to puzzle over the answer to the question "Where did the water come from?" They should think about the question and figure out how to settle it. The lesson also fails to make students distinguish their observations from conclusions.

Strategies Used to Remodel

S-1   fostering independent thinking

S-17 making inferences

S-21 exploring implications

REMODELLED LESSON PLAN

In order to present the problem, rather than the solution to the problem, this lesson should begin, not with colored, but with clear ice water. *S-1* Ask students to observe the container and describe what they see. Tell them that this lesson will focus on the question "Where did this water come from?" Allow discussion. Ask, "Why do you think so? How could we find out?"

To help students develop an experiment ask (allowing discussion after each question): "Why can't we tell just by looking at the water? Does the water outside look like the water inside? Could we make the water inside different? How?" Have students choose one or more methods which use available materials (e.g. the water could be colored or flavored).

When students have conducted their experiments, ask *S-17* "What do you observe? What can you conclude? Why? Is the water outside like the water inside? Where did the water come from?"

The student text could be read and discussed as a sum up. Or the class could discuss what they found out in this lesson. Possible discussion questions include the following *S-21* : What have we learned about water? Air? What questions could we ask? (Does all air have the same amount of water in it? What are the differences between regular water and water in the air? What effect does the water that is in the air have?)

Understanding component teaching strategies that parallel the component critical thinking values, processes and skills: What are the basic values that (strong sense) critical thinking presupposes? What are the micro-skills of critical thinking? What are the macro-processes?

Measuring Air

(Science - 1st Grade)

Objectives of the Remodelled Lesson

The student will:

- practice using critical terms 'conclude' and 'assume'
- practice stating and evaluating an assumption

ORIGINAL LESSON PLAN

Impress upon your class that a gas, too, can be measured. Just as we can measure a solid and a liquid, we can also measure a gas. The Measure exercise, page 36, establishes a special unit for measuring gas. The unit equals the air spaces in a sponge. First, have a pupil fill a small sponge with water. Then have him squeeze the water into a measuring cup. How much water drains into the cup? Next, have a pupil squeeze the water from a large sponge into the measuring cup. How much water does the large sponge hold? Make a comparison.

Explain to your class that the water displaces the air in the sponge. That is, the water takes the place of the air which filled the spaces in the sponge. The amount of water which is squeezed from a sponge serves as a measure of the amount of air which the sponge held. Give all the boys and girls in your class a chance to measure the air in a sponge. The experiment will help them to develop the concept of volume and of a gas as matter. A gas, like all matter, has mass and takes up space.

Student Text: There is air in a sponge. How much air is in the little sponge? How much air is in the big sponge?

from *The Young Scientist Observing His World*. John Gabriel Navarra, et al. Harper & Row Publishers. © 1971. pp. 36, T33. Used with permission. All rights reserved.

Critique

To tell the students they will measure air and have them measure water instead seems unnecessarily confusing. The reason for measuring water should be made clear before the measurements are carried out. This lesson misses the opportunity to have students use analytical vocabulary, and make an assumption explicit for critique. Students need practice evaluating good, as well as bad, assumptions.

Strategies Used to Remodel

S-1　fostering independent thinking

S-10　integrating critical vocabulary

S-14　making assumptions explicit

S-22　evaluating assumptions

REMODELLED LESSON PLAN

The teacher should repeatedly squeeze and release a sponge. Then ask the following questions **S-1** : "Does this sponge have anything in it? Does it have air in it? (yes, when released; no, when squeezed) How much? Can we measure the air?" (Allow discussion.) If any students have ideas, allow them to conduct tests. Later, compare the results to those obtained by the experiment below.

Suggest that maybe we would have to measure the air indirectly. Point out (or elicit through questioning) that now the air fills all the holes and pockets in the sponge. If the sponge is soaked in water, then all those spaces would be full of water. The amount of water that the sponge holds would be easy to measure.

Have the students take the suggested measurements. Ask, "What did we measure? (How much water the sponges hold.) What did we find? (Give amounts.) How much air do the sponges hold?"

Say **S-10** "We saw that this sponge holds x water. We concluded that it holds x air. How can we say how much air the sponges hold when we didn't measure air, we measured water? What did we assume? **S-14** (That the sponge holds the same amount of air as water.) Was this a good assumption? **S-22** Why or why not?" Discuss at length.

Finally, have the class discuss the following questions: What did we learn about air? What does "empty space" mean? Is there empty space in this room? Allow discussion and disagreement. (See "At Work on the Earth" and "Two Concepts of Soil" for discussion of the distinction between scientific and ordinary concepts.)

What is remodelled today can be remodelled again. Treat no lesson plan as beyond critique and improvement.

Looking and Learning
(Science - 1st Grade)

Objectives of the Remodelled Lesson

The student will:

• make inferences from pictures

• distinguish guesses, direct observations and inferences

• practice using critical thinking vocabulary

ORIGINAL LESSON PLAN

Abstract

The students look at two pictures of children at the beach, and make observations. The teacher discusses the pictures with the students, attempting to bring out a number of predictable observations. Questions are asked to elicit more detail and to connect student observations to their personal experience. Most of the observations and questions suggested by the text deal with what the students directly observe; others require students to guess about what is happening; a few require inferences.

from *Today's Basic Science,* John Gabriel Navarra, et al. Harper & Row Publishers. © 1971. pp. 36, T33. Used with permission. All rights reserved.

Strategies Used to Remodel

S-18 supplying evidence for conclusions

S-17 making inferences

S-10 integrating critical vocabulary

REMODELLED LESSON PLAN

As students make observations ask, "How do you know that?" **S-18** Elicit distinctions between cases in which they merely guess (e.g. the children are at the beach on a class outing), make direct observations (e.g. there are three children looking at a shell), and infer **S-17** (e.g. we can tell it must be fairly warm out by the way people are dressed). In each case ask, "What makes you think so?" **S-18**

If students do not make inferences, elicit them by asking questions like "What kind of a day is it?" followed by "What makes you think so?"

Repeat their remarks back to them using the vocabulary **S-10** (e.g. "You saw that people were playing at the beach dressed only in bathing suits. You inferred that it is a nice day.")

If a staff becomes proficient at critiquing and remodelling lesson plans, it can critique and 'remodel' any other aspect of school life and activity, and so become increasingly less dependent on direction or supervision from above and increasingly more activated by self-direction from within.

Making Things Move

(Science - 1st Grade)

Objectives of the Remodelled Lesson

The student will:

• practice forming categories

• discuss the reasons for categories

• recognize that energy is required to make anything move

• compare and contrast different forms of energy

ORIGINAL LESSON PLAN

Abstract

This unit attempts to develop the concept that "energy must be used to set an object in motion or to alter its motion." Each section provides an example or two to illustrate a particular form of energy (electrical, chemical, mechanical, etc.) In each case these examples are contrasted with a human powered or living counterpart (e.g. motorcycle vs. bicycle).

from *Concepts in Science.* Paul F. Brandwein, et al. Harcourt Brace & World, Inc. 1980. pp. 2-8. Used with permission.

Strategies Used to Remodel

S-1 fostering independent thinking

S-7 recognizing reasons underlying categories

REMODELLED LESSON PLAN

To allow students to give their own examples, begin the unit with a brainstorming session in which students mention anything they can think of that moves. **S-1** Record these responses. Afterwards, go through the list encouraging students to form their own categories by asking "Does anything else mentioned earlier have the same source of movement as (x)?" (Choose any item on the list that can be grouped easily with other items.) Continue this process until as many of the items as possible have been put into categories. Ask, "How are the items in this first category different from those in the second? Third?" and so on. *S-7* Have the students label the groups.

Then ask "What do all of these groups have in common?" If necessary remind students that the criteria they used for coming up with items was "anything that moves" and the criteria they used for forming categories was "things that are moved the same way." *S-7* Then go back through the original lesson, asking of the examples given "Do we already have a category that this would fit, or do we need a new category? What would you call this category?"

Sum up the lesson by asking "What did we learn about how things move? What are some of the different ways things move? What do all of these have in common?"

Critical thinkers distinguish what they know from what they don't know. They are not afraid of saying "I don't know" when they are not in a position to be sure of the truth of a claim.

What the Scientist Does

(Science - 2nd Grade)

Objectives of the Remodelled Lesson

The student will:

- develop basic ideas about what science is
- probe into reasons for doing science
- practice reciprocity regarding reasons for doing science
- discuss how different scientific questions can be settled
- practice forming categories

ORIGINAL LESSON PLAN

Abstract

We have selected introductory and concluding lessons from a unit on "What the scientist does." In the first lesson, students list and discuss their ideas about what scientists do. The middle lessons develop the idea that scientists observe, experiment, read, keep records, and discuss their work, in order to learn. Each lesson has pictures of scientists engaged in scientific activities in various fields, and pictures of children doing the same. The text tells the students what the scientists are doing, why, and that children can do the same. Some lessons suggest specific activities. The final lessons summarize the ideas covered, and encourage students to do science.

from *Today's Basic Science 2*. John Gabriel Navarra, et al. © Harper & Row, Publishers. 1967. pp. 6-7, T1-3, 8-9. Used with permission. All rights reserved

Critique

This unit has several strengths. It encourages students to see themselves as scientists. The unit gives a fuller description of science than most texts when it mentions reading and discussion as part of science. The material, however, is incomplete.

The students do not contrast science with other disciplines, and so do not develop the distinction between science and non-science. Students are not given an opportunity to come up with a more complete list of the objects of scientific study. The unit also has no material about why people study science, or how scientists focus on questions and problems.

S-12 clarifying ideas

S-6 exploring underlying purposes

S-3 fostering reciprocity

S-1 fostering independent thinking

S-11 clarifying issues

REMODELLED LESSON PLAN

The teacher may want to have this series of discussions at both the beginning and end of the year. The ideas covered in this lesson should be re-introduced whenever they seem relevant to a specific discussion during the year.

Begin by asking, "What is science?" (Discuss at length.) Have students compare science to other subjects *S-12*. Then lead a discussion about why people do science *S-6*. Be sure that the following ideas are among the responses: curiosity, the need to solve specific problems, desire to improve the quality of life. Encourage extended discussion about the reasons. If students disagree, ask them to explain each other's positions *S-3*.

Ask, "What do scientists study?" *S-1* Have students brainstorm examples. List all responses. Then have students categorize their responses. (For instance, if one item is 'frogs' and another 'living things,' a student may point out that the first is a specific instance of the second.)

Then have the students select a few of the items and brainstorm questions a scientist could ask about the subject. List the questions. For each question ask, "How could we find out?" *S-11* (If students answer, "By reading about it." ask, "How could we find out for ourselves?" or, "How did the people who wrote the books find out?" or similar questions.) Then have the students discuss similarities and differences between processes of settling different questions.

Finally, conduct a discussion of the following questions: What do you like about science? Dislike? What areas of science do you find the most interesting?

Breakfast
(Science - 2nd Grade)

Objectives of the Remodelled Lesson

The student will:

- practice developing criteria for evaluating breakfasts
- evaluate breakfasts

ORIGINAL LESSON PLAN

Abstract

Students discuss the importance of a good breakfast, identify different breakfast foods, and mention which breakfast foods they like best. They learn that good breakfasts keep you warm, help you be ready for work and play, and include fruit, milk and grain. They learn the importance of sugar and fat in the diet, and discuss the different forms that these take. They also learn what people in other cultures eat for breakfast.

from *Searching In Science.* William J. Jacobson, et al. © American Book. 1965. pp. 134-143, G82,-91.

Critique

The text provides students with examples of good breakfasts, rather than having students suggest and discuss examples. By talking only about good breakfasts they neglect to discuss bad breakfasts (i.e., breakfasts that either harm you or don't help you.) Furthermore, the discussion of good breakfasts is limiting. To suggest that a good breakfast necessarily includes milk is false (especially considering the number of people who are allergic to milk, and that its nutritional value can be found elsewhere.) Students are in no position to distinguish foods that are good for you, foods that are bad for you, and foods that have both good and bad qualities. Students are asked to investigate what people in other cultures eat for breakfast. We suggest students also practice evaluating the strengths and weaknesses of different breakfasts, using widely accepted criteria such as low fat, high fiber, essential vitamins and minerals, etc.

Students discuss "energy" foods that contain fat or sugar, and the importance of having both these in your diet is stressed, but the vastly different forms are not compared or evaluated from a nutritional standpoint. (e.g., both fresh fruit and cake are treated as equally valuable sources of sugar.)

Strategies Used to Remodel

S-1   fostering independent thought

S-15 developing criteria for evaluation

S-12 clarifying ideas

REMODELLED LESSON PLAN

The teacher should begin by facilitating a discussion of what makes a good breakfast. Ask "Can anyone give me an example of a good breakfast? *S-1* What does this breakfast do for your body?" (Keep a list of the criteria students come up with.) *S-15* After eliciting several responses the teacher should ask "Can anyone give me an example of a bad breakfast? *S-12* Why is that a bad breakfast? Does such a breakfast harm you in any way? Does such a breakfast not meet certain needs you have?"

After students have investigated a number of different cultures to see what they eat for breakfast, ask them to apply the criteria previously developed. Ask of each different breakfast "Is this a good breakfast? Why do you think so? How does it compare with the breakfasts common in our culture?" Encourage students to discuss the strengths and weaknesses of both their own culture's typical breakfast, and that of others.

When discussing foods containing sugar and foods containing fat ask students, "Which sugar and fat foods do you think are better for you? Why?" The teacher may need to introduce the distinction between processed and unprocessed sugars; and animal and vegetable fats; and provide students with a general idea of how each affects the body.

Sum up the lesson by asking, "What are some of the criteria of a good breakfast? Give me some examples of different kinds of good breakfasts." (Encourage students to see that different cultures may meet their needs in different ways.) Ask students to give examples of strengths and weaknesses of specific breakfasts by using criteria suggested earlier. (e.g., I think this breakfast is good because it has a lot of fiber but bad because it has a lot of processed sugar.)

Comparing Man to Animals

(Science - 2nd Grade)

Objectives of the Remodelled Lesson

The student will:

- practice giving evidence for claims
- probe the similarities and differences between man and animals

ORIGINAL LESSON PLAN

LESSON CAPSULE

1. How are all the animals in these pictures alike? Have children compare number of eyes, ears, heads; discuss ways each animal moves, gathers food, breathes; ask if any of the animals make noises and how this is done. Review how each animal's body is supported. Which ones have bones? Review the names of the five senses and have children share ideas about whether or not each animal has all the senses and how the senses are used.

2. Read with children the information and questions on page 135. In discussion, bring out the ideas that man walks upright on two feet, wears clothing, can do many things with his hands, has a language, and is able to learn many kinds of things. Questions similar to the following may be used in guiding the discussion. What kinds of activities can man carry out that animals cannot? Could a frog cook its dinner? Why? Could a crab tie a shoelace? Why? Could a fish draw a picture? Why? Could a giraffe sing a song? Why? Could a ladybug build a road? Why? Do you suppose some animals might learn to do some of the things man can do? Which animals? Who would teach them?

3. Have children begin picture collections showing the kinds of activities man can carry out and animals cannot. Children might list ideas they want to illustrate - e.g., playing musical instruments, operating equipment (cars, planes, tools), cooking, sewing, growing food and preserving it, reading, writing, playing checkers and other games, and activities they perform at school.

4. To show how important language is in communication, ask a child to give a command to another without talking to or touching the latter. The command could be to sharpen a pencil, dust an eraser, empty a wastebasket, etc.

from *Science: Understanding Your Environment*. George G. Mallinson. Silver Burdett. ©1978. pp. 134-135. Used with permission. All rights reserved.

Critique

This lesson is a missed opportunity to have students practice giving evidence in support of their beliefs, and to probe deeper into questions concerning the differences between animals and man.

Although students are asked "to share ideas about whether or not each animal has all the senses and how the senses are used" it is not clear how or if the teacher encourages them to support their claims. Furthermore, activity 4, on communication, is not integrated with the lesson, since it is in no way related to questions about animal communication.

Strategies Used to Remodel

S-18 supplying evidence for a conclusion

S-1 fostering independent thinking

REMODELLED LESSON PLAN

For each student response concerning the similarities and differences between animal and human senses, ask "What makes you think so? *S-18* Did you learn it yourself or from someone else? What did you observe and conclude?" If the students say they learned it from someone else ask "What could you do to test this claim for yourself?" *S-1*

In the exercise on communication, add, "Do you think animals communicate? What makes you think so?" *S-18* If yes, "How do they communicate? What are the different ways humans communicate? How are these similar to or different from how animals communicate?"

Add further thought provoking questions time providing, e.g., "How do animals learn? Do they have anything like school? What makes you think so? What does it mean to think? Do animals think? How do you know? *S-18* What kinds of things do animals communicate to each other? ('I'm hungry! I'm scared! Food! Get away!') What are some similarities and differences between what we and animals communicate?" The class could also discuss how much human language dogs 'understand.' (Although such questions are difficult, even for adults, there is no reason that children can't begin to ponder them early. This gives them valuable practice in asking further questions to clarify a problem, and distinguish what they know from what they are unsure of.)

Rocks of the Earth

(Science - 2nd Grade)

Objectives of the Remodelled Lesson

The student will:

• practice developing questions about rocks

• practice discussing how scientific questions can be answered

• categorize questions

ORIGINAL LESSON PLAN

Abstract

The first lesson introduces a unit on rocks. The student page has a picture of two children by a stream in the mountains. The text draws attention to sizes and shapes of rocks. The students describe and discuss rocks they have found, compare their rocks to the picture, and discuss where rocks are found. The second lesson, which sums-up the unit, focuses on the following questions: What sizes and shapes are rocks? In what places can you find rocks? Are some rocks softer than other rocks? How can you find out which rocks are softer? Are some rocks harder than other rocks? How can you find out which rocks are harder? How can you find out if a rock is limestone? How can you make crystals? What do crystals look like? How are rocks used?

from *Discovering Science*. Albert Piltz, et al. Charles E. Merrill Publishing Co. © 1973. pp. 2, 13T-14T Used with permission. All rights reserved.

Critique

The unit misses the opportunity to have students develop their own questions, and, in many cases, reflect on how to settle them. The text provides the teacher with the questions, and suggests specific ways that experiments should be conducted. Students should be allowed to develop and explore their own questions, about problems they are most interested in, and practice seeing how these questions guide their means of inquiry, i.e. what kinds of things they need to do to answer the questions. This unit further misses the opportunity to have students practice classifying and discussing types of questions, i.e. comparing and contrasting the ways in which different questions are answered.

Strategies Used to Remodel

S-1 fostering independent thinking

S-11 clarifying issues

REMODELLED LESSON PLAN

Begin the lesson by asking students, "What do you know about rocks?" Then ask, "What would you like to find out about rocks?" **S-1** Help students recognize how good questions are an important part of scientific inquiry by asking, "Do you know what to do to answer this question? **S-11** Is the question clear?" (Do you know what it means or do you need to ask further questions?) Then, "How would you find out? Do you need facts? Do you need to do an experiment? Do you need to measure or count? How should you measure? Is there any other way you can find out? Is one way better than another? Why do you think so?" Record specific methods students suggest for answering questions.

After you have completed this process for at least several of the students' questions, encourage students to think about their responses and ask "Are any of these questions similar in the way you find out the answers? Which ones? What would you do to answer the first question mentioned? What would you do to answer the second question mentioned? How are these similar?" The teacher should begin grouping the questions on the board. After a group of two questions has been formed ask, "Are any of the other questions similar to these? How so?" When the students have exhausted their choices for the first group ask of the remaining questions "Are any of these questions similar? What would you do to find out the answer to the first? What would you do to find out the answer to the second? How are these similar?" Continue this process until the students have grouped as many questions as they can. If the teacher sees an obvious similarity that students have overlooked they should probe the relationship between the two questions by asking "How did you say we could find out the answer to this question? And the other question? Are these at all similar?"

To sum up, ask, "What are some of the kinds of things we decided that we must do to find out the answers to our questions about rocks? Were some questions harder than others? Can someone give me an example of a question they think is hard to answer? Why do you think so? Can anyone give an example of a question

177

that is easier to answer? Why do you think so?" Conclude by mentioning that whatever problem they are trying to solve, it helps to think about what they must do to answer the questions they have about it.

For the rest of the unit, the students should try to answer the questions they find most interesting. (They may need to supplement their experiments with reading.)

We can never become fairminded unless we learn how to enter sympathetically into the thinking of others, to reason from their perspective and eventually to try seeing things as they see them.

Plant and Animal Products in Food

(Science - 2nd Grade)

Objectives of the Remodelled Lesson

The student will:

- develop and discuss criteria for evaluating foods
- be introduced to the idea of criteria for evaluation
- apply the criteria to actual cases

ORIGINAL LESSON PLAN

CONCEPT: Man depends on plants and other animals for food.

BEHAVIORAL OBJECTIVES: The child will be able: (1) to classify common foods as plant product, animal product, or a combination of both and (2) to show how the energy in foods all animals eat can be traced back to the sun.

VOCABULARY: Text: energy, strong

MATERIALS NEEDED: Step 1: Labels from hot dog and roll packages. Step 2: Empty food containers--boxes, cans, jars, bags, and envelopes. Step 3: Resources for food picture collections; materials for bulletin board display.

LESSON CAPSULE: 1. The boy at the right is eating a hot dog. To find out what plants and animals are used in making the hot dog and roll, plan a class or committee visit to the grocery store (or school cafeteria) and record the ingredients as listed on the packages. 2. Have children bring empty food containers or labels to class. Compare the ingredients lists of different brands of the same food. Most labels list ingredients in order by percent of weight, from greatest to smallest percent. Have children group the containers to show plant products, animal products, and combined plant and animal products. Discuss where and how each product is grown, how it reaches the producer, and how it is prepared.

STUDENT TEXT: You need much energy every day. You need energy to run and jump. You need energy to grow strong. You need energy to think. The energy you need comes from the food you eat. People use many plants and animals for food. What is this boy eating? What plants and animals does this food come from?

from *Science: Understanding Your Environment.* George G. Mallinson. © Silver Burdett. 1978. p.142. Used with permission. All rights reserved.

Critique

This lesson provides the teacher with a natural place to introduce evaluation of food products, but instead it focuses only on the distinction between plant and animal products. This constitutes a missed opportunity to have students develop criteria for choosing foods to eat, and apply the criteria to specific foods.

Strategies Used to Remodel

S-16 distinguishing relevant from irrelevant facts

S-15 developing criteria of evaluation

S-3 fostering reciprocity

REMODELLED LESSON PLAN

The class should discuss what is relevant to deciding which foods to choose. *S-16* The teacher should ask "What are some of the things we should know about food before deciding to buy it?" *S-15* List these responses. Allow room for disagreement and discussion. One student, for example, may argue that how food tastes is the most important factor; whereas another student believes that the food that is cheapest is best. If disagreement doesn't arise naturally ask "What does your partents think is most important when choosing a breakfast cereal for you to eat? *S-3* What do you think? What criteria do your partnets use to decide? What criteria did you use? Who do you think is right? Why?"

Then have students look at the ingredients, and list several pairs of different brands of the same foods. Have students evaluate two brands of the same food using the criteria each thinks are most important. Then have them evaluate the foods using their parents' criteria. *S-3*

If what we do in a remodel is unclear, review the critique and strategies for guidance.

At Work on the Earth

(Science - 3rd Grade)

Objectives of the Remodelled Lesson

The student will:

- distinguish ordinary usage of 'work' from the scientific usage
- distinguish work from play
- recognize that human purposes determine how words are used

ORIGINAL LESSON PLAN

Abstract

Students begin the lesson by observing a picture of children pushing a raft down a river, and discussing what the children are doing. The text asks, "Would you say they are doing work?" Students say what they think 'work' means; then they are introduced to the scientific meaning of 'work.' Each child is asked to demonstrate an action that verifies his understanding of the scientific meaning. Other children observe and identify the force that is applied and the motion that results.

Next students are asked whether water can do work, and distinguish between forces used to do work (e.g. child raking leaves vs. boy holding hose still while the water moves the leaves.)

from *Concepts in Science*. Paul F. Brandwein, et al. Haracourt Brace Jovanovich, Inc. 1980. pp. T8-T11.

Critique

This lesson provides an important introduction to the idea that the same word can have different meanings, and that scientists, especially, can have special meanings for ordinary words. Unfortunately, however, this lesson fails to give students valuable practice in moving up and back between different meanings of the same word, and recognizing and generating examples of when one, both, or neither meaning applies. Instead of moving back and forth, this lesson moves immediately to the scientific usage of the word 'work' and assumes it throughout the lesson. Students should be encouraged to struggle with the different meanings, and recognize the relationship of one's purpose to one's use of words.

Strategies Used to Remodel

S-12 clarifying ideas

S-13 distinguishing ideas

S-6 exploring underlying purposes

REMODELLED LESSON PLAN

Students can probe further into their own understanding of work by distinguishing it from the contrasting idea of play. *S-12*   Have them generate several examples of both work and play. Write these on the board in separate columns. Go back over the list and ask students to comment on what seems to be intrinsic to their idea of work, i.e., what do all the examples on the board have in common. Go through the same process for 'play.' To probe the more subtle distinctions between the two concepts ask, "Can anyone give me an example of when work seems more like play? What should we call it then?" (There are no 'right answers' here, but it is important that students practice giving as much support for their answers as possible.) Then ask, "Can anyone give me an example of when play seems more like work?" If students need help recognizing the more subtle distinctions, ask questions like the following: Why might you call running in the park play and someone else call it work? Is having fun a very important aspect of play? Do you ever have fun when you're working in the yard? What should we call it then, work or play? Do you always have fun when you play? What else makes it play?

Next, introduce the idea that scientists have a special meaning for the word 'work.' Provide an example of a force making something move. Ask students to generate further examples. Ask them how these examples are different from the ones they suggested earlier. Review the examples of work and   play generated at the beginning of the lesson and ask, "Does the scientific idea of 'work' apply to these cases? *S-13*   Which ones would the scientist call an example of work being done? For the scientist, is 'play' the opposite of 'work'? What is?"
Encourage students to see how our purposes guide how we use words by asking, "Is one of the uses of the word 'work' right and one wrong, or are both right? Why do think so? Why does the scientist have a different meaning of 'work'? *S-6*   Why don't they just use the ordinary meaning of the word? Should we always use 'work' the way scientists do?"

Air Has Weight
(Science - 3rd Grade)

Objectives of the Remodelled Lesson

The student will:

- develop experiments to settle a question
- practice distinguishing observations from conclusions

ORIGINAL LESSON PLAN

Abstract

Students learn that air has weight by doing two experiments: balancing two full balloons on a yard-stick and letting air out of one; comparing the weights of an empty and full basketball. Students are also introduced to the word 'conclusion,' and are encouraged to check their conclusions.

from *Today's Basic Science*. John Gabriel Navarra, et. al. © Harper & Row Publishers. 1967. pp. T16-17, 26-27 Used with permission. All rights reserved

Critique

This lesson presents experiments rather than raising a question and letting students try to develop experiments to settle it. Also, the lesson introduces the concept 'conclusion' without contrasting it with its companion concept 'observation'. It misses the opportunity to have students distinguish what they observe from what they conclude, and reflect on the process of moving from observation to conclusion.

Strategies Used to Remodel

S-1 fostering independent thinking

S-18 supplying evidence for a conclusion

S-14 making assumptions explicit

REMODELLED LESSON PLAN

Rather than using the text, raise the issue "Does air weigh anything?" Allow discussion. Then ask, "How could we find out?" *S-1* Allow discussion. If the students can't think of an experiment, lead them to see that they can compare the weights of equivalent containers, one with, one without air.

Have the students conduct their experiments. Then ask, *S-18* , "What did you observe? What did you conclude? How did the experiment settle the issue?" Have students explain their reasoning as fully as possible *S-14* . (I saw that the balloons were balanced. Then, when I pricked one, I saw it shrink up. The air must have left it. Then I saw that the balloons weren't balanced anymore. The full balloon went down. I concluded that it was heavier. The heavier object on a balance goes down. The balloon that lost air went higher, was lighter, than the other. Since the balloons themselves weigh the same, and the balloon with air in it is heavier, I concluded that air does have weight.)

The students can read and discuss their texts as a sum up activity.

Thinking critically involves the ability to reach sound conclusions based on observation and information. Critical thinkers distinguish their observations from their conclusions.

A Living System
(Science - 3rd Grade)

Objectives of the Remodelled Lesson

The student will:

- develop hypotheses about how rocks are broken into soil
- design and conduct experiments to test their hypotheses

ORIGINAL LESSON PLAN

Abstract

We selected lessons from a unit on soil. In them, students are introduced to the topic, examine soil samples, and conduct experiments designed to show how rocks are broken down. Students are shown how rubbing rocks together breaks pieces off. They record contents of soil samples. They rub two pieces of sandstone together for five minutes and count the pieces. Students are told how air, water, plants, and temperature changes break rocks.

from *Concepts In Science*. Paul F. Brandwein, et al. Harcourt Brace Jovanovich, Inc. 1980. pp. T32-T34, 53-54, 56-58, 63-64.

Critique

By presenting the processes by which rocks are broken down, and the experiments which illustrate them, the lessons discourage students from struggling with an issue and developing their own hypotheses and experiments.

Students are told to count the pieces of rock they have broken off, yet there is no reason for learning how many pieces are broken off by five minutes of rubbing. Students shouldn't be asked to measure or count unless doing so helps settle some issue of interest. Measuring and counting, in themselves, are pointless. The idea that scientists run around counting and measuring everything in sight, for no reason, is a stereotype. Students need to learn how to use quantification as part of the process of settling questions. They need to learn to distinguish times when such activities are useful from times when they are not. This part of the lesson should be dropped.

REMODELLED LESSON PLAN

Before students read page 63, which covers a number of ways in which rocks are broken up, they should have a chance to reason about the issue, "How are rocks broken up?"

First, remind students that one thing they found in their soil samples was rock. Ask, "Where did the little pieces of rock come from? How did big rocks get broken into pieces?" Ask them to recall partly broken, crumbling, or cracked rocks they have seen. Ask them if they know or could guess the cause. *S-1* Let the students brainstorm possible answers. Make a list. Allow discussion. Choose several responses and ask, "How could we find out if this breaks rocks?" Allow discussion. The class could be split into groups, each of which can design and conduct experiments to test the hypotheses and report the results to the rest of the class.

To summarize the lesson, have the class read and discuss the relevant passages in the text, or have students write about how rocks change.

School time is too precious to spend any sizeable portion of it on random facts. The world, after all, is filled with an infinite number of facts. No one can learn more than an infinitesimal portion of them. Though we need facts and information, there is no reason why we cannot gain facts as part of the process of learning how to think.

Two Concepts of 'Soil'

(Science - 3rd Grade)

Objectives of the Remodelled Lesson

The student will

 • practice distinguishing the scientists' concept of 'soil' from that of farmers.

 • compare the two concepts

ORIGINAL LESSON PLAN

Abstract

Seven pages from the student's text, and one page from the teacher's edition, were selected from a unit on soil. The first page distinguishes the scientists' concept of 'soil' (all of the earth's covering is soil) from the farmers' concept (soil is the part of the land in which crops can grow.) The rest of the students' pages cover the following topics: kinds of soil, makeup of soil, layers of soil, and soil conservation. The last page (from the teacher's edition) has review questions for the unit.

from *Concepts in Science*. Paul F. Brandwein, et al. Harcourt Brace Jovanovich, Inc. 1980. pp. 55, 60, 79, 81-83, 86, T41.

Critique

After introducing the distinction between the two concepts of soil, the text simply uses the word 'soil' without saying which sense of the concept is meant. Furthermore, the text fails to mention how purposes determine how a word is used.

Strategies Used to Remodel

S-6 exploring underlying purposes

S-13 distinguishing ideas

REMODELLED LESSON PLAN

When discussing the page on which the distinction between 'soil' (science) and 'soil' (farming) is made, ask students to think about the two concepts. Ask: How are the concepts similar? Different? Which concept covers more examples? Is one concept clearer than the other? Which concept is more familiar to you? Why do scientists and farmers use the same word differently? **S-6** Is one use right and the other wrong? (No, the uses suit their different purposes.)

For the other pages, ask students which concept of 'soil' is meant. **S-13** Have them explain how they know. (For instance, on page 60, the scientific concept is used. Sand is one kind of soil, and sand isn't 'soil' to a farmer. On page 79 the text probably means the farmers' concept because it says "good soil" -- which probably means 'good for people to use.')

When using the review questions, again, have the students explain which concept is meant each time 'soil' occurs.

In order to think critically about issues we must first be able to state the issue clearly. The more completely, clearly, and accurately the issue is formulated, the easier and more helpful the discussion of its settlement.

Parts of a Wave

(Science - 3rd Grade)

Objective of the Remodelled Lesson

The student will discover the parts of waves and learn the standard terms applied to them.

ORIGINAL LESSON PLAN

Parts of a Wave: Having observed the waves in a rope, your pupils can now proceed with a lesson on the parts of a wave. As the textbook explains, a wave has two main parts, a trough and a crest. The distance from one crest to the next crest in a wave train is known as wavelength. One complete wave consists of one crest and one trough. Refer to the drawing, "A Wave and Its Parts," page 134. Compare this drawing with the drawings which the boys and girls made while they were observing the waves in a rope.

Student Text: Let's go through your experiment with the rope again. Set up some waves. Observe the motion. Observe carefully the up-and-down movement of the rope. Now, look at the point at which you tied the rope to the post.

Again, set up some waves. Note that a part of each wave moves above the point at which the rope is tied. This is the high point of the wave. This high point is called the crest. Every wave has a crest. Another part of the wave moves below the point at which the rope is tied. This is the low point of the wave. The low point is called the trough. Every wave has a trough.

One crest and one trough make a complete wave. The length of a wave is the distance from one wave crest to the next crest. This measure is called the wavelength. The length of every wave can be measured.

from *The Young Scientist*. John Gabriel Navarra, et. al. © Harper & Row, Publishers. 1971. pp. T63, 134 Used with permission. All rights reserved.

Strategy Used to Remodel

S-1 fostering independent thought

189

REMODELLED LESSON PLAN

Before using the text, the teacher should give the students a chance to discover the parts of waves for themselves, rather than presenting the answers to them. **S-1**

Draw several different looking waves on the board. Focus students' attention on the wave parts by asking the following questions: How are these waves different? Similar? What parts do they have? How could we describe these waves? How could we distinguish them? Where could we measure them?

Lead the students to point out the high points, low points, and the distance between repeating patterns. (They may also mention the distance up-and-down.)

If the students don't know the standard terms, introduce them, relating each to the students' descriptions (the up-and- down length is 'amplitude.')

Point out that, although the wavelength could be measured from any two corresponding points (trough, crest, half-way between, etc.,) it is standard practice to measure it from crest to crest.

Lesson plan remodelling is well done when the person doing the remodel understands the strategies and principles used, when the strategies and principles are well thought-out, when the remodel clearly follows from the critique, and when the remodel teaches critical thinking better than the original.

Some Vocabulary and Distinctions

Critical Thinking: refers to

    a. a body of intellectual skills and abilities which (when used in keeping with the dispositions and values below) enable one rationally to decide what to believe or do.

    b. a body of dispositions

    c. a set of values: truth, fair-mindedness, open-mindedness, empathy, autonomy, rationality, self-criticism

Uncritical Person: refers to one who has not learned the intellectual skills above (naive, conformist, easily manipulated, dogmatic, closed- minded, narrow-minded).

Critical Person: refers to any person who in a weak or strong sense uses the intellectual skills above (a critical person may or may not significantly embody the dispositions or be committed to the values of critical thinking. Some critical persons use the intellectual skills to justify or rationalize whatever beliefs they uncritically internalize and do not hold themselves or those they ego-identify with to the same intellectual standards to which they hold those they disagree with or disapprove of.)

Weak Sense Critical Thinker: refers to

    a. one who does not hold himself or those he ego-identifies with to the same intellectual standards to which he holds "opponents"

    b. one who has not learned how to reason empathically within points of view or frames of reference with which he disagrees

    c. one who tends to think monologically

    d. one who does not genuinely accept, though he may verbally espouse, the values of critical thinking

    e. one who uses the intellectual skills of critical thinking selectively and self-deceptively to foster and serve his vested interest (at the expense of truth)

Strong Sense Critical Thinker: refers to

    a. one who holds himself and those he agrees with to the same intellectual standards to which he holds those he disagrees with

    b. one who thinks empathically within points of view or frames of reference with which he disagrees (one who is able to see some truth and insight within opponents points of view as well as weaknesses within his own)

c. one who is able to think multi-logically and dialogically

d. one who genuinely strives to live in accordance with the values of critical thinking (hence one who can see occasions in which he or she has failed so to live)

e. one who uses the intellectual skills and abilities of critical thinking to go beyond those beliefs which serve his or her vested interests and to detect self-deceptive reasoning

Critical Society: refers to the notion of a society which rewards adherence to the values of critical thinking and hence does not use indoctrination and inculcation as basic modes of learning (rewards reflective questioning, intellectual independence, and reasoned dissent.)

Monological Thinking: refers to thinking that is conducted exclusively within one point of view or frame of reference.

Monological Problems: refers to problems that can be rationally solved by reasoning exclusively within one point of view or frame of reference (many technical problems can be solved by monological thinking.)

Multi-logical Thinking: refers to thinking that goes beyond one frame of reference or point of view.

Multi-logical Problems: refers to problems which to be rationally solved require that one entertain and reason empathically within more than one point of view or frame of reference.

Dialogical Thinking: refers to thinking that involves a dialogue or extended exchange between different points of view or frames of reference.

Dialectical Thinking: refers to dialogical thinking conducted in order to test the strengths and weaknesses of opposing points of view (court trials and debates are dialectical in nature.)

Dialogical Instruction: refers to instruction that fosters dialogical or dialectic thinking.

Socratic Questioning: refers to a mode of questioning that deeply probes the meaning, justification, or logical strength of a claim, position, or line of reasoning. Socratic questioning can be carried out in a variety of ways and adapted to many levels of ability and understanding.

Reciprocity: refers to the act of entering empathically into the point of view or line of reasoning of others; learning to think as others do and by that means to sympathetically assess that thinking. (Requires creative imagination as well as intellectual skill and a commitment to fair-mindedness.)

Additional Vocabulary

evidence: The data on which a judgment or conclusion might be based, or by which proof or probability may be established.

premise: A proposition upon which an argument is based or from which a conclusion is drawn; logic -- one of the first two propositions of a syllogism, from which the conclusion is drawn.

assumption: A statement accepted or supposed as true without proof or demonstration; unstated premise.

conclusion: A judgment or decision reached after deliberation.

inference: A conclusion based on something known or assumed; derived by reasoning.

reasoning: The mental processes of one who reasons; especially the drawing of conclusions or inferences from observations, facts or *hypotheses*. The evidence or arguments used in this procedure.

truth: Conformity to knowledge, fact, actuality, or logic: a statement proven to be or accepted as true. Not false or erroneous.

fallacious: Containing or based on a fallacy; deceptive in appearance or meaning; misleading; delusive.

prove: To establish the truth or validity of something by presentation of argument or evidence; to determine the quality of by testing.

implication: A claim which follows from other stated claims; an indication which is not said openly or directly; hint; what is hinted or suggested by what is said or done.

egocentric: A tendency to view everything else in relationship to oneself: one's desires, values and beliefs (seeming to be self-evidently correct or superior to those of others) are often uncritically used as the norm of all judgment and experience.

ethnocentric: A tendency to view one's own race (culture) as central, based on the attitude that one's own group is superior.

sociocentric: When a group or society sees itself as superior and thus considers its way of seeing the world as correct; there is a tendency to presuppose this superiority in all of its thinking and thus to serve as an impediment to open-mindedness.

Appendix: Original Lesson Plans

In the following pages, O-53 to O-183, most of the original lesson plans are printed. The purpose of including them is to aid the reader in understanding the process of critique and remodel. The reader should also note that these originals are excellent resources for critical thinking infusion. The original lesson plans for which we were granted permission are numbered in accord with the page in the text where they are first cited. For example, the original for "Places to Play," which occurs on page 53, is listed as "O-53," the original for "Air has Weight," which occurs on page 183, as "O-183," etc.

We gratefully acknowledge the following publishers for their generosity in allowing the excerpts to be reprinted:

Harcourt Brace Jovanovich
Holt, Rinehart and Winston
Silver, Burdett & Ginn Inc.
The Economy Company
Bowmar Noble Publishing, Inc.
The Bobbs-Merrill Company, Inc.
Houghton Mifflin Company
Laidlaw Brothers, A Division of Doubleday & Company, Inc.
Addison-Wesley Publishing Co.
J. B. Lippincott Co.
D. C. Heath and Company
Charles E. Merrill Publishing Co.
Silver Burdett Company
Harper & Row Publishers
Harcourt Brace & World Inc.

Places to Play

(The following teaching suggestions apply to both pages 2 and 3.)

Purpose

To develop positive attitudes toward oral language activities; to develop good listening habits.

Procedure

1. Introduce the lesson by calling attention to the pictures on pages 2 and 3. Say: **The pictures show boys and girls playing. Which pictures show boys and girls playing in the city? Which pictures show boys and girls playing outside the city?**

2. Ask: **How can you tell which pictures are city pictures? How can you tell which pictures are not city pictures?** After the children have responded, ask them to look closely at the pictures on both pages so that they will be ready to tell what the boys and girls are doing.

3. To help organize the children's responses, point to one picture at a time. Ask the pupils to tell what the children in the picture are doing. Then ask the pupils to tell of their own, similar play experiences. An example:

Look at the first picture. What are the girls on the steps doing? What are the other children doing? Do you play with dolls? Do you play with a ball? Have you ridden a scooter? What else can you ride? What else can you do outdoors? Tell us about it.

Repeat the process with the other two pictures.

4. Discuss the play activities on page 3 the same way. Bring out differences between urban and coun-

try/suburban scenes by asking questions such as: Where would you see farm animals? Where would there be more cars to look out for? Where would there be more trees and grass?

5. After you have established the difference between urban and non-urban places, draw attention to the similarity between the games being played in both types of places. Say: **The children in the pictures live in different places. Are they all playing different games? Are some of the games the same?** Playing ball, going on a swing, jumping rope, riding, and making believe are common to both pages.

6. Early in the learning activity, begin to encourage good speaking and listening habits. Establish the rule

2

from *Let's Talk and Listen.* Yellow Level *Language for Daily Use* Mildred A. Dawson, et al. Harcourt Brace Jovanovich. 1973. pp. 2-3. Used by permission.

times to talk about things we like to do. We will remember to talk one at a time, to listen courteously, and to speak loudly enough so all can hear.

that *one* child speaks at a time. Illustrate this by pointing to the pictures of the girls jumping rope and the children playing tag-ball. Note that *one* child is the center of attention. Stress the point that a good listener pays careful attention to the speaker.

7. Some pupils may make errors in usage. It is best not to make the children self-conscious or inhibit their spontaneous expressions by insisting on correctness so early. Speak slowly and clearly so that you may be easily understood. The children will often imitate your pronunciation and diction, as well as your usage. By providing a model, you can influence their usage without insisting on correctness.

Use of Page 34

(1) To use pictures to motivate discussion; (2) to help children anticipate outcomes and draw inferences; (3) to help children compose two- and three-sentence oral stories; (4) to provide review in using capital letters in writing names of people.

MATERIALS NEEDED

(1) Chalk.

HOW TO USE THE PAGE

Have the children locate page 34.

Help the children discover that Susan, Tom, and Betty are the children in the pictures. Elicit the generalization that all the pictures in the top row show Susan doing different things; those in the middle row show Tom; and those in the last row show Betty.

Interpreting the pictures. Help the children to interpret the action in each set of pictures. Encourage them to tell about action which may have preceded each pictured episode and to anticipate action which may follow it.

Here are suggested questions to use with each picture.

First row of pictures. Call attention to Susan's name beside her picture.

1. Why is Susan running after the dog? Have you seen this dog before? Where? What is its name? Why do you think Susan's dog is running away with her doll's clothes? Where do you think he got them? What do you think the dog will do with them? What do you think Susan will do?

2. What has happened to Susan in this picture? What do you think caused the skate to come off? Do you think it is broken? What do you think will happen after she gets in the house? If the skate is broken, who may repair it? Have you ever broken a toy? Tell us about it. Who helps you repair your toys if they are broken?

3. What is Susan doing here? Who probably asked her to get the newspaper? Do you think the family will be able to read the whole newspaper? Do you have a newspaper left at your door each morning or evening? Does anything ever happen to it? What?

Second row of pictures. Have the children identify the boy and frame his name.

1. What is Tom doing here? (Decorating his bicycle.) Why do you think he decided to do this? Where do you think he will go when he finishes decorating his bicycle? (To a parade.) Have you ever been in a parade? Tell us about it.

2. Where is Tom in this picture? What is he doing? Is his father just leaving or returning? Where do you suppose his father has been? How do you think the family will show they are happy to have Father at home?

3. What is Tom doing? Where do you think he is? Why did he decide to paint his wagon? Why do you think Tom looks worried? What do you think will happen when his mother or father looks at the floor? Did you ever have an accident with paint? How can Tom get the paint off the floor? How could newspapers have prevented this accident? (Put old newspapers under the paint.)

Third row of pictures. All of these pictures are about the same person. Who is it? Find her name. What is it? With what capital letter does it begin?

1. What is Betty doing here? To whom is Betty bringing the flowers? Where did she get them? Do you think someone suggested she bring them to the teacher or did she think of it herself? What time of year do you think it is?

2. What is Betty doing here? Do you think the dress is a surprise for Betty? What makes you think the family may have bought it for her? What makes you think Betty may not have many new dresses? Where do you think she will wear the dress?

3. Where has Betty been? Where did she get the money for the ice cream cone? Do you think she has been in the ice cream shop for quite a long time? What does her mother think about the length of time? Do you ever spend part of your allowance for ice cream cones?

Drawing inferences. After the discussion, help the children draw inferences about the characters. Use questions such as the following:

Susan. What do the pictures in the first row tell about Susan? What kind of girl is she? What makes you think she is thoughtful? careful? careless? Does anything tell you that she can do things well for herself or does she often need help? In what ways might she have helped herself in these pictures?

Tom. What kind of boy is Tom? Does he like to take part in things? What makes you think that he is good at thinking of things to do? Is he usually busy? Is he helpful? Is he careless? What makes you think he sometimes does things too quickly?

Betty. What kind of girl is Betty? What makes you think she is thoughtful of others? Do you think she appreciates things people do for her?

Writing names. Have the names beside the rows of pictures pronounced. Ask: "What kind of letters do we use to begin names of people? What capital letter do you see at the beginning of each name?"

Say: "I am going to write a name on the chalkboard. See if you can read the name I write here." Write *Susan.* Have the name pronounced. (Capital *S-u-s-a-n.*) Call for several volunteers to write the word.

Follow the same procedure in writing *Tom* and *Betty.*

Composing two- and three-sentence stories. Help the children compose oral stories about the characters on this page. Several may be recorded.

> Betty is good.
> She has a new dress.
> Her family loves her.

PRACTICE BOOK

Use page 22 of *My Practice Book.*

* * *Lesson may be divided here.* * *

From Teachers' Edition of Book I-1 of GINN ELEMENTARY SERIES. © Copyright, 1963 by Silver, Burdett & Ginn Inc. Used with

Susan

Tom

Betty

O-65

34

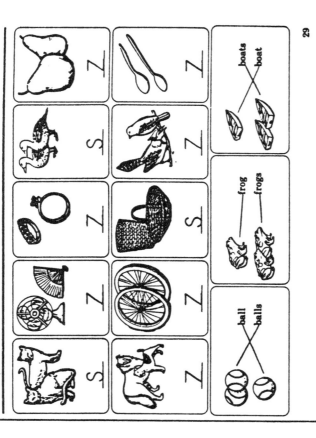

We work with words.

S   Z   Z   S

S   Z   Z   S

ball —×— balls   frog —×— frogs   boats —×— boat

29

We work with words.   Sound the words.

(77a)jumps stops runs plays   wants
b) (40)mash trick trap trip   tried
(40)brain brave brace bring   broke

A Toy for Mike

"Mike will like this toy," Ann said.
"He wants a big ball. 3
He wants a ball like this."

"I know Mike will like it," Pat said. 1
"Now we have the ball.
And we have the string.
But can we tie it?" 4

30

from *Tag In And Out All Around*
Theodore L. Harris et al. The Economy
Company, © 1973. pp. T204-205. Used by
permission.

Page 29

Directions   Sounding words with the ending **s**
Have pupils identify each picture and write **s** for /s/
or **z** for /z/ to indicate the sound **s** stands for in the
word. For the second part, have them match each word
with the appropriate picture.

**Developing
Comprehension
Page 30
Word Study**

Assist the children in analyzing the words in "We work
with words" and "Sound the words." To be sure the
children understand the meanings of the new words,
have them use the words in sentences.
    Challenge words: fix, made, tie

*Story
Motivation*

Display several odd-shaped toys such as a top, a baseball bat, and a sand bucket and shovel. "If you were
going to a birthday party, you might take one of these
toys as a gift. But what would you need to do to it first?"
(wrap it) If time allows, provide paper and ribbon and
let a child attempt to wrap one of the toys. Encourage
pupils to observe and discuss the difficulties involved.
"Read the story title and look at the picture. Who is
Mike? Do you see a toy for him?"

*Guided
Reading*

Have pupils read the page silently to find out what the
girls are saying.

*Discussion
and Rereading*

1. Who is Ann's friend?
2. What are Ann and Pat doing?
3. What gift do they have for Mike?
4. Read the question Pat asks. What do you think she
   means?

204   In and Out

O-67

Guided Reading

Direct attention to the first picture on page 31. "What do you think has happened?" Have the children read the first half of the page silently.

Discussion and Rereading

1. Who tries to wrap Mike's toy first? (Pat)
2. Why can't Pat wrap the basketball? (She can't get the string tied.)
3. What happens when Ann tries to wrap the toy? (The string breaks.) Find her words and read them the way you think she would say them.
4. Why is Ann so upset? (It is time to go.)
5. Do you think Pat has a plan for wrapping the gift? What does she say that lets you know?

Guided Reading

"Do you think Pat's idea will work?" Have pupils finish reading the story silently.

Discussion

1. Do you think Pat's plan is a good idea? Why or why not?
2. What things do Pat and Ann use to wrap the ball? (sack and crayons)
3. How do Pat and Ann feel about the present? Do you think Mike will feel the same as they do?

Conclusion

1. What was the best part of Pat's idea?
2. What else could they have used to wrap the toy?
3. Was there any part of the story that could not have happened?
4. Have you ever had a problem like Pat and Ann's? Tell what happened.

Page 32 *Directions*

Choosing solutions to problems
Have pupils read each story and put X by the two best solutions. Then let them discuss their choices and suggest other solutions.

"See, Ann," said Pat.
"This will work.
And you and I made it.
We made it for Mike.
We can go now.
Mike will like this!"

Pat tried to tie the string.[1]
She tried and tried to tie it.
Ann tried to tie the string.
But the string broke.

Ann said, "Oh, no! [3]
The string broke.
It broke, Pat!
And now we have to go."[4]

"Wait, Ann!" said Pat.
"Look! The ball can go in this![5]
We do not have to tie this
with a string."

Think about It

It is time for work.
But Dad can not go.
Dad will ———.

X ——— walk to work
X ——— fix it
——— wait for the rain to stop

Up high went the kite.
But down it went.
Bob will ———.

——— go up and get it down
X ——— run with the string
X ——— have Dad get it down

Ann wants to walk with Max.
But Max is not here.
Ann will ———.

X ——— look for Max
——— splash Max
X ——— wait for Max

A Toy for Mike   205

Splash! Splash!

Kevin ran down to the pond.

Kevin went to the pond and looked in.

Jan met Kevin at the pond.

A little duck was in the pond.

A big turtle was in the pond.

33

Sandy ran to the pond.

Splash! A big jump, and Sandy was in the pond.

The splash was very big.

The big splash got Kevin and Jan very wet.

34

Sandy went after the wet duck.

The duck went down very fast.

"The little duck got away," said Jan.

"Sandy lost the duck in the pond," said Kevin.

35

Introducing "Splash! Splash!" (Pages 33–37)

Setting purpose for reading Distribute copies of *A Happy Morning*. Then write the title *Splash! Splash!* on the chalkboard and have it read. . . . Call attention to the exclamation points.

Ask: **What does the word *splash* make you think of?** . . . **Where might the story take place?** . . . Continue: **Does the title tell us what made the splash?** . . . **Does it tell us if anyone got splashed?** . . . **We must read the story to find out. Turn now to page 33.**

Silent Reading

—Read page 33 to see if you can find out what made the splash.

Page 33
—What did Kevin do? Whom did he meet at the pond?
—What animals were in the pond?
—Did we find out on this page what made the splash? Read the next page to see if you find out there.

Page 34
—Who made the splash?
—What happened to Jan and Kevin when Sandy jumped into the pond?
—Why do you think Sandy jumped into the pond? Read page 35 to find out if you are right.

Page 35
—Did Sandy get what he jumped into the pond after? Why not?
—Who was watching Sandy? How do you know that Jan and Kevin were looking at Sandy?
—Sandy lost the duck. Let's read the next two pages to find out if he ever caught anything in the pond.

Then Sandy went after the
big turtle.

The big turtle went down in
the pond.

"Sandy lost the turtle," said Jan.

36

Kevin was still very wet.

Jan was still very wet.

Kevin and Jan sat on the grass.

Sandy went up to Kevin.

Then Sandy sat down.

Kevin and Jan and Sandy sat
in the morning sun.

37

Pages 36–37

—Did Sandy catch anything in the pond? Why not?

—What did Sandy do after he lost the turtle?

—What were Jan, Kevin, and Sandy doing at the end of the story?

Story Interpretation and Extension

—Why is "Splash! Splash!" a good title for this story?

—How do you think Jan and Kevin felt toward Sandy when he splashed them? What might they have said to Sandy?

—Do you think that Sandy was afraid of the duck or the turtle? How do you know he wasn't?

—Were the duck and the turtle afraid of Sandy? What makes you think they were?

Oral Reading

Recognizing the same idea stated in different words After pupils have turned to the first page indicated below, read the sentence that follows in the list. Ask pupils to find and frame the sentence which means almost the same thing as the sentence you have just read. Have the sentence from the book read aloud.

—**Page 34.** Sandy jumped into the pond with a loud splash. (*second*)

The water splashed all over Jan and Kevin and got them wet. (*last*)

—**Page 35.** The duck swam down to the bottom of the pond. (*second*)

Jan said, "The duck escaped." (*third*)

—**Page 37.** Sandy came out of the pond. (*fourth*)

Sandy sat in the morning sun with Jan and Kevin. (*last*)

Enjoying oral reading Read the entire story aloud to pupils. Have children notice how punctuation tells you when to pause or when to vary your intonation for questions and exclamations. Then have every pupil read the story with a partner.

Since children have now completed approximately half of *A Happy Morning,* you may wish to evaluate their oral reading. Have each pupil sit beside you, apart from the group, as he reads "Splash! Splash!" or one of the previous stories. Check such aspects of oral reading as: (1) phrasing, (2) attention to punctuation, (3) word recognition, (4) natural expression in the reading of dialogue.

Group Activities

Consonant substitution Write the word *wet* on the chalkboard and have it read. Tell pupils that

Pages 24 and 25

Guided Reading and Comprehension: Have the children read pages 24 and 25 silently.

Discussion and Rereading: Guide the discussion with the following questions:

1. Have Toby and Cleo lived on the block all their lives? (no) Read lines that prove your answer.
2. What things do they like about the city?
3. What problem do they have?

Toby and Cleo walked along the street carrying their ice skates. There were many things to see. Cleo liked to look in the store windows, and Toby liked to watch the building machines.

1 "I like this block more than I thought I would," said Cleo. "I thought there would be nothing for us to do but sit around in
2 the apartment. But with the park on our block, we can ice skate!"

2 "Another thing I like about living here is that Dad has work all the time now," Toby said.

"But I don't feel like we really belong," said Cleo. "So far we don't have any good friends on our block."

24

4. How do Toby and Cleo plan to work out their problem?
5. What did Toby and Cleo do to get ready for the race? Can you think of anything else besides practice that might help? (It would help to eat and sleep properly to avoid illness, to keep ice skates in good condition, and to think of the best plan for skating in a group race.)
6. Which boys and girls will be most likely to win the races on Sports Day? (Those who have practiced regularly, own good skates, have long legs, and have a strong desire to win will have an advantage.)
7. Do you think Cleo and Toby will have some competition in the race? Read the lines that show this.

Motivation: "What can Cleo do to make up for being smaller than some of the other girls?" Allow time for pupils to set purposes for reading.

"I know," said Toby. "The other kids talk to us. Mr. March is nice to us at the park.
4 But if we could race on Sports Day, maybe we could make some new friends."

5 Both Toby and Cleo skated every day after school. They wanted to win their races.

7 Toby saw other boys skating. Some of them were good skaters that would be in the race with Toby.

"I hope I can win that race!" Toby said. On Sports Day, Toby and Cleo hurried to the
7 park. Cleo's race was first. When the girls lined up to race, Toby saw one girl much bigger than Cleo.

25

44

TWO WAYS TO WIN

"Well, that tallest girl will win," Toby thought. "With those long legs, she will be fast. Too bad for Cleo!"

But Cleo got off to a good start. **The** 1 tall girl could not keep up with her. Then a girl named Sue started to pass all of the skaters. Soon she was just behind Cleo, skating very fast. Suddenly Cleo hit a big crack in the ice and fell. She jumped up quickly and skated hard. But Sue didn't fall, and she won the race.

All the girls were laughing and talking as they rushed over to Sue.

"You did it! You did it!" they shouted over and over again.

Cleo skated away from the girls. Toby came to her and asked, "Did you hurt your leg?"

Cleo shook her head, and she sat down on 3 a bench. "I lost my race," she said. "Now, Toby, you will have to win your race. If you don't win, we won't get to know any new people around here."

26

It was time for Toby to get ready for his race. A tall boy named Dave lined up beside Toby. The race started! Toby skated very fast, and he was ahead of many of the boys. He was able to pass everyone but Dave. Toby could not catch him.

All at once something happened! Dave's skate hit the same crack in the ice that Cleo had hit. Down he went! 4

There was a snap! Toby saw Dave 5 frowning and holding his leg. Toby stopped beside Dave. But all the other skaters rushed by. "Don't get up," Toby said to Dave. Then he shouted, "Mr. March! Mr. March!"

27

Pages 26 and 27

Guided Reading and Comprehension: Have the children read pages 26 and 27 silently.

Discussion and Rereading: Ask questions about the purposes set. Continue the discussion with these questions:

1. Did the tall girl turn out to be Cleo's main rival in the race? (no) Read the lines that prove this.
2. How do you think Cleo felt after the race? What things made it hard for her? (The other girls rushed over to Sue. Cleo felt that she had let Toby down. She probably had hurt her arm or leg when she fell.)
3. Read aloud the last paragraph on page 26. Do you think Cleo's statement is true?

4. When Dave hit the crack in the ice, what happened to him that did not happen to Cleo?
5. Why do you think Dave did not get up after he fell?
6. In what ways did Toby use good judgment? (He stopped to help Dave, cautioned him about moving his injured leg, and called the park supervisor for help.)

Motivation: "In the meantime, what do you suppose is happening in the race?" Have the children set purposes for reading the rest of the story.

Page 28

Guided Reading and Comprehension: Have the children read page 28 silently.

Discussion and Rereading: Ask questions about the purposes set. Continue the discussion with these questions:

1. Do you know who won the race? (no)
2. Read what Tim said about Toby. What does "a good sport" mean?
3. Why did Toby get so much attention even though he hadn't won the race?
4. How do you think Cleo felt at the end of the story? What made her feel good?
5. What two ways to win did Toby and Cleo find?
6. Is there magic involved in winning friends?

Conclusion: Ask the pupils to open their books and find the sentences that show these things:

1. Cleo was happier than she thought she would be in her new home. (page 24)
2. Their father had a job. (page 24)
3. Toby and Cleo had something to do after school. (page 25)
4. The boys did not race first. (page 25)
5. Cleo was not badly hurt when she fell. (page 26)
6. Toby was off to a good start. (page 27)
7. Dave took a bad fall. (page 27)
8. Toby was the only skater who stopped to help Dave. (page 27)
9. Carl wanted Dave to stay around for a long time. (page 28)

Extending Comprehension

Display a picture of one animal chasing another. Ask the children to plan a make-believe (fanciful) story about these animals. Guide them to develop the three parts of their story with these questions:

1. Who are the characters in this story? Why is one chasing the other?
2. What does the animal being chased plan to do? What problem comes about during the chase?
3. How is the problem solved? What is a good ending for this story?

After the story has been developed, invite children to act it out. Some children may feel less inhibited if they use puppets. Then discuss other possible solutions to the problem posed in this story.

📖 Activity Book, Page 7

Mr. March rushed over. When he saw Dave's leg, he said, "Maybe you broke a bone! It's a good thing you didn't get up."

"Toby could have won that race," said Bill. "But he stopped to help Dave."

"What a good sport!" Tim added.

Then Sue and Carl walked over to Cleo. "Are you Toby's sister?" Sue asked.

"Yes, I'm Cleo," she answered.

"You're a good skater!" said Sue. "And your brother is really a good sport!"

Carl nodded. "I hope Toby plays ball. We will need a good catcher next spring."

When Cleo heard Carl, she thought, "There is more than one way to win!" And then she rushed over to tell Toby.

28

Individualizing Instruction

Exploration

1. Have two groups of children plan a bulletin board one side of which will show winter sports and the other, summer sports. One group may find pictures of sports played primarily in the summer, such as swimming, baseball, and tennis. The other group may find pictures of sports played in winter, such as hockey, football, and skiing.
2. Play the game "Ready, Set, Go." With brown wrapping paper make three race tracks ten to twenty feet long. Draw lines across the track at intervals of two feet. Put the tracks on the floor and have each racer stand behind the first line. Instruct each racer that he must be the first to answer a question card in order to move to the second line. Have a leader read prepared cards that contain such questions as these: What is taller than a house? What is faster than a car? What is longer than a bus? What is lighter than a marshmallow? Let the winner of the race be the leader for the next game.
3. Lead a discussion about the good sport in the story. On a chart write down the characteristics of a good sport as suggested by the children.

Page 40

Guided Reading and Comprehension: Have the children read page 40 silently.

Discussion and Rereading

1. Read the sentence that tells the main idea of these paragraphs.
2. What message is discussed on this page and shown in the illustration? Read the sentence aloud.
3. What message do you get from the catcher? (Where did it go?)
4. Read the question that asks about something you have experienced. Then answer the question.
5. Do you see messages without words on the other boys' faces?

Motivation: "What other kinds of messages without words do you think the author will discuss next?" Have the children set purposes for reading.

1 Did you ever get a message without words? When you came to school today, did the look on someone's face say, "I'm happy!" If you ever got mud on the floor, what was the message on your mother's face?

2 If a baseball goes past the catcher, he may scratch his head as he looks for it. Do you understand his message?

Did you ever think of a smile or a frown or a scratch as a message?

Page 41

Guided Reading and Comprehension: "Look at the illustration. What do you think has happened?" (The blue-capped team has won. The red-capped team has lost.) "What helps you know how they are feeling?" (facial expressions, gestures, body movements) Have the children read page 41 silently.

Discussion and Rereading: Ask questions about the purposes set. Continue the discussion with these questions:

1. What sentence tells the main idea of these paragraphs? Does the illustration show this?
2. What body movements in the illustrations show that the blue-capped team won? (arms raised, climbing on back of player, picking up and swinging a player, jumping in the air, heads raised) What body movements show that the other team lost? (looking toward the ground, sitting in slumped position, bending over, leaning on one another, heads resting on fists)
3. Read and answer the last question on page 41.
4. Why does the author ask questions? (The author wants the reader to start thinking of ways to send messages without talking.)

Many times the way someone moves sends
1 a message. When you see a boy running, he seems to say, "I'm in a hurry."

You've seen the boys on a baseball team jump up and down when the game is over. Did you get a message from that? The way they moved seemed to say, "Our team won!"

3 What messages do you get when you see your friends wave to you?

from *Mustard Seed Magic*, Theodore L. Harris et al. Economy Company. © 1972. pp. T62-63. Used by permission. All rights reserved.

There are so many ways to send messages without words.

A wave of the hand can mean "Hello!" A policeman does not have to say anything when he sends the message, "Stop!" He can hold up his hand, and you will obey. Yes, you do get his message! The lady at the library may send you a message by putting her hand over her mouth. Do you get the message? Will you obey?

Now tell about some other ways you've seen messages sent without words.

Extending Comprehension

Introduce the game "Ask the Computer." To program the computer, have the children read orally "Messages without Words." Explain that the information from the selection is now programmed in the computer. Have the child chosen to be the computer wear paper-bag gloves with **Yes** written on one and **No** on the other. Let the pupils ask questions of the computer who should raise the **Yes** or **No** glove to answer the question according to what the author has said in this selection. Instruct the computer to shake his body if the question isn't programmed. Allow the children to take turns being the computer. If desirable, extend the game by programming the computer with new information.

Recall the earlier class discussion about messages without words. Help pupils recognize that the emphasis was on facial expressions, gestures, and body movements. Ask a child to read the last sentence in this selection. Encourage the children to think of ways to send messages without words, such as using trail markers, international signs, smoke signals, pictures, drums, flags, fog horns, and light beams. If desirable, illustrate these techniques on a chart.

📖 Activity Book, Pages 14 and 15

Page 42

Guided Reading and Comprehension: "Look at the illustration. What messages do you get from these people?" Have the children read page 42 silently.

Discussion

1. What three messages were discussed on this page? (Hello, Stop, and Shhh)
2. Tell about other people you see who sometimes send messages without words. (teachers, firemen, bus drivers, parents, safety patrolmen, milkmen)
3. What kind of selection is "Messages without Words"? (factual)
4. Summarize in one sentence what the author says in this selection.

Individualizing Instruction

Exploration

1. Suggest that pupils find out about the history of communication from primitive drawing to the printing press, telegraph, telephone, radio, television, and satellite system.
2. Ask the group to consider how individuals who are blind and others who are deaf manage to communicate. Many pupils will be fascinated by the use of Braille and sign language.
3. The game "Draw a Riddle" may be used to help children utilize details in illustrating a riddle. Have the children divide a piece of newsprint into six boxes. Read each clue aloud and pause after each so that the children may draw what the clue suggests to them. Point out that each clue offers another detail which may alter succeeding drawings. At the conclusion check to see who was able to draw the riddle first. Use a riddle similar to the following:

   1. I have four legs.
   2. I am brown.
   3. A family owns me.
   4. Sometimes I sit beside a desk.
   5. I am wooden.
   6. You can sit on me while you write at the desk.

63

Pages 20-22

Story Motivation: Encourage the children to discuss their own collections and different kinds of collections they have seen or heard about.

Guided Reading and Comprehension: Ask the children to read pages 20-22 to discover what Eddie collects and to find out how his parents feel about the collection.

Discussion

1. What does Eddie collect? (junk)
2. How does Mr. Wilson feel about Eddie's "valuable property"? (He thinks it is junk.)
3. Did Eddie's father think the telephone pole was worthless? Why not? (He could use it.)
4. Do you think Eddie's mother likes the junk? Why?
5. Where did Eddie go with his father and mother one Saturday? (antique shop)
6. Why did Eddie think his father had said "Aunt Teek"? (He didn't know the word **antique**.)
7. What did Eddie consider to be junk that his father thought was valuable property? (antiques)
8. What are some things that Eddie might have seen on the shelves of the antique shop?

Never a week went by that Eddie Wilson didn't bring home a piece of something he called "valuable property." But his father called it junk.

All the family knew when Eddie brought home some of this valuable property. At dinner he would always say, "I had a very enjoyable day today."

"Now, see here, Eddie!" said his father one day. "This junk collecting has to stop! Every week the neighbors put out all their rubbish, and every Saturday you bring most of that rubbish to our house. Now I'm tired of it."

"You were glad when I brought home the telephone pole," Eddie said.

"Well, that was different," Mr. Wilson said. "I could use that pole. But this junk collecting has got to stop. We'll never get all that junk out of your room."

"But, Dad!" said Eddie. "It's my valuable property."

"Valuable property!" said Eddie's father. "Junk! All you bring home is junk!"

"Even the telephone pole?" said Eddie.

20

"Well," his father said, "that's the only thing we were ever able to use."

The next Saturday Mr. Wilson took Mrs. Wilson and Eddie shopping. They drove for a while before Mr. Wilson stopped in front of a shop. Over the door of the shop was a sign that said ANTIQUES. Eddie was able to read most signs. But he couldn't read that one.

"What does that sign say?" he asked.

"Antiques," answered his father.

"Are we going to see Aunt Teek?" Eddie asked. "Does she own this shop?"

"Not Aunt Teek," laughed Mr. Wilson. "But antiques. Antiques are old things. The sign means that this shop has all kinds of old things to sell."

21

"You mean junk?" asked Eddie.

"Certainly not!" said Mr. Wilson. "Eddie, antique things are very valuable. They sell for a lot of money."

Eddie and his father and mother walked up to the shop. Boxes on the front steps were full of all kinds of old things.

"It looks like junk to me!" said Eddie.

The inside of the shop was full of more old things. "I can find a piece of very valuable property here!" Eddie thought.

Eddie's father and mother talked to the shopkeeper while Eddie wandered around. He looked at shelf after shelf of old things. Then he wandered through a door into the back of the shop.

22

from *Air Pudding and Wind Sauce.*
Theodore L. Harris, et. al. © The Economy Co.
1972 pp. T37-41. Used by permission. All rights reserved.

38

"Hello, son!" said a man stacking boxes. "Can I help you?"

"I'm just looking around," said Eddie.

Then all at once Eddie saw something that looked like valuable property. High on a shelf stood an old carriage lamp. It was rusty and covered with dust.

"Do you want to sell that lamp?" Eddie asked the man.

"Oh, I guess we could," he answered.

"How much is it?" asked Eddie.

"Oh, twenty-five cents would be enough," said the man.

Eddie took his money from his pocket. He had seventy-five cents. "Okay," he said. "I'll take it!"

23

Pages 23 and 24

Motivation: "What do you think Eddie will find in the back of the antique shop?"

Guided Reading and Comprehension: Have the children read pages 23 and 24 to check their predictions.

Discussion and Rereading

1. What did Eddie buy? (carriage lamp, coffee grinder)
2. Read the paragraph aloud that tells what Eddie did with his purchase. (page 24) Why did he hide the box? (He didn't want his father to see it.)

Motivation

1. Do you think Eddie's father will find the box in the trunk?
2. If you were Eddie's father, what would you do if you found the box in the trunk?

The man took the lamp from the shelf.

Just then Eddie saw something with wheels. "What is that?" he asked.

"That's an old coffee grinder," the man answered.

"Those are swell wheels on it!" Eddie said. "What's the price?"

"Oh, I guess you can have it for about two quarters," the man replied.

"Then I'll take it, too," said Eddie.

The man blew the dust off the carriage lamp and put it into a box with the coffee grinder. The end of the lamp wouldn't go in, but he covered the box with a lid and tied a piece of string around it. "I guess that'll do," he said.

"Thank you!" said Eddie. He gave the man his seventy-five cents.

2 Eddie decided to slip out the back door with his bundle. When he got to the car, he quickly opened the trunk. Then he set the box inside.

Eddie returned to the front steps just in time. When his father and mother came out, he was looking at a rusty old lock.

24

"Hey, look at the swell old lock!" called Eddie as if nothing had happened

"It's a piece of junk!" said Mr. Wilson. "Put it down and come along, son!"

They all got into the car and drove off. Eddie sat in the front seat between his father and mother. For some time Eddie said nothing. Suddenly he said, "Well, I had a very enjoyable day today."

Mr. Wilson stopped the car with a loud screech. Slowly he turned around and looked on the back seat. Nothing was there.

"What did you say, Eddie?" he asked as he started the car.

"I just said I had a very enjoyable day today," Eddie replied.

Again Mr. Wilson stopped the car with a screech. Then he got out and opened the trunk. There was Eddie's box.

Pages 25-28

Guided Reading and Comprehension: Have the children read pages 25-28 to learn what happens to Eddie's "new junk." Tell them to read and think about the questions on page 28 when they have finished reading the story.

Discussion

1. Did Mr. Wilson know Eddie had gotten more junk? How? (Eddie said, "I had a very enjoyable day today.")
2. What happened to Eddie's junk? (He sold it.)

Rereading: Ask one child to be Eddie and another to be Eddie's father. Let them read orally several lines of dialogue. Then let other children take turns reading the parts. Remind them to read only the words in quotation marks. On the last page check their understanding of the dash as a signal to pause.

Think about This: Ask the children to read the questions on page 28. Let them express their thoughts. For the first question it may be helpful to consult the dictionary to obtain exact definitions of junk and antiques. Before answering the last question, the children may wish to reread parts of the story.

"Please, Dad!" Eddie begged before Mr. Wilson could open the box. "That isn't junk. It's valuable antique property."

"Eddie," said his father, "no more junk, and I mean it!" He carried Eddie's box to a rubbish can on the street.

As he set the box down, Mr. Wilson saw the end of the carriage lamp. He took off the string and opened the box.

"Say!" Mr. Wilson said. "This could be a good carriage lamp! A little oil polish will make this rusty lamp shiny. Then I'll set it on that post by the door."

"But I bought it, Dad," said Eddie. "I gave a quarter for it."

"Well, I'll give you a dollar for it, son," said his father. "How is that?"

"Okay," said Eddie.

"Look, Mother!" Mr. Wilson said. "Look at this carriage lamp."

Mrs. Wilson was looking inside Eddie's box, too. "Why, look at this old coffee grinder!" she said. "Oh, I want this! A little red paint is all it needs. It'll make a beautiful antique lamp!"

26

"But I bought it, Mom," said Eddie. "I gave my quarters for it."

"I'll give you a dollar for it," she said. "Is a dollar all right?"

"Oh, Mom!" said Eddie. "I like the swell wheels on that old coffee grinder."

"Well, then I'll give you two dollars for it," said his mother. "Two dollars is a lot of money, Eddie."

"Okay," Eddie said.

Later, as they drove home, Eddie said, "Dad, guess what I'm going to do when I grow up. I'm going to sell junk! I can make a lot of money selling junk."

27

"You sure can!" said Mr. Wilson. "How about us selling junk together?"

"Okay, Dad," said Eddie. "Will we have a shop of our own?"

"Certainly!" said Eddie's father. "And we'll have a big sign that says WILSON AND SON—ALL KINDS OF JUNK."

Think about This:

1 What is the difference between junk and antiques?
2 What do you think Eddie's father did with the telephone pole that Eddie brought home?
3 Why do you suppose Eddie and his father think that they can make money selling antiques?

28

40

Extending Comprehension

Discussion of the Selection: The following discussion is to help children understand inferences. "While reading 'Any Old Junk Today?' we learned several things that the author did not tell us about in detail. For example, we learned that Eddie did not know the meaning of **antique**. We also learned that Eddie did not want his father to know that he had purchased the coffee grinder and the carriage lamp.

"There are other things we can learn from the story that the author did not tell us in detail."

1. How much money did Eddie have after he sold the antiques to his parents? ($3)
2. How did the author tell us that Eddie had $3? ($1 from his father, $2 from his mother)
3. Did Eddie make money or lose money? (made money)
4. How much did Eddie make? ($2.25)
5. The author didn't tell us this. How did you know? (He started with 75¢. Now he has $3.)
6. How do you think Eddie felt about the deal?
7. Was anything in the story considered valuable property by both Eddie and his father? (telephone pole, carriage lamp)
8. How did you know? (Eddie brought the pole home, and his father used it. Both paid money for the carriage lamp.)

Exercise 7: Main idea

What Is the Main Idea?

Write **X** before the group of words that best tells the main idea of "Any Old Junk Today?"

1. Eddie's father did not like Eddie's junk.
2. Eddie took a collection to school.
3. Eddie bought a coffee grinder.

X 4. Eddie found something that was valuable both to him and to his father.

5. Eddie had an enjoyable day.

Directions: Distribute copies of the exercise and have the children complete the exercise independently. Encourage the children to **discuss** their answers.

📖 Activity Book, Pages 8 and 9

The Horse Was in the Parlor:
Page 114

Setting the Stage

This amusing story is based on the serious, but almost hidden, theme of "Keeping up with the Joneses."

The following words and expressions may need to be developed: *stone's throw, lonesomelike, carriage, down her nose.*

Show the children where Ireland is on a map or a globe. Explain that this story has an Irish background even though the characters speak English. Have the children read the title, look at the opening pictures, and guess what the story will tell.

Perceptive Reading

Have the children read the story silently. Then ask the following questions to help them recall interesting incidents: What did Pat and Nora decide to do with their old house? What different animals did they put in the house? What happened when Aunt Bridget went to the door of the house? How did she feel later?

Sharing the Story

Choose several children to read the story aloud. Ask one child to read the narrative sections and others the conversation.

Stimulate discussion by asking the following questions: What kind of person do you think Nora was? Was Nora snobbish? What kind of person do you think Aunt Bridget was? Was Aunt Bridget snobbish? Which of the two did you like better?

Expressional Activities

Help the children develop a puppet show including the following characters: Pat, Nora, Aunt Bridget, and Uncle Daniel. Suggest that they make large drawings of the old and new houses for background.

Have different children read aloud the parts of the story that they think are the funniest or the most amusing.

from *Fun All Around,* Nila Banton Smith et al. The Bobbs-Merrill Company, Inc. © International Reading Association.1964. pp. T25,114-120. Used by permission. All rights reserved.

THE HORSE WAS IN THE PARLOR

It was moving day for Pat Mooney and his wife, Nora, but they were not moving far. Their new house, which Pat had built, was only a stone's throw from their old house.

As Nora started to cook supper in the new kitchen, she looked through the window at the old house. It was dark and empty.

"The dear old place looks lonesomelike, so it does," she said. "What are we going to do with it, Pat?"

"Sure, and we'll use it for a barn, Nora, dear," answered Pat. "We've been wanting a horse and a cow and a pig all these years, but never had a place to keep them."

Nora clapped her hands. "Oh, Pat, what a grand place we'll have!" she cried. "How I wish our proud Aunt Bridget could see how well we're getting on in the world."

"I thought you never wanted to see Aunt Bridget again," Pat exclaimed. "No more do I, after the way she looked down her nose at us when visiting in the old house."

"With our fine new house and a barn full of animals, we'll be as grand as she is," said Nora. "How soon do you think we could get ourselves a few animals, Pat?"

"Mike Maguire has a good horse he wants to sell," Pat answered thoughtfully. "We could put her in the parlor."

Nora laughed. "If we give the horse the parlor, the cow must have the kitchen," she said. "The pig can have the bedroom."

The old house made a fine barn. Soon the Mooneys had a horse in the parlor, a cow in the kitchen, and a pig in the bedroom.

One morning, soon after the animals were settled in the old house, the mailman came by with a letter for Pat.

"Aunt Bridget and Uncle Daniel plan to visit us next Wednesday afternoon," said Pat as he handed the letter to Nora.

"Ah, but that's grand news, Pat," cried Nora. "Aunt Bridget doesn't know a thing about our new house. What a surprise the fine lady will be having!"

Nora cleaned and swept and dusted the new house. The she baked fruitcake and white cake and cookies. Aunt Bridget would find only the best at the Mooneys' house.

"Is everything ready?" asked Pat right after lunch on Wednesday.

"Everything but the special sauce for the fruitcake," said Nora. "It must be made at the last minute, you know, and I'm after starting it right now."

Pat went upstairs to change his clothes, and Nora started the sauce. It was a hard job, for she had to beat the sauce for ten minutes. There was no stopping for a rest, either, or the sauce would be spoiled.

In the middle of the ten minutes' beating, she happened to look out the window. There was Aunt Bridget going to the old house. Nora hadn't heard the carriage drive up.

"Pat!" she cried. "Pat! Come down here this very second. Aunt Bridget is here, and I can't leave my sauce."

Pat could not come, however, for he was without his trousers and his shoes.

In the meantime Aunt Bridget knocked on the front door of the old house in a most ladylike way. Nobody answered, of course, for how could a horse say anything?

Aunt Bridget knocked again. Still getting no answer, she opened the door and walked in. Such a scream as there was then!

The noise brought Pat flying downstairs carrying his trousers. Nora almost dropped her spoon and spoiled the sauce.

Aunt Bridget, very red in the face, came back to the doorway. "There's a horse in the parlor," she called to Uncle Daniel, who was waiting in the carriage.

"Sure, Nora must be in the kitchen," said Uncle Daniel. "Try the kitchen door."

Aunt Bridget tried the kitchen door and came face to face with the dear old lady of a cow. When the cow lowered her horns, Aunt Bridget jumped back into the driveway and hurried to the carriage.

"If Pat and Nora want to live with their animals, they can!" she said angrily. "They will get no visit from me, however, if they choose to live in a barnyard."

By this time Pat had his good clothes on and had stepped out to the carriage. "I'm surprised, Aunt Bridget, that you'd take Nora and me to be living in a barnyard."

Aunt Bridget stared at Pat and the new house, too ashamed to say a word.

When the proud lady spoke at last, it was in a very quiet voice. "Is this new house yours, then?" she asked. "Brand-new it is, and you never told me about it at all."

Then she turned to her husband. "Daniel," she said, "where are your manners? Come, let us look at this fine new house."

Sure, it was a fine tea party the Mooneys gave their aunt and uncle after that. When it was over and the carriage had driven off, Pat and Nora smiled at each other.

"Did you notice, Pat," said Nora happily, "that Aunt Bridget never looked down her nose at us once all afternoon?"

Unit: Tricks, Traps, and Deals

ON THE LOOSE

Pages 8-10

Guided Reading and Comprehension: When the children have given their ideas, ask them to read the first three pages of the story to see how their ideas compare with the story in the book.

Discussion: Ask the following questions to guide the discussion:

1. How is this story like the one you would have written? How is it different?
2. Where did this story take place?
3. Why didn't Kate have a phone? (just moved)
4. What is Kate's problem? If this were your problem, how would you solve it?

Motivation: "What will you want to find out as you finish the story?" List the children's questions on the board. Explain that they will probably think of other questions as they read. Some of the inquiries should involve the story title, Kate's problem, and the trucks.

Guided Reading and Comprehension: Ask the children to finish reading the story to find answers to their questions.

Kate and the Big Cat

On the Loose

Kate set a large sack on the table. "Mom, can't I please stay here while you and Dad go back to get the new kitchen curtain?" she asked.

"Stay here alone? In this **2** apartment?" her mother replied. "Why, Kate, there's no one else around, and we have no phone."

"Oh, Mom, I'm not a baby," Kate said. "Besides, if I stay here, I can get started unpacking. Oh, please, can't I stay?" Kate added, turning to her dad.

"Well, if you could start unpacking, it would be a big help, Kate," said Dad. "But besides getting a new kitchen curtain, we need to get someone to put in our phone. So we may be gone for some time."

"I'll be okay, Dad. I'm sure I will," replied Kate. "I've started unpacking some of these boxes already. And I can put away the fresh meat, too."

"Well, I guess you may stay," replied her mother. "But don't leave the building."

8

Kate went with Mother and Dad to the car. "Remember. Don't leave until we get back," Dad said as they drove away.

"Okay," said Kate. But she did wish her mother and dad wouldn't treat her so much like a baby. "They're the same as always," she thought.

Kate sighed softly as she watched the car pull onto the highway. She had thought that things would really be different when she moved to this new place. **4** "But if they're going to treat me like a baby, everyone else will, too," Kate thought. "It'll be just like it was at the old apartment." And she sighed once more.

9

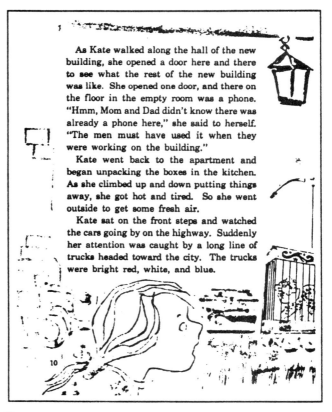

As Kate walked along the hall of the new building, she opened a door here and there to see what the rest of the new building was like. She opened one door, and there on the floor in the empty room was a phone. "Hmm, Mom and Dad didn't know there was already a phone here," she said to herself. "The men must have used it when they were working on the building."

Kate went back to the apartment and began unpacking the boxes in the kitchen. As she climbed up and down putting things away, she got hot and tired. So she went outside to get some fresh air.

Kate sat on the front steps and watched the cars going by on the highway. Suddenly her attention was caught by a long line of trucks headed toward the city. The trucks were bright red, white, and blue.

10

"Those are circus trucks!" Kate cried.

Kate stared as the trucks moved along. She knew each truck carried cages of circus animals. If she stared hard enough as they passed by, she might be able to see the animals inside the cages.

Suddenly Kate stared at only one truck. The door on its cage kept sliding open and shut! Then the door stayed wide open. A large animal poked its head out the door, and Kate saw its yellow and black stripes. "A tiger!" she whispered softly.

The big animal looked all around. Then it jumped from the truck and headed into the tall grass along the highway.

The circus trucks kept moving slowly on. "Oh, my! No one else saw what happened!" cried Kate. "What can I do?"

11

The tiger crept out of the tall grass and headed toward the apartment buildings. Then it crept into a large clump of bushes near the apartments. "What can I do?" Kate kept saying over and over.

Then Kate thought of the phone in the empty room. Quickly she ran down the hall and picked up the phone. She heard a dial tone hum in her ear, and she quickly began spinning the dial.

"Give me the police, please!" Kate almost shouted.

A second later a steady voice said, "This is Officer Brown."

"Tiger! There's a tiger in some bushes in front of our apartment," cried Kate.

"Did you say 'tiger'?" the policeman asked. Then he said, "Look, little girl, I don't have time for games. Why don't you just go outside and play? You know better than to play with the phone."

Then Kate heard the dial tone again. The policeman did not believe her! ^BKate was all alone with a real tiger walking around just outside her apartment building.

12

Pages 11 and 12

Discussion: Direct attention to the questions on the board. Encourage the children to tell the answers they found. As each child tells an answer, let him erase the corresponding question.

During the discussion the following points should be brought out:
1. A tiger has escaped from a circus truck.
2. The tiger is near Kate's apartment.
3. Kate called the police, but they thought she was playing a trick.

If some questions remain on the board, point out that they may be answered in the first part of this story.

Extending Comprehension

Rereading and Discussing the Selection: Lead the children in discussing the two story problems.
1. Read aloud the sentence on page 9 that tells what Kate's first problem was. (Kate felt she was being treated like a baby.) At what times have you been treated like a baby?
2. Read the sentence on page 12 that tells Kate's other problem. (Kate was alone with a tiger.)
3. Which of Kate's problems do you think was more important? Why?

Exercise 3: Distinguishing between important and unimportant details

---

The Important Thing to Say

Kate called to ask the police to capture' the tiger. Write **X** before each important thing the police needed to know to capture the tiger.
   1. The tiger had stripes.
X 2. Kate lived at 1005 West Third Street.
   3. The tiger had gotten out of a circus truck.
   4. No one was there but Kate and the tiger.
   5. Kate lived in an apartment building.
   6. Kate's mom and dad would be coming home soon.
   7. The apartment's phone number was 345-7782.
(Other answers may be acceptable if supported by logic.)

Directions: Have the children complete the exercise independently. Then encourage them to discuss their answers. Help the children understand that the reasoning that led to the answer is more important than the answer itself.

📖 Activity Book, Pages 2 and 3

sound, and the other is silent. Work with the other words in this group in the same manner. If necessary, you may remind the children that ge and dge represent /j/.

Note: At another time during the day, work individually with pupils who are having difficulty with any of the phonetic principles presented in this lesson.

Exercise 4: Recognition of long and short vowel sounds

Mark the vowel letter you hear in each word.

bāse	fōam	crēak	jŭdge	sāge
băt	hĕdge	tīde	stōnes	hĭnt
hūge	stēep	sŏck	lŏdge	găps

Directions: Read the directions with the children. Have the children mark the vowel letter to show the sound heard in each word. Let various children pronounce the words. If time permits, have them use the words in sentences.

Activity Book, Page 4

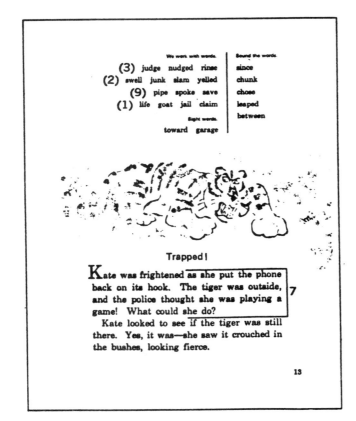

Reading the Selection

Page 13

Word Study: Help the children analyze the words in each row under "We work with words" and "Sound the words." Ask them to look at the first row of words.
1. How many vowel letters are in the word judge?
2. How many consonant letters separate the vowels?
3. What vowel sound will we hear in each word?
4. What sound will the e stand for in each word?

Have the children take turns sounding the words. "Look at the second row of words. How many vowel letters are in each word?" Let the children sound these words. In working with the last two rows of words, the children should remember the vowel sounds presented in Plan 1.

Direct the children's attention to the words under "Sound the words." Let each child sound a word and use it in a sentence. Continue until all of the words have been identified.

Direct attention to the sight words. Pronounce each word and ask the children to repeat it. On the board write **The car moved slowly toward the garage.** Ask the children to read the sentence silently. Have one child underline the sight words and have another read the sentence orally. Encourage the children to make sentences with the sight words.

Challenge words: bang, chunks, eaten, Kate's, pans, pound, prove, rushing, thoughts

Note: Challenge words are new in each story. Most children should be encouraged to read these words in context; however, some children may need to sound selected words and discuss their meanings before reading the story.

Story Motivation: Introduce "Trapped!" by reviewing the problem Kate had at the end of the first part of the story. "What do you think Kate will do?" Guide the children in making predictions by directing their attention to the title and asking who or what was trapped.

Guided Reading and Comprehension: Have the children read the entire story to see if their predictions are correct.

What if a small child came along? And how were Mother and Dad going to get inside when they came home? |8

Then Kate saw the line of garage doors that lay between her and the tiger. Mother and Dad had left their garage door open. Since that garage door could be locked from the outside, Kate decided she might be able to capture the fierce tiger.

She went rushing to the kitchen and chose a ham from one of the boxes. 1Then she ran to the garage. She threw the ham inside and then hurried back to the apartment. Quickly she opened some fresh meat. She cut one pound into chunks, then another. 2Then, one by one, she threw the chunks of meat onto the driveway.

14

Soon the meat made a trail between the tiger and the garage door. Then as hard as she could, 3Kate threw a chunk of meat out toward the tiger. The meat plopped near the driveway, right in front of the bushes.

Everything was still. Then the fierce tiger leaped out of the bushes. And in one bite the hungry animal ate the chunk of meat. Then it sniffed from side to side for more. 4Kate threw another chunk near the open garage door. The tiger leaped again. Now it was on the driveway.

Little by little the hungry animal came across the driveway, eating each chunk of meat. Soon it had eaten its way to the garage door. Would it smell the ham inside?

15

"Oh, no!" Kate moaned as the tiger stopped just outside the garage. Like a big cat, it curled up and began to clean its paws.

"Tiger! Tiger! Don't go to sleep!" Kate begged softly. "Go on inside!"

But the tiger seemed to have eaten enough already. It stretched and looked sleepy. What could Kate do now? She had to get the tiger into the garage.

Then Kate's thoughts went back to the pots and pans she had put away. But if she stood in the door making noise with those pots and pans, the tiger was sure to see her. "You said you were not a baby. Now prove it," she told herself.

So she ran to the kitchen and chose two large pans.

16

5Kate threw one pan out onto the driveway and beat the other with her hand. At the loud clang, the tiger leaped to its feet. Then it ran inside the garage.

In a second Kate was outside. 6She yanked on the rope of the garage door, and the door came down with a bang. She quickly turned the handle to lock it. At last she had the tiger in her trap!

Before long, Kate's mother and dad came home. Kate was watching for them. 9"Oh, Kate! You're safe!" her dad called as he drove into the driveway. 10"We just now heard that a circus tiger got away near these new apartment buildings."

"I know all about the tiger," Kate said, still a little frightened, "since I have him caught there in the garage."

17

Pages 13-18

Discussion

1-6. Tell how Kate captured the tiger.

Rereading: As you read the following statements, ask the children whether they are true or false. Have the children read aloud the parts of the story that make them think as they do. (The numbers in parentheses are page numbers.)

7. Kate knew that she was in danger. (13)
8. Kate cared about the safety of others. (14)
9. Kate's father was worried about her. (17)
10. Kate's mother and father knew that the tiger was loose. (17)
11. Her father no longer thought of Kate as a baby. (18)
12. Kate felt that things would be different now. (18)

Extending Comprehension and Study Skills

Discussion of the Selection

1. How did capturing the tiger solve both of Kate's problems? (tiger no longer a danger; Kate no longer considered a baby)
2. At what times in the future might Kate feel that she is being treated like a baby?

Exercise 5: Interpreting a pictograph

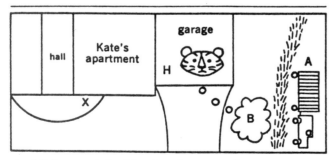

A. Make an **A** beside the circus truck.
B. Make a **B** on the bush the tiger hid behind.
C. Make an **H** to show where Kate threw the ham.
D. Make **O's** where Kate threw the meat chunks.
E. Make an **X** to show where she was banging pans.
F. Draw a tiger's head where the tiger was trapped.

Directions: Distribute copies of the exercise and help with the interpretation of symbols. Ask the children to complete the exercise.

Activity Book, Pages 5 and 6

34

"There? In the garage?" her mother and dad said at the same time. Then, from inside the garage, they heard the soft footsteps of the tiger, then an angry roar.

"Yes, there in the garage," Kate replied, trying to sound as if she had not done a thing important. "I decided to capture him myself."

Kate told her dad about the phone that had been left in the apartment building. And Dad went rushing inside to call the police. Soon a circus truck came and took the tiger away.

When all was quiet again, Kate's mother had a new, proud look in her eyes. "I can't get over that child," she kept saying to Dad. "What was she trying to prove when she decided to capture that tiger alone?"

"Child, nothing!" Kate's dad answered. "Anyone who can trap a tiger by herself is not a child. We'll have to treat Kate like a lady from now on." **11**

12 Kate felt warm inside when she saw that proud look in her dad's eyes, too. This was going to be a great place to live!

18

Individualizing Instruction

Word Perception: Recognition of long and short vowel sounds

In each row underline the words that contain the same vowel sound as the word shown at the beginning of the row.

dust	rug	rule	rusty	dollar
mild	alive	rid	ribbons	dimes
lot	spoke	rows	hops	copy
pace	pain	rake	dart	stall
huge	fuse	must	mule	rules
test	peace	shed	neat	edge

Directions: Read the directions with the children and help them work the first row. Have them complete the page independently.

Exploration: Encourage the children to present the dramatization activities suggested in Plan 1.

Poor Little Puppy: *Page 24*

Setting the Stage

The children will greatly enjoy this story about Lady, a dachshund puppy. First, they will sympathize with her as Sam and Sally try to teach her how to do tricks. Then they will be delighted to find that she is good for something after all.

The following words may need to be developed: *proud, ladder, clever, ashamed.*

Let the children read the title of the story and look at the pictures in the story. Encourage them to discuss the kind of puppy shown in most of the pictures. Write the word *dachshund* on the chalkboard and explain its German origin.

Perceptive Reading

Have the pupils read the story silently. While they read, write the following on

the chalkboard. Then let the children take turns reading the questions aloud and answering them orally. What kind of body and legs did the puppy have? What did Sam say about the size of her body and legs? What did Sally say about her head and tail? What did Sam and Sally name their puppy? Why did they give her that name? What things did the big boy say that Lady could not do? What rhyme did the big boy make up about her?

What could Ginger, Polly Brown's dog, do well? What could Cookie, Billy Hillman's dog, do well? What was the first trick Sam and Sally tried to teach Lady? What was the next one? What happened when they tried to teach her to climb a ladder? What trick did she learn to do all by herself?

Sharing the Story

Select one child to read the narrative sections of the story. Select other children to read the parts of Sam, Sally, the big boy, and the little boy's mother.

Ask these questions to help the children discuss important ideas in the story: Why were Sam and Sally proud of Lady even before she could do any tricks? What kind of boy was the big boy who made fun of Lady? What would you have said if someone had made fun of your dog? Why did Lady not learn to do the tricks that Sam and Sally tried to teach her? Why was digging for a ball a trick she did not have to learn?

Expressional Activities

Invite the children to bring snapshots of dogs that they own or magazine pictures of dogs that they would like to own. Encourage the children who own dogs to tell how they care for their dogs, and why they are proud to have them for pets.

Help the children make up a simple tune for the jingle:

> "She's two dogs long and half a dog tall.
> She's good for play and that's about all."

Have one child sing the tune jeeringly for the big boy, and another child sing it sadly for Sam. Then have all the children sing the following jingle merrily:

> "She's two dogs long and half a dog tall.
> She's good for play and for finding a ball!"

Make available for the class to read the delightful book about another dachshund, *Noodles*, by Munro Leaf with illustrations by Ludwig Bemelmans.

Sam and Sally were highly excited about a puppy that their father had just given them. This puppy was the kind that had a long body and short legs.

"Her body is almost long enough for two puppies, but her legs are not long enough for one puppy," laughed Sam.

"Her head is a long way from her tail," said Sally, "but her head and tail aren't very far from the floor."

"What shall we name her?" asked Sam.

"Why not call her Lady, since she is so pretty?" said Sally.

"All right," said Sam.

As time passed the children found that Lady made a good pet, and they became very proud of her. Finally something happened that made them wonder whether they should be proud of her or not.

One day a big boy stopped on the front sidewalk and began to tease the children about Lady. "She's two dogs long and half a dog tall," he shouted. "She's good for play, but that's about all."

The children, taken by surprise, didn't reply, so the boy went on talking. "She's not good for watching things, because she can't chase people away."

"I guess that's right," said Sam, half to himself. "She can chase people in play, but she can't chase people away from the house and yard."

"She's not good for doing tricks," said the boy. "She can't jump up high, and she can't sit up on her hind legs."

"That's so, too," thought Sally.

Finally the big boy walked on, and Sam said, "Come to think of it, what that boy said about Lady is right."

"Yes," said Sally. "She's two dogs long and half a dog tall. She's good for play, but that's about all."

The children began to talk about other dogs that they knew. Every dog, it seemed, was good for something besides play.

"Polly Brown's dog, Ginger, is good for chasing strangers away," said Sally.

"Lady never could become a watch dog," said Sam. "Her legs are far too short for chasing strangers away."

"Billy Hillman's dog, Cookie, is good at doing tricks," said Sally. "Maybe we can teach Lady to do tricks, too."

"That's a good idea," said Sam. "We'll start to teach her tomorrow. She's clever, so she should learn easily."

While the children talked, Lady watched and listened. She didn't understand what they were saying, of course, but she knew that they were talking about her.

Always when Lady was happy, she wagged her tail, but now she stopped wagging it. She became a sad little puppy, wondering what was wrong.

That evening Sam and Sally picked out a number of tricks to teach Lady. The next morning after breakfast they hurried into the yard to begin teaching her.

First, they tried to teach her to jump over a stick, but she wouldn't jump. She just walked under the stick.

They tried to teach her to sit upright, but whenever they let go of her, she fell over on her side. She fell over time and time again.

By now the children were about ready to give up. "Let's try to teach her one more trick," said Sam. "Maybe we can teach her to climb a ladder."

Sam put her about half way up a ladder, but when he quit holding her, she fell to the ground. Again he placed her half way up the ladder, but this time when he let go of her she jumped to the ground.

Sam could not get Lady to stay on the ladder. Each time she fell or jumped off.

Poor Lady couldn't understand what the children were trying to do with her. She wondered and wondered because they never had acted this way before.

The children soon left Lady and went in the house. "She's not clever enough to do tricks," said Sam. "Either that or else her body is too long."

"Yes," said Sally. "She's two dogs long and half a dog tall. She's good for play, but that's about all."

Before long a little boy and his mother came walking by the yard. The little boy, who was only two or three years old, was carrying a pretty red ball.

When the little boy saw Lady in the yard, he was greatly excited. All at once he dropped his ball, and it rolled into a deep hole.

The little boy tried to reach the ball, but his arm was far too short for the deep hole. Then his mother tried to reach it, but she couldn't get it either. "We can't get your ball," she said at last.

The little boy began to cry. "I want my ball," he said between sobs.

All this time Lady had been watching from the yard. Now she ran to the hole and tried to crawl into it. The hole was too small, so she began to dig it larger.

Her little paws almost flew, and soon she had the hole big enough to put her head in. Deeper and deeper she dug until her body was almost out of sight.

Sam and Sally came running from the house to see what was happening. "Lady, Lady," they shouted. "What are you doing?"

"She is digging to get my little boy's ball, which rolled into a deep hole," the boy's mother explained. "She certainly is a wonderful puppy."

In a few minutes Lady came backing out of the hole with the ball in her mouth. She ran to the little boy and dropped it right in front of him.

"Now, isn't that clever!" cried the boy's mother. "You must be proud of her."

Sam and Sally were ashamed to think that they hadn't always been proud of Lady.

"She's a very helpful dog, too," said the boy's mother. "Some dogs are good only for doing tricks, but she's a dog that can dig. Her short legs and her long body make her a fine dog for digging."

"That's right," cried Sam. "We thought that she was good for nothing but play, but now we know better."

Sally nodded happily and said, "She's two dogs long and half a dog tall. She's good for play and for digging out a ball."

—so human that children will almost forget that they are animals.

The following words and expressions may need to be developed: *camel, jackal, gentleman, crabs, sugar cane.*

Let the children read the title of the story and look at the opening pictures. Ask these questions to introduce the story: What two animals do you see in the pictures? What do you think is likely to happen?

Perceptive Reading

Have the children read the story silently. Then ask the following questions to help them recall interesting details: Why did the jackal want to go to the other side of the river? How did he persuade the camel to take him across the river? What trick did he play on the camel in the sugar cane field? What trick did the camel play on the jackal in the river? What lesson did the jackal learn from his experience?

Sharing the Story

Have three children read the story aloud, one child reading the narrative sections and two others the conversation.

Ask the following questions to stimulate discussion: Which animal do you think was the smarter, the jackal or the camel? Which animal did you like better?

Expressional Activities

Help the children prepare a comic strip based on the story. Divide the class into groups and ask each group to illustrate one of the incidents. Suggest drawing balloons around the conversational parts.

Place several collections of make-believe stories on the reading table, including: *The Tall Book of Make Believe* by Robert Bright and Carl Sandburg.

The Camel and the Jackal: *Page 200*

Setting the Stage

The camel and jackal in this old folk tale are almost human in their virtues and vices

from *Fun All Around*, Nila Banton Smith et al. The Bobbs-Merrill Company, Inc. © International Reading Association.1964. pp. 200-3, T35. Used by permission. All rights reserved.

THE CAMEL AND THE JACKAL

A big camel and a little jackal lived by a river. The camel was quite a gentleman, but the jackal liked to play tricks.

Every day the jackal went to the river to eat crabs. After a while, he had eaten all the crabs he could find. Then he said to himself, "I know there are more crabs on the other side of the river. I cannot get them, because I cannot swim."

Now the jackal knew that the camel liked sugar cane more than anything else. He also knew that the camel could swim. So he ran to the camel and said, "I know where there is good sugar cane. Do you want some?"

"Oh, yes," said the camel. "I should like very much to have some. Where is it?"

"On the other side of the river," replied the jackal. "If you will take me on your back and swim over, I will show you."

"Very well," said the camel.

The jackal climbed on the camel's back, and the camel swam across the river. First the jackal took the camel to the field of sugar cane. Then he went to eat crabs.

Soon the jackal had eaten all the crabs he wanted, and he was ready to go home. The camel was still hungry.

"I will make the camel go home," said the jackal. So he ran into the sugar cane field and began to laugh and sing.

Some people heard him. "A jackal is in our sugar cane," they cried. They picked up sticks and stones and ran to the field.

The little jackal hid, and the people saw only the camel. They hit him with sticks and stones and drove him away.

When the people had gone, the jackal came out of hiding. "Are you ready to go home?" he asked the camel.

"Why did you laugh and sing?" asked the camel. "The people hit me with sticks and stones and drove me from the field."

"Oh," said the jackal, "I always laugh and sing after dinner."

"I see," said the camel. "Well, let's go back home now."

He took the jackal on his back and began to swim. Out in deep water he stopped. "I'm going to roll over," he said quietly.

"If you do that," cried the jackal, "I will fall into the water. Why do you want to roll over anyway?"

"Oh," said the camel, "I always roll over after I have had my dinner."

The camel rolled over, and off went the jackal. He didn't drown, but he learned a good lesson. Never again did he try to play a trick on the camel.

ACTIVITY SHEET 56

LESSON 1   1 or 2 days

What Tools Are in My Classroom?

FOCUS

This lesson develops children's understanding of themselves as human beings. It focuses on tools found in a kindergarten classroom.

The learning experiences in this lesson help to develop the skills of conceptualizing, comparing, classifying, inferring, and acquiring and reporting information from direct observation, pictures, and charts. The lesson also fosters self-awareness.

PERFORMANCE OBJECTIVES

The student should be able to:

- Conceptualize *tool* by identifying objects made or adapted by human beings and used by people in performing certain tasks.

- Compare the tools pictured on the activity sheet with those found in his or her classroom.

- Classify the tools pictured on the activity sheet by indicating which are found in his or her classroom and which are not.

- Infer from a chart that his or her classroom contains many tools.

MATERIALS

Activity Sheet 56

a sheet of paper, pencils or crayons, scissors, paste, butcher paper for chart

Prepare a chart like the one shown in the diagram below.

TOOLS IN OUR ROOM	TOOLS NOT IN OUR ROOM

BACKGROUND INFORMATION

This lesson is designed to introduce kindergartners to the concept *tool* and to acquaint them with tools found in their classroom. The lesson also serves as a foundation for further exploration of the special ability to make and use tools that is shared by all human beings.

from *Me,* Harlan S. Hansen et al. Houghton Mifflin Company. © 1976. pp. 140-143 Used by permission. All rights reserved.

STRATEGIES

Opening the Lesson   Hold up a sheet of paper and begin tearing it into two part . Ask: *What tool would make this job easier?* Begin carrying water in the palm of you hand

to a plant or animal in another part of the classroom. Ask: *What tool would make this job easier? Why do people use tools?*

Developing the Lesson   Distribute Activity Sheet 56   Direct the children's attention to the photograph in the front of the activity sheet. A k: *What is this girl doing? What tools is she using? How does each of these tools help her to paint?* Elicit responses. Help the children to see that the table is a surface on which to work, the paper is a surface on which to paint, the paint is a medium for expressing ideas, the tray holds tools are in the classroom and then record that information on their activity sheets. Be sure that classroom tools are out where they can be seen when the children begin this activity.

Provide pencils or crayons for the children. To establish the procedure to be used in recording information on the activity sheet, ask: *Do we have scissors in our classroom? Draw a circle around the picture of the scissors if we have that tool in our classroom.* Circulate among the children, helping those who are having difficulty.

Ask: *Do you think there are tools in our classroom that are not pictured on the activity sheet?* Accept responses and then direct the children's attention to the empty space on the activity sheet. Say: *If you see a tool that is not shown on the activity sheet, you can draw a picture of that tool in this space.*

Allow the children to choose partners and move around the classroom as research pairs, recording what tools they observe. You may have to remind the class that the picture of a tool is marked only once, no matter how many examples of that tool are found in the classroom.

When the children have had time to record the data about tools in their classroom, ask the student research pairs to cut apart the pictures of tools. Have them sort the pictures, putting those they have in their classroom in one pile and those they do not have in their classroom in another pile.

Bring out the chart prepared earlier. Help the children to understand the headings on the chart. Ask: *Which tools belong in the top space on the chart?* You might consider asking the children to follow this procedure in putting the pictures in the top space on the chart. Have one member of a research pair select a picture of a tool they observed and paste it in the appropriate category. Ask the second member of that research team to point out to the other members of the class where the tool was observed, and then describe or demonstrate one use of the tool. Continue this procedure until all the tools found in the room have been placed on the chart. Involve as many student research pairs as possible.

When the first category of tools is complete, ask: *Where do the other pictures from the activity sheet go?* Have the children paste in the proper position on the chart the pictures of tools they did not find in their classroom.

Summary and Evaluation   Have the children look at the chart and make up sentences describing what is shown. Some appropriate sentences are: We found ten tools in our room today; we found most of the tools on the sheet; we found some tools in our classroom that were not on the activity sheet.

After the children have described what the chart shows, ask: *Why do people use tools? What is one tool we have in our classroom? Why do people use that tool? What is one tool we do not have in our classroom?* (If the children have difficulty with this question, refer them to the chart.) *Which of the tools not found in this classroom would you like most to have? Why?*

PROVISION FOR INDIVIDUAL DIFFERENCES

Ask each child to bring a small tool from home and demonstrate to the class how the tool is used.

Make a collage of pictures of tools. Encourage the children to identify the tools and tell how each of them is used.

The book *The Toolbox* by Anne and Harlow Rockwell (Macmillan) may be used to reinforce and enrich this lesson.

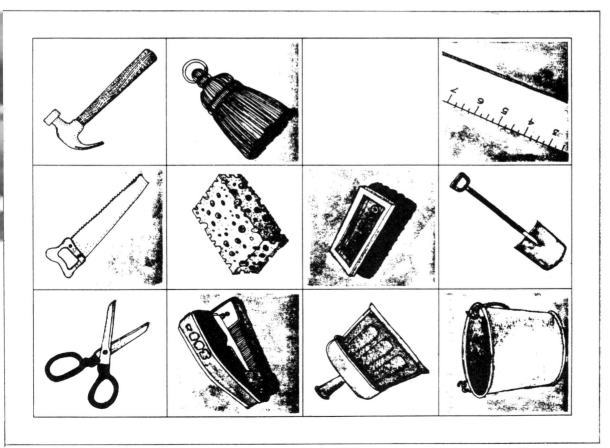

the paint, and the paintbrush enables the girl to transfer the paint from the container to the paper.

Have the children look at the back of Activity Sheet 56. Direct their attention to the picture in the top left corner. Ask: *What is this tool? What job does this tool help people do?*

Follow the same procedure with the other tools pictured on the activity sheet. When all the tools have been identified, ask: *Which of these tools do we have in our classroom? How can we find out?* Help the children to see that they can observe which

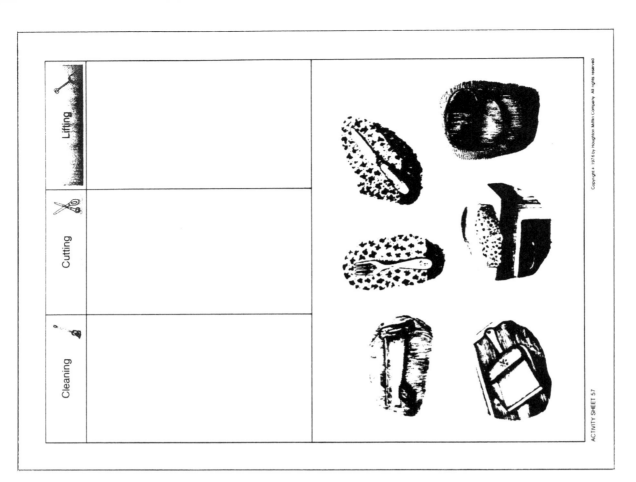

Cleaning	Cutting	Lifting

ACTIVITY SHEET 57

LESSON 2   1 or 2 days

How Are Tools Used?

FOCUS

This lesson develops children's understanding of themselves as human beings. It focuses on classification of tools according to the work the tools facilitate.

The learning experiences in this lesson help to develop the skills of evaluating, classifying, comparing, and acquiring and reporting information from pictures and charts. The lesson also fosters self-awareness and tolerance of uncertainty.

PERFORMANCE OBJECTIVES

The student should be able to:

- Evaluate tools and classify them according to how they are used.

- Compare the way he or she classifies the tools with the ways other people in the class classify them.

- Exhibit tolerance of diversity by explaining why a classmate placed a particular tool in a category different from the one in which he or she placed the tool.

MATERIALS

Activity Sheet 57

scissors, paste

BACKGROUND INFORMATION

All young learners need to develop the ability to classify. This skill enables them to pull together intellectually those things that share common attributes. Thus they are better able to deal conceptually with the phenomena in their environment. In the previous lesson the students identified tools found in their classroom. No attempt was made, however, to differentiate among these tools on the basis of how each of them is used. In this lesson the children will classify various tools according to the work each tool facilitates.

STRATEGIES

Opening the Lesson Ask a member of the class to locate and hold up a tool found in the classroom. Have the child name the tool and describe or demonstrate how the tool is used. Continue this procedure until a variety of tools have been identified. Ask: *What are some jobs that tools help people do? Do you think a tool can be used for more than one kind of job? What reasons can you give for your answer? Do you think different kinds of tools can be used to do the same job? What reasons can you give for your answer?* Accept responses and then explain that the class is going to find out more about different kinds of tools used for particular jobs.

Developing the Lesson Distribute Activity Sheet 57. Explain to the children that the words and pictures at the top of the three columns on the activity sheet describe different kinds of jobs that people do. Ask: *What job does a broom help people do?* Accept

responses. Establish the fact that a broom helps with cleaning. Help the children read the word printed beside the picture of the broom. Follow the same procedure with the pictures and words at the top of the two remaining columns.

Direct the children's attention to the pictures of the tools shown. Ask the children to identify each of the tools shown. Distribute scissors and have each child cut apart the activity sheet, following the line between the chart and the pictures of the tools. Ask the children to put the chart aside while they cut out the pictures of the tools.

O-100

Plan a bulletin board display of pictures of tools. Group the tools according to the work for which they are used, e.g., cutting, lifting, cleaning. Encourage the children to identify each tool and to suggest alternative ways of classifying those tools that may serve more than one purpose.

The book *Pick It Up* by Sam and Beryl Epstein (Holiday) may be used to reinforce and enrich this lesson.

When all the children have cut out the pictures of the tools, say: *You are going to classify these tools. Put the picture of each tool in the column on the chart that shows the job for which that tool is used.* Work with the children to establish this procedure. Say: *Find the picture of the saw. Is a saw used to clean, to cut, or to lift?* Establish the fact that the saw is used to cut and should, therefore, be put in the column for cutting tools. Continue working with the children until all of them understand what to do. Then allow the children to work independently.

Circulate among the children as they work, helping those who are having difficulty. When all the children have finished classifying the tools, have them paste the pictures in the proper columns.

Ask several students to show their charts and tell what their selections are for each of the three categories. There should be disagreement regarding the classification of several of the tools. For example, a fork can be used for both cutting and lifting. Encourage the students to identify the tools that different students have placed in different categories. Ask: *Why did some people say the fork is used for lifting? Why did some people say the fork is used for cutting? Which answer is the right one?* Establish the fact that both answers are acceptable.

Summary and Evaluation   Display all the classification charts and give the children an opportunity to look at them. Ask: *What are two tools that are used for the same kind of work? What is one tool that can be used for more than one kind of work? Do all the charts look like your chart? What reason can you give for your answer? Which chart is right? Why do you think so? What are some other ways in which these tools could be classified?* (Hard tools/soft tools, dangerous tools/tools that are not dangerous, metal tools/tools that are not made of metal are some suggested classifications.)

PROVISION FOR INDIVIDUAL DIFFERENCES

Have the children make toolboxes from cardboard cartons such as shoe boxes. Each child can use paints, crayons, contact paper, or cutouts to give his or her toolbox a personal touch. (See illustrations below.) Have each child cut out pictures of tools and store them in his or her toolbox. These pictures of tools can then be classified according to the work each tool facilitates. Old magazines, catalogues, and newspaper advertisements are good sources of pictures.

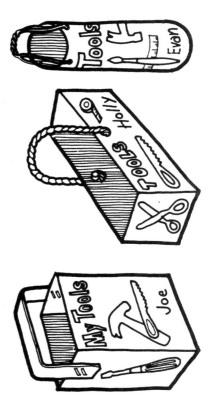

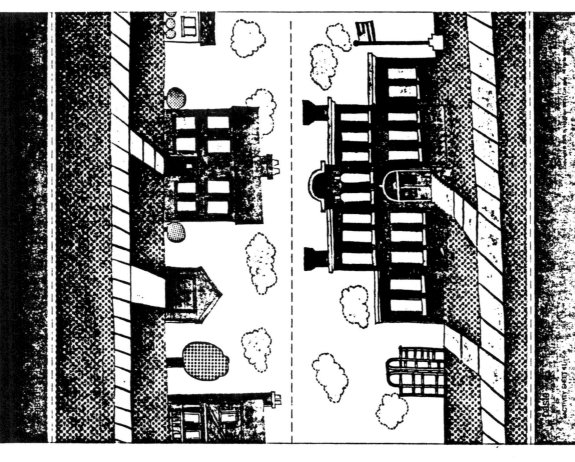

LESSON 7   1 or 2 days

How Is My School Like My Home?

FOCUS

This lesson develops children's understanding of themselves as members of groups. It focuses on the fact that both home and school help satisfy the basic needs of a kindergartner.

The learning experiences in this lesson help to develop the skills of conceptualizing, classifying, comparing, hypothesizing, and acquiring and reporting information from pictures and charts. The lesson also fosters self-awareness and respect for others.

PERFORMANCE OBJECTIVES

The student should be able to:

• Identify basic needs, using pictures.

• Classify situations in which basic needs are being met by indicating whether the need is being satisfied by the home or by the school.

• Hypothesize that both home and school help to satisfy his or her basic needs.

• Demonstrate decreasing egocentricity by describing how home and school help him or her satisfy basic needs.

MATERIALS

Overhead Visual 5 (see below), Activity Sheets 41–42

paste, scissors, thumbtacks or pins, bulletin board, overhead projector

Cut out the pictures on pages T171 and T173 to use in making a bulletin board display.

STRATEGIES

Opening the Lesson   Project Overhead Visual 5. Say: *When we talked about families, we learned that everyone has certain needs. Look at this overhead visual. What are those needs?* (Overhead Visual 5 shows the symbols for love, food, shelter, clothing, and help that were shown on Activity Sheet 20 and used in Unit 2, Lesson 5.)

After the children have indicated that everyone needs love, food, shelter, clothing, and help, ask: *Who helps you get the things you need?* Arrive at the conclusion that

BACKGROUND INFORMATION

Children may not be aware that the school does much more than provide instruction. The school helps to meet the basic needs of children. This lesson is designed to broaden the children's understanding of common concerns of home and school.

Fold along the dotted line in the center of your activity sheet.

Hold the activity sheet so you can see the picture of a house. Fold up along the dotted line below the picture. Put a little paste at each corner of the fold where the words "paste" are, and then hold the fold down until you count to ten.

Turn the activity sheet over. Fold up along the dotted line below the picture of the school. Put a little paste where the words "paste" are, and then hold the fold down until you count to ten.

Here is what you have. Set it aside until later.

Distribute Activity Sheet 42. Direct the children's attention to the picture in the upper left corner of the sheet. Ask: *What is happening in this picture? Who is helping a child get what he or she needs? Is this help being given at home or at school? How do you know?*

Follow the same procedure with the other pictures on Activity Sheet 42. When both the need and who is helping to meet it have been determined for each picture, tell the children to cut apart and classify the pictures, using the sorter made from Activity Sheet 41. Have the children put in the pocket below the house the pictures that show the home helping to meet a need. The pictures that show the school helping to meet a need should be put in the pocket below the school. Allow the children to work independently, alone or in groups. Circulate among them, helping those who are having difficulty.

After all the children have finished sorting the pictures, ask: *Do both home and school help meet needs? How do you know?* (There are pictures in the pocket below the house and pictures in the pocket below the school.)

Summary and Evaluation Help the children summarize what they have learned. Put on the bulletin board the pictures of the house and school (page T171). Then hold up a picture from Activity Sheet 42 (page T173). Ask: *Should this picture be placed below the house or below the school? Why?* Put the picture in the position indicated. Follow this procedure with the other pictures from Activity Sheet 42. After all the pictures have been pasted, ask the class to think of a title for the bulletin board. "Home and School Help Meet Needs" would be an appropriate title.

Ask: *What is one need the home helps you satisfy? What is one need the school helps you satisfy? How are home and school alike? How are they different?*

PROVISION FOR INDIVIDUAL DIFFERENCES

Have the children cut out and classify pictures showing how schools and homes satisfy basic needs. Old magazines are good picture sources.

Invite a parent to visit the classroom and tell how home and school cooperate to meet the basic needs of children.

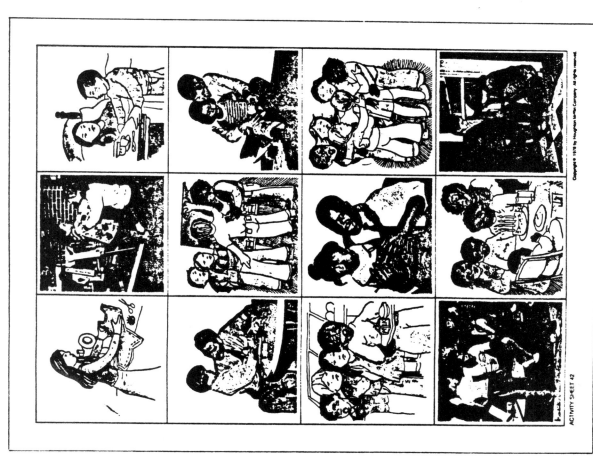

ACTIVITY SHEET 42

their families help them get what they need. Ask: *Do you think your school also helps you get what you need?* Accept responses and then tell the children they are going to find out if both home and school help kindergartners get what they need.

Developing the Lesson Distribute Activity Sheet 41 and provide paste and scissors for the children to use. Explain that everyone has some folding, pasting, and cutting to do before he or she can find out if both home and school help meet needs. Give the children these directions and demonstrate each step.

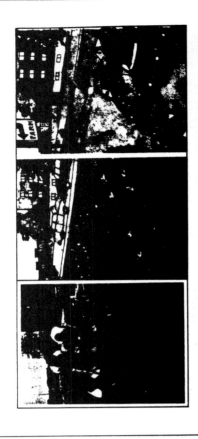

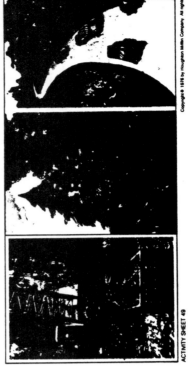

ACTIVITY SHEET 49

LESSON 4   1 or 2 days

Do Communities Change?

FOCUS

This lesson develops children's understanding of themselves as members of groups and inhabitants of Earth. It focuses on how communities change.

The learning experiences in this lesson help to develop the skills of inferring, evaluating, comparing, conceptualizing, imagining, hypothesizing, and acquiring and reporting information from pictures. The lesson also fosters self-awareness, tolerance of uncertainty, and respect for the natural environment.

PERFORMANCE OBJECTIVES

The student should be able to:

- Evaluate a particular action and select the change that will probably result, using pictures.

- Demonstrate tolerance of change by telling why he or she feels a particular way of bringing about change in a community is good.

- Compare two photographs taken several years apart and note changes that have occurred in a building and its environs.

- Use his or her imagination to describe changes that might occur in a community.

- Cite evidence to support the hypothesis that communities change.

MATERIALS

Activity Sheet 49
pencils or crayons

BACKGROUND INFORMATION

In previous units, the children have been introduced to the concept *change.* This lesson is designed to broaden their understanding of that concept by focusing on various changes that might occur within a community. The lesson also serves as a foundation for the next lesson in which the kindergartners identify specific changes within their own community.

from *Me,* Harlan S. Hansen et al. Houghton Mifflin Company. © 1976. pp. 126-7 Used by permission. All rights reserved.

STRATEGIES

Opening the Lesson   To help the children review changes that have occurred in their lives, play a game. Tell the children to stand if a statement you make is true. Some statements you might make are: *You are now taller than you were last year. You weigh more than you did last year. You have more skills now than you had when you were a baby.* Ask the children how they know that these statements are true.

Shift the children's thinking toward future changes in their lives. Some statements you might make are: *You will learn to read. You will get taller. You will learn to drive a car.* Ask the children why they think these things will happen.

Help the children to see that each of the statements you made was about change. Ask: *Does each individual change? Do you think communities also change?* Accept responses and then explain that the class is going to find out what the answer to that question is.

Developing the Lesson   Distribute Activity Sheet 49 and provide pencils or crayons for the children to use. Direct the children's attention to the photograph in the upper left corner of the activity sheet. Ask: *What is happening in this picture? Why*

O-104

will be and have marked the drawing that shows the result. Ask: *What are your feelings about this kind of change?*

Have the children look at the back of the activity sheet. Ask: *What do these pictures show? Are these pictures of the same building? How do you know?* Establish the fact that the two photographs are of the same bank, but that the top photograph was taken a long time before the bottom one was. Ask: *What changes do you see?* Give the children time to compare the photographs and indicate changes they see. Have each child check the changes as they are discussed. Some of the changes are: wings were added to the building; the sign was removed; a street light and mailbox were added; a traffic island and road sign were added and the markings for the crosswalk were changed; the sidewalk and street were resurfaced; a parking meter was removed; new shrubs were planted; the ivy was removed; the curb was painted. Some children may also note that one photograph was taken in spring, the other was taken in winter. When all the changes have been identified, ask: *How do you feel about this kind of change? Pretend that you have been away from our community for a long time. What changes do you think you would see when you return home?*

Summary and Evaluation   Ask: *Do communities change? Why do you think so?* (The activity sheet showed pictures of change in a community.) *What is one way of changing a community? What feelings do you have about this kind of change?*

PROVISION FOR INDIVIDUAL DIFFERENCES

Invite the principal to tell the class about changes that have been made in the school building. Display photographs that show the changes, if such photographs are available.

Have the children make suggestions for changes in the arrangement of the classroom. Ask the students to explain why they think such changes would be beneficial.

Display "Before" and "After" photographs of buildings and other community sites. Encourage the students to identify the changes that have occurred.

These books may be used to reinforce and enrich this lesson: William Kotzwinkle, *The Day the Gang Got Rich* (Viking Press); Paul Tripp, *The Little Red Flower* (Doubleday); Janice Udry, *The Sunflower Garden* (Harvey).

do you think these people are making a garden? What change will take place? Have the children look at the two drawings to the right of the photograph. Say: *Put a mark on the picture that shows the change that took place.* When the children have marked the result of the action shown in the photograph, ask: *How do you feel about this kind of change in the community?*

Follow the same procedure with the other photographs on the activity sheet. One photograph shows a building being demolished; the other shows a wooded area being cleared. In each case after the children have determined what the result of the action

LESSON 18   1 or 2 days

Why Did the Girl Say, "No"?

FOCUS

This lesson develops children's understanding of themselves as human beings. It focuses on how decisions reflect what is important to an individual.

The learning experiences in this lesson help to develop the skills of inferring, imagining, comparing, hypothesizing, and acquiring and reporting information from pictures and role-playing. The lesson also fosters self-awareness, respect for others, and tolerance of uncertainty.

PERFORMANCE OBJECTIVES

The student should be able to:

- Acquire and report information about a decision-making situation, using pictures.

- Use his or her imagination to role-play possible courses of action open to the person in the decision-making situation.

- Infer from the course of action the person chose what was important to that person.

- Cite evidence to support the hypothesis that a person's decision reflects what is important to that person.

- Demonstrate increasing empathy by telling why the decision another person makes might differ from one he or she makes.

MATERIALS

student text pages 84–85

a worn, comfortable-looking pair of shoes; a fashionable, not-too-comfortable-looking pair of shoes; display of decision-making exercise from Lesson 16

BACKGROUND INFORMATION

This lesson is an exercise in value clarification. The children will be asked to examine a decision and ascertain what was important to the person who made that decision. Hopefully, these learning experiences will increase the children's awareness that the decisions a person makes reflect what is important to that person. Because different things are important to different people, not everyone chooses the same course of action in a particular decision-making situation.

Value clarification is an ongoing process. Whenever possible during the school year, reinforce and extend what the children will be learning in this lesson, providing additional opportunities for each child to consider what is important to him or her and to ascertain how these values affect the decisions he or she makes.

STRATEGIES

Opening the Lesson Appear before the children wearing a worn, comfortable-looking

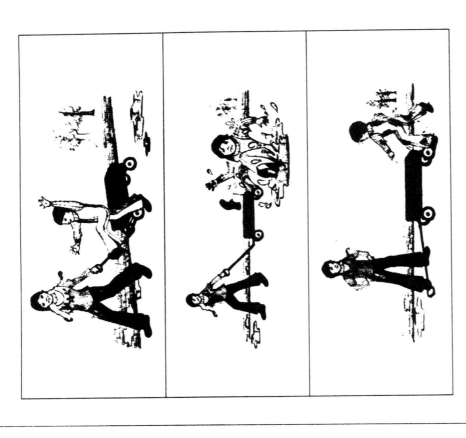

84

Ask the students to look at your shoes and describe them. Explain to the children that one shoe (point to it) is comfortable; the other shoe (point to it) looks pretty but makes your foot hurt. You must decide which shoes to wear.

Make your choice. Bring out the second shoe of the pair you have decided to wear and put it on. Ask: *What decision did I make? What was important to me? Why do you think so? Do you think you can tell what is important to a person by looking at decisions that person makes? Why or why not?* Accept responses and then explain that today the class will be finding out more about this question.

Developing the Lesson Have the class turn to pages 84–85 of the student text. Tell the

Ask: *What did the girl say?* Have the children read what is printed at the bottom of page 85 and respond to the question. Ask: *What was important to the girl?* If you are using the consumable texts, have each child mark what he or she thinks was important to the girl.

Have the class look again at student text pages 78–79. Ask: *What was important to the girl? In that case, what was important to the girl?* Follow the same procedure with pages 80–81 in the student text.

What do you think the girl did with her money? What was important to you?

Ask the children to look at their decision-making exercises from Lesson 16. Ask: *What decision did you make? What was important to you?*

Ask: *What do people do when they make decisions?* (People think and choose.) *How may a decision show what is important to a person? Do all people think the same thing is important? Why or why not? How do you feel about people making decisions that are different from the decision you would make?*

Have each child draw a picture of one decision-making situation he or she has experienced. Have the child show what courses of action were open and then indicate what he or she chose to do. Question each child about what was important to him or her in that situation, as reflected by his or her decision.

These books may be used to reinforce and enrich this lesson: Evaline Ness, *Sam, Bangs, and Moonshine* (Holt); Crosby Bonsall, *It's Mine, A Greedy Book* (Harper & Row); Masako Matsuno, *Taro and the Tofu* (World); Barbara Hazen, *The Gorilla Did It* (Atheneum).

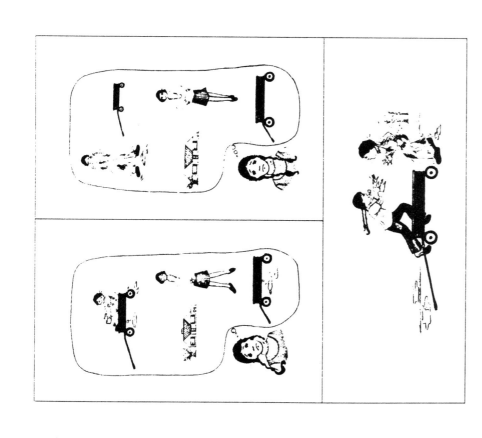

Why did the girl say, "No"?

85

A girl is pulling a shiny new red wagon down the sidewalk. Her little brother is skipping along beside her. The brother falls in a mudhole. He cries and asks to ride in the shiny new wagon. The girl thinks. If she says "Yes," her brother will stop crying, her mother will be pleased, but the wagon will be a muddy mess. If she says "No," her brother will continue to cry, her mother will be unhappy; but the wagon will be shiny and clean. The girl says "No."

Ask: *What happened in the story? What choices did the girl have? What would happen if the girl said, "Yes"?* Allow time for the children to role-play the results of this course of action. Ask: *What would happen if the girl said, "No"?* Again, allow time for the children to examine through role-play, the results of the particular course of action.

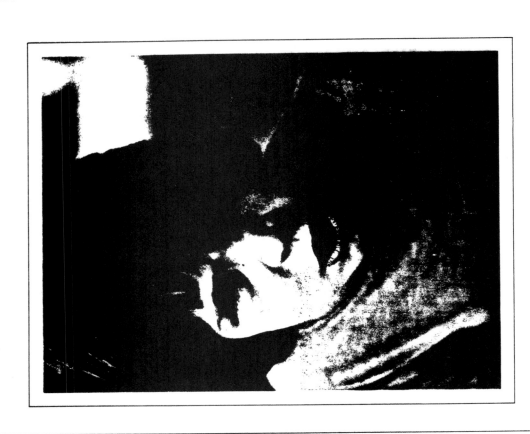

LESSON 12   1 or 2 days

When Do We Feel Angry?

FOCUS

This lesson develops children's understanding of themselves as individuals. It focuses on what causes people to feel angry.

The learning experiences in this lesson help to develop the skills of conceptualizing, inferring, hypothesizing, and acquiring and reporting information from direct observation and pictures. The lesson also fosters self-awareness and respect for others.

PERFORMANCE OBJECTIVES

The student should be able to:

• Conceptualize *anger* by identifying situations in which this emotion is being displayed.

• Infer from facial expression and attitude which people are angry.

• Exhibit increasing empathy by explaining why some of the people pictured in the student text feel angry.

• Cite evidence to support the hypothesis that everyone is sometimes angry, but that different things make different people angry.

MATERIALS

student text pages 32–33

from *Things We Do*, Frank L. Ryan, et al. Houghton Mifflin Co. © 1976. pp. T66-9. Used by permission. All rights reserved.

VOCABULARY

angry

BACKGROUND INFORMATION

This is the first of three lessons designed to help children cope with their feelings of anger. It explores the idea that there is nothing "wrong" with having such feelings and with expressing them in nondestructive ways. Anger is an emotion that everybody experiences.

STRATEGIES

Opening the Lesson   Write *happy*, *sad*, and *afraid* on the chalkboard. Ask a volunteer to pantomime one of these feelings. Have the other members of the class identify the emotion being portrayed and give reasons why a person might feel that way. Continue this procedure until all three of the emotions that have been discussed in previous lessons are reviewed.

Developing the Lesson   Have the children turn to page 32 in the student text. Ask: *How does this boy feel?* Establish the fact that the boy looks angry. (If the children say *mad*, accept that term, but encourage them to use the word *angry*.) Add *angry* to the list of words on the chalkboard. Have the children pronounce the word

Ask: *How do you know the boy is angry? Do you ever feel this way? What makes you angry?* Accept responses. Give all the children who wish to contribute to the discussion an opportunity to tell what makes them angry. Ask: *Do you think everyone feels angry sometimes?*

Tell the children to look at page 33 of the student text. After the children have read what is printed there, direct their attention to the set of pictures at the top of the page. Ask: *What is happening in the first picture? What is happening in the second picture? Who do you think is angry?* If your class is using the consumable edition of the student text, have each child circle the people he or she thinks may be angry.

Ask: *Why do you think the people in these pictures are angry?* (The girls may be angry because the boys have the ball. The boy in the yellow shirt may be angry because

Have the children role-play situations that provoke anger. Points to be considered in planning role-playing are found on pages T62-T63.

These books may be used to reinforce and enrich this lesson: Russell and Lillian Hoban, *The Sorely Trying Day* (Harper & Row), Charlotte Zolotow, *The Hating Book* (Harper & Row).

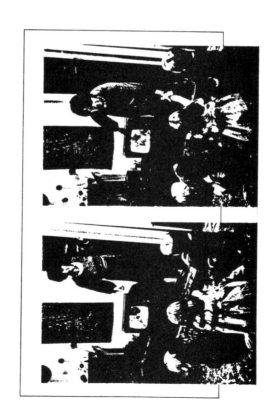

When do we feel this way?

the other children are trying to get the ball. The boy in the red jacket may be angry because he is not getting an opportunity to play with the ball.

Follow the same procedure with the set of pictures at the bottom of page 33. (The woman may be angry because the little girl is not willing to leave the group watching television. The little girl may be angry because she must leave the group. The other children may be angry because their television viewing is being interrupted by the conflict between the little girl and the woman.)

Ask: *What are some things that make people angry? What are some things that make you angry? Do you think that everyone is angry sometimes? Why do you think so?*

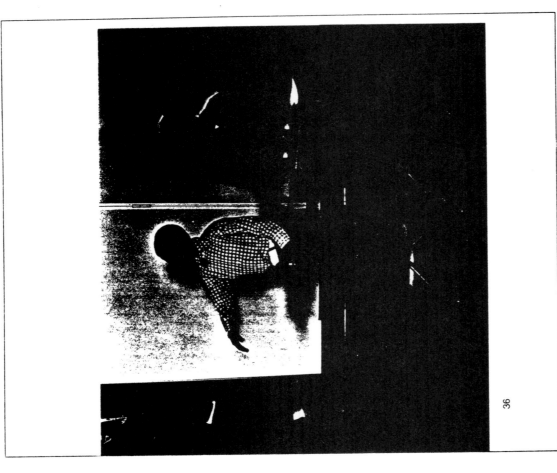

36

LESSON 14

2 or 3 days

How Can We Keep from Being Angry?

FOCUS

This lesson develops children's understanding of themselves as individuals. It focuses on how children and adults can cope with situations that make them angry.

The learning experiences in this lesson help to develop the skills of inferring, imagining, evaluating, and acquiring and reporting information from pictures and role-playing. The lesson also fosters self-awareness and respect for others.

PERFORMANCE OBJECTIVES

The student should be able to:

- Exhibit increasing empathy by telling how he or she thinks other people feel in anger-provoking situations.

- Identify ways to reduce feelings of anger, using pictures and role-playing.

- Evaluate ways to reduce feelings of anger and select the one he or she would use in a particular situation.

MATERIALS

student text pages 36–37

pencils or crayons

BACKGROUND INFORMATION

How does an individual cope with feelings of anger? One approach is to reduce the frequency of his or her involvement in anger-provoking situations by becoming aware of what these situations are and avoiding them. A second approach is for the individual to make the best of anger-provoking situations when they do arise, by adopting a course of action that will reduce feelings of anger. This lesson provides opportunities for children to explore both ways of coping with anger-provoking situations.

STRATEGIES

Opening the Lesson   Ask: *Do you like being happy better than you like being angry? What reasons can you give for your answer? If you like being happy better than you like being angry, do you think there are some ways to keep from being angry?* Accept responses and then tell the children they are going to find out more about ways to keep from being angry.

Developing the Lesson   Have the children turn to pages 36–37 in the student text and read what is printed there. Direct the children's attention to page 36. Ask: *What is happening in this picture? How do you think the girl who is being told to stay away feels? Why?* Help the class to see that the girl probably feels angry because she is not being allowed to participate in the group project. Ask: *What could the girl do to keep from being angry?*

Direct the children's attention to page 37. Explain that the pictures on this page show two ways the girl might keep from being angry. Ask: *What is the girl doing in the top picture?* (She is offering additional materials for the project and asking to join the group.) *How do the other children feel about what the girl is doing? Do you think the girl is keeping herself from being angry? Why might this be a good way to keep from being angry?* Accept responses. Allow the children to interpret the situation in various ways. Help them to see that the girl is reducing her feeling of anger by taking positive action to help with the project and thus to gain admission to the group.

Direct the children's attention to the picture at the bottom of page 37 in the student text. Ask: *What is happening in this picture?* (The girl is playing by herself with other materials.) *Do you think the girl is keeping herself from being angry? Why might this*

Suggest other situations and have the children tell what could be done to reduce feelings of anger. Here are two situations you might like to use:

A father is telling his child to clean up the bedroom. The child sees friends playing outside. Who may be angry? Why? What can the child do to keep from being angry?

Some children are behaving in a boisterous manner at the breakfast table. Mother is telling them to calm down. A glass of milk is sitting very near the edge of the table. Who may be angry? Why? What can the children do to help prevent an anger-provoking situation?

Summary and Evaluation Say: *Raise your hand if you like being happy better than you like being angry. What can you do to keep from being angry? What can you do to keep other people from being angry?*

PROVISION FOR INDIVIDUAL DIFFERENCES

Have the children collect pictures of situations that make people angry. Ask the children to role-play how they would keep from being angry if they were in those situations.

Ask each child to draw a picture of something that makes him or her angry. Let each child show his or her drawing and tell how he or she might keep from being angry the next time that situation arises.

These films can broaden the children's understanding of how people can cope with anger-provoking situations: *Our Angry Feelings* (BFA Educational Media, 11 minutes); *A Walk in the Woods* (Coronet Films, 6 minutes); *A Rock in the Road* (Bailey Films, 6 minutes); *The Fence* (Bailey Films, 7 minutes).

What can we do to keep from being angry?

be a good way to keep from being angry? Accept responses. Help the children to see that the girl is keeping from being angry by avoiding the group that is excluding her and by concentrating on doing something else.

To help the children test the courses of action suggested in the student text, have them role-play the situation and the two solutions to the problem. Points to be considered in planning for role-playing are found on pages T62–T63.

When the children have fully explored two courses of action the girl might follow, ask: *If you were the girl in the picture, which would be the better way for you?* If your class is using the consumable edition, have each child mark the course of action he or she thinks is better. Ask: *Why do you think the choice you made would keep you from being angry?*

LESSON 6   2 or 3 days

How Would You End the Conflict?

FOCUS

This lesson develops children's understanding of themselves as members of groups. It summarizes the three basic types of conflict and provides children an opportunity to review ways to resolve such disagreements.

The learning experiences in this lesson help to develop the skills of conceptualizing, inferring, evaluating, hypothesizing, and acquiring and reporting information from direct observation and pictures. The lesson also fosters self-awareness and tolerance of uncertainty.

PERFORMANCE OBJECTIVES

The student should be able to:

- Conceptualize *conflict* by identifying situations in which people are in conflict.

- Infer from pictures what the causes of particular conflicts are.

- Evaluate ways of settling disagreements and draw pictures of the ones he or she prefers for the conflict situations shown in the student text.

- Cite evidence to support the hypothesis that conflict can be resolved in different ways.

- Demonstrate tolerance of diversity by explaining why another person prefers a way that is different from the way he or she prefers to resolve a particular conflict.

- Exhibit increasing self-awareness by describing how he or she can help resolve conflicts.

MATERIALS

student text pages 100–101

pencils or crayons, copies of the worksheet on conflict resolution

Make for each child a copy of the worksheet on conflict resolution. The pattern for the worksheet is provided on page T196 and on Duplicating Master 12.

VOCABULARY

conflict

from *Things We Do*, Frank L. Ryan, et al. Houghton Mifflin Co. © 1976. pp. T132-3. Used by permission. All rights reserved.

BACKGROUND INFORMATION

Three types of conflict were identified in Lessons 3–5 — conflict over who will have or use scarce resources, conflict over who will bear a social cost, and conflict over what to do. Each of these types of conflict is incorporated in this lesson. The children are asked to identify the conflicts shown in the student text, indicate what is causing each of them, and then draw a picture showing one way to end each of the disagreements. There are no right or wrong solutions. The children may choose competitive or cooperative ways to resolve conflict. And, in the case of conflict over scarce resources, they may also

indicate that the scarce resource be isolated. What is important is that the child be given an opportunity to weigh different approaches to conflict resolution and decide which he or she prefers.

STRATEGIES

Opening the Lesson   Ask the children to turn to pages 100–101 in the student text. Have them read and respond to the first question on page 101. Ask: *How many conflicts (disagreements) do you see?* Tell the children to study the picture carefully before answering the question. If you are using the consumable texts, have each child circle the people who are disagreeing with one another.

Allow time for the children to do their drawings. Circulate among the children as they work, questioning individuals about their reasons for selecting particular solutions for the conflict situations.

When everyone has completed this activity, display the drawings. Be sure the children have put their names on their work. Give the children an opportunity to examine the drawings and question one another about the solutions they chose for each conflict situation.

Ask: *How could the conflict between the two boys be ended? Why do you think that would be a good way to end the conflict? Did others in this class choose a different way to end the conflict? Why do they think another way of ending the conflict is better than the way you chose?*

Follow the same procedure with the other conflict situations. Ask: *How can these ways of ending disagreements help you? How does knowing how to end conflict make you feel?*

Have the children recall stories or television programs that contained conflict situations. Have the children describe the conflict and tell how it was resolved. Ask the children how they think the people felt when the conflict was resolved in that way.

Ask the children to watch for conflict situations on the playground. The children can then share with each other the types of conflict observed. The class can discuss various ways of ending such conflicts.

Have the children role-play other conflict situations and ways of ending these disagreements.

Have each child draw pictures showing some conflict situations he or she has experienced and how that disagreement was resolved.

These books may be used to reinforce and enrich this lesson: Joan Potter Elwart, *Daisy Tells* (Steck-Vaughn); Judith Viorst, *Rosie and Michael* (Atheneum); Berthe Amoss, *Tom in the Middle* (Harper & Row).

101

What is happening?

What would you do?

O-109

Say: *Point out the people who are disagreeing with one another.* (There are three conflict situations.) *What is causing conflict between the two boys?* (They both want the same book at the same time.) *What is causing conflict between the older boy and girl?* (Neither wants to straighten up the clutter of games and toys.) *What is causing conflict between the man and woman?* (They disagree about what to do.)

Have the children read the second question on page 101. Instead of accepting responses, give each child a copy of the worksheet on conflict resolution. Tell the children to think about ways to settle conflict and then, in the spaces provided on the worksheet, draw pictures showing how they would end each of these conflicts. Tell the children that pages 94–99 in their textbook suggest ways to end the conflicts.

Student objectives

The students should learn that:
1. We need rules to get along with others.
2. Rules are important for the good of everyone.

Vocabulary and concepts

rules   think
beach   other
safe

Student attitudes

Awareness that rules foster efficiency, safety, and justice and are to be respected and obeyed

Creating interest

Ask the children what they think rules are. Write *rules* on the board. Discuss their ideas. Then ask if they can think of a reason why we have rules. One of the answers should be to keep people safe. Write *safe* on the board. Ask if they follow rules when they eat. Discuss and conclude that rules help us get along in the world.

Say that another reason for having rules is so that everyone will have a chance to live a good life. Ask if rules help people get their fair share? Do rules help to give everyone a turn when on the playground? Do we need rules inside the school? Think about it. Write *think* on the board. What would happen if you didn't have to raise your hand before talking? Raising hands is one kind of rule. What other rules can you think of? Write *other* on the board.

Ask the students if they think people have always had rules to live by. Point out that rules give guidance so

that people can live in peace. How would it be if everyone always crossed the street at any time and at any place? How would it be if people drove their cars any way they pleased? How would it be if people always thought only about themselves?

Guiding reading and learning

Ask the children to turn to page 34 to find out about the importance of rules. Tell them this is a story about a trip to the beach. Write *beach* on the board. Have the entire class join

you in reading the title and the first four lines. Then ask a boy to read Ben's part and a girl to read Alice's part. Ask what reasons Alice gives for needing rules. [Safety; to insure turns] Have students read page 35 together, and then ask for another reason for having rules. Discuss in detail.

Rules are important

"Let's take a trip," said Mrs. Linder.
"Let's visit the park at the beach.
We will need rules for our trip.
Why do we need rules?"

"We have lots of rules," said Ben.
"There are rules for the playground."

"Rules help keep us safe," said Alice.
"Rules help everyone get a turn."

Classroom rules

"Our class has rules," said Ann.
"Some rules are about when to talk."

"Other rules tell when to listen," said Joe.
"We have to think of other people.
Rules help us think of others."

From Teachers' Edition of *At School* of TIEGS-ADAMS: PEOPLE AND THEIR HERITAGE, © Copyright 1983 by Silver, Burdett & Ginn Inc. Used with permission.

Student objectives

The students should learn that:
1. Rules and laws are similar.
2. Laws are usually established by the government.

Vocabulary and concepts

laws

Student attitudes

Awareness that laws are the responsibility of everyone

Student objectives

The students should learn that:
The role of the police in our society is to help us.

Vocabulary and concepts

police

Student attitudes

Awareness that law and order hinge on law enforcement and our respect for it

Career awareness

law enforcement positions

Guiding reading and learning

Have students turn to page 37 and describe what is happening in the pictures. Then have the class read the page aloud with you. Discuss with children the ways in which the police help us.

Rules everywhere

Our world has many people.
We all need rules, or laws.
We need laws to be safe.
We need rules to be happy.

Who helps us
keep rules?

The police

Police help us keep laws.
How do they help us?

Creating interest

Review the fact that every community has police to help make sure that laws are obeyed. Write *police* on the board. These men and women do more than just arrest people who break the law. The police protect us when there is danger.

If you were able to get a police officer from your community to talk with the class, introduce the officer at this time.

Reinforcement and enrichment activities

1. Have the class make a mural showing the work of the police.
2. Write a group letter of thanks to the police officer who visited the class.
3. Arrange to have the class visit a police station. If possible, arrange for a ride in a police car.

Creating interest

Help children recall why rules are important in the school and on the playground. Then tell them that it is well that they learn about rules early in life because there are rules everywhere in the world. The world is run by rules. Some people call them laws. Write *laws* on the board. Have them list some laws grown-ups must obey.

Guiding reading and learning

Have the children turn to page 36 and look at the pictures. Ask them if these pictures give them any ideas about why laws are necessary. After discussion, have the children take turns reading a line at a time. Repeat the question in the last line and encourage discussion. After a while, use the term "laws" in place of "rules." Conclude that police and training by parents and teachers help us keep laws.

Student objectives

The students should learn that:
1. It is important for families to have rules.
2. There are different rules for different families.

Student attitudes

Awareness that rules promote family unity
Consideration for others

Student objectives

The students should learn that:
If a school trip is to be safe for everyone, it is necessary to have good rules and to keep them.

Vocabulary and concepts

soon

Student attitudes

Acceptance of responsibility for maintaining order on buses

Career awareness

transportation

Creating interest

Remind children that they have been reading about rules that are followed in the classroom, on the playground, in the community, and in families. Ask if there are special rules to be followed when taking a bus trip or bus ride. What are some rules people who ride buses must follow? Say that students will soon read about bus rules. Write *soon* on the board.

Do you have rules
in your family?
How do they help
your family?

Creating interest

Ask the class to recall the three big sets of rules they have been studying. They were rules for the classroom, the playground, and the community. Do those same rules apply anywhere else? Where do we all first learn to keep rules? Accept answers such as church and home, but keep asking until you get "family" as a response.

Guiding reading and learning

Tell the children to turn to page 39. Have the class read the story aloud with you. Then ask what the rules are that the children told Mrs. Linder to write on the board. Afterwards, have them discuss Mrs. Linder's list of rules. Are they good rules? The teacher, the bus driver, and the children made those rules. All have the responsibility of keeping them. Conclude that the safety of a school trip depends on the cooperation of many people. Discuss the importance of a bus driver's job and its value as a career.

Bus rules

"We know why we have rules,"
said Mrs. Linder.
"Soon we will go to the beach.
We must have a safe trip.
What bus rules do we need?"

Rules in homes

Families have rules, too.
Rules help keep the family safe.
They help keep the family happy.

Guiding reading and learning

Ask children if they can tell from the pictures on page 38 if these families have rules. Discuss the rules. Have individuals read the lines at the top of the page. Ask for what two reasons a family must have rules. [For safety and happiness] Have the lines at the bottom of the page read aloud. Have the questions answered. Discuss the rules a family might have. These could include rules for TV watching, bedtime, household chores, letting parents know where you are, caring for clothes, and fire drills. Conclude that a family keeps rules for the good of all.

Reinforcement and enrichment activities

1. Have the children draw pictures to show the rules that must be kept by bike riders, pedestrians, or passengers in cars. Have the students talk about their pictures before displaying them in the classroom.
2. Suggest that children draw a picture that shows a bus driver obeying a safety rule.

Our country's birthday

Our country has a birthday.
It is on July 4.

Long ago our country was part of England.
People wanted to be free from England.
They said this on July 4, 1776.

July 4 is a holiday for us.
We have picnics and parades.
Many people fly flags.
We are proud to be Americans.
We are proud to be free.

Student objectives

The students should learn that:

1. Long ago our country was not free and many brave people had to fight to make it free.

2. The founders of this nation sent a Declaration of Independence to the King of England stating that this nation was free.

3. The birthday of our country is called Independence Day, and we celebrate this holiday each year, honoring the many people who made it a free nation.

Vocabulary and concepts

Independence Day
England
proud
free

Student attitudes

Awareness of pride in being an American and appreciation of being free

Creating interest

Say that July 4 is our country's birthday. Mark it on the calendar. Explain that long ago America belonged to England but wanted to be free. Write *Independence Day* and *England* on the board. Say that America wanted its own government so a Declaration of Independence was sent to the King of England. We are proud of the many people who worked and fought to make our country free. Write *proud* on the board.

Guiding reading and learning

Have the children turn to page 81 and look at the pictures. Explain that the picture at the right shows the bell that was rung to tell people about the Declaration of Independence. Ask how people in the United States celebrate Independence Day. Then read the page with the class.

After the reading, help the children understand the meaning of being free. Bring out that with freedom comes responsibility. Discuss what happens to nations whose people take their freedom for granted and do not assume the responsibility for safeguarding it. [Tyrants take over; corruption and poverty bring misery to all.] Point out that ours is a government of the people, by the people, and for the people—that is why we are free.

From Teachers' Edition of *At School* of TIEGS-ADAMS: PEOPLE AND THEIR HERITAGE, © Copyright 1983 by Silver, Burdett & Ginn Inc. Used with permission.

Martin Luther King, Jr.'s birthday

The birthday of Martin Luther King, Jr.
is January 15.

He was a leader of black people.
He worked to make his dream come true.

His dream was about a better life
for his people.

He wanted all people to live together
in peace.
He was given the Nobel Peace Prize.

Student objectives

The students should learn that:
1. Martin Luther King, Jr., was one
of the great leaders of this country.
2. Martin Luther King, Jr., was a
black leader who worked for civil
rights; he is loved by many people.

Vocabulary and concepts

Martin Luther King, Jr.
dream
better life

Creating interest

Say that on January 15 a famous
black American leader was born.
Explain that this man's name is very
well known because he led the civil
rights crusade in the United States
and in 1964 received the Nobel
Peace Prize, an award given to people who do something valuable for
the good of humanity. Ask who this
man was. Write *Martin Luther King,
Jr.*, on the board. Add his name to
the calendar.

Guiding reading and learning

Have the children discuss the picture of Dr. King on page 92. Tell
students that he made an inspiring
speech in Washington about his
dream for a better life for people.
Write *dream* and *better life* on the
board. Explain that the speech was
recorded and is broadcast on his
birthday in his honor. Have the children read the page with you and then
discuss why this man was followed
by so many people. Point out that his
teachings of nonviolence were in
accord with his Christian beliefs as a
Baptist minister.

Reinforcement and enrichment activities

1. Find an appropriate book in the
library on the life of Martin Luther
King, Jr., and read it to the children.
2. Have the children role play a part
of the book about Dr. King. Have them
emphasize his stuggle for black equality.
3. Relate the story of Dr. King's
participation in the bus boycott in
Montgomery, Alabama. Blacks refused
to ride the buses if they had to sit only
in the back of a bus. As a result of the
boycott, blacks were finally allowed to
sit anywhere on the buses.
4. Show a filmstrip on Dr. King.

92

3. Schools in India

Most children in India go to school.

But not all children do.

There are not enough schools for everyone.

The children in the picture are learning
  to read.

Their classroom is outdoors.

Their village has no school building.

from *Families and Social Needs,* Frederick
M. King et al. By permission of Laidlaw
Brothers, A Division of Doubleday &
Company, Inc.. 1968. pp. 119-121,
T107-109.

JUST FOR FUN

Learn to say "Good morning" in Hindi.

The word *namaste* means "Good morning."

You say it this way: nah-mah-stay.

TEACHING HELPS—Section Introduction, page 119

CONCEPTS

1. There is a great need for increased school facilities in India.
2. All the children cannot attend school, but many children between six and eleven attend school.
3. Many schools are held outdoors because of lack of school buildings.

Background Information

Although India has made great progress in recent years, it still does not provide an education for all of its people. Only about one fourth of the people can read and write. The lack of school buildings and teachers is critical, almost one third of the children not having the advantage of attending school for even a few years. And the schools that the Indians do have for the most part do not compare favorably with those in many other parts of the world, even though the Indians are trying hard to improve the educational opportunities in India.

Recommended Procedure

Getting Started Help the children find India on a globe. Bring out the idea that the climate in much of India is warmer than that of Switzerland. Lead them to suppose that the schools in India might be quite different from those in Switzerland, which they have just finished studying.

Have the children review village life in India as they page through Section 3 of Units 4 and 5.

Developing the Lesson After the children have turned to page 119 and have read the section title, have them talk about the picture briefly before reading the page.

Say, "Read page 119 to find out why this school is being held outdoors. Read the part that tells why." *(sentence 6)* Then have them read the part that tells what the children in the picture are doing *(sentence 4)*, and the sentence that tells why some children do not go to school. *(sentence 3)*

Help the children understand that India does not have enough schools for everyone because there are many poor people in India. The Indians don't have enough money to build enough schools or to pay enough teachers.

Discuss the picture in terms of the annotations, stressing the fact that it would be very tiring to sit on the hard ground and in the sun for a long time.

Concluding the Lesson Help the children carry out the "Just For Fun" activity. Bring out the thought that although other languages also are spoken, Hindi is the official language of India because the government passed a law making it the official language.

Also help the children understand that the Indian people realize the importance of education and they are working hard so that everyone in India can learn to read and write.

Going Further Help the children find pictures of schools or outdoor classes in India and make a display of them. Have someone show the pictures to the class and tell about them.

How are village schools used?

Some mothers and fathers
had no school.
They did not learn to read
and write.
Now they can go to school.

They can go at night.
They can learn to read
and write.

The people are learning to write, usin
the language of their own state, not
hindi.

Who can go to your school?

TEACHING HELPS—page 120

CONCEPTS

1. Schools in India may be used by children during the day and by adults at night.
2. Many adults in India learn to read and write at night school.
3. Many new village schools are being built throughout India because Indians realize the importance of education.

Recommended Procedure

Getting Started Talk with the children about how schools are built in our country—who pays for the buildings and who builds them. Review with the children the fact that all grown-ups in our country pay taxes, and that part of the taxes are used to help build and maintain schools. The schools are built, however, by many different kinds of workers.

Developing the Lesson Have the children turn directly to page 120. Guide the reading of the first group of sentences by giving directions such as these: "Read to find out about the school at the top left of the page. Who built the school? *(sentence 2)* Why did they build it?" *(sentence 3)*

Then have the children read the next group of sentences to find out how the school pictured at the bottom of the page is being used. *(by the parents)* Discuss what the parents are learning. Also discuss why they never learned to read and write when they were children. *(There weren't enough schools for everyone to go to school.)* Be sure that the children don't get the idea that *all* parents in India were deprived of an education as children.

Have someone read page 120 aloud while the other children listen for two ways in which Indian village schools are used. *(for children during the day and for parents at night)* Point

out that school can be held anywhere a teacher can meet with some students. You may wish to help the children recall some schools in our country, which were held in the teacher's home.

Discuss the pictures on page 120, bringing out the points in the annotations. Stress that the interior of the school would be dark since the windows are small and there aren't many of them. Stress the fact that glass is expensive, and also that there isn't electricity in many areas of India. Also, electricity would be too expensive for many of these people. Thus many classrooms remain rather dark inside.

Concluding the Lesson In discussing the concluding question, help the children note that only children go to classes in their school during the day. Many of their schools also hold evening classes for adults. You may wish to discuss what kinds of things adults study at night school in this country and compare these with things that Indian adults learn at night school.

Going Further Help the children think of reasons why people want to learn to read and write.

Help the children make a list of the school supplies Indian children have in their schools. Compare these supplies with those in your classroom.

Have the children pretend they are attending an Indian school and have a reading and a writing lesson, using only school supplies that Indian children have.

EVALUATION

Have someone read aloud Sentence 3 on page 120. Have the children take turns telling what they think this sentence means. Note understanding of the concepts developed in the lesson.

This village has a new school.

The fathers of the children

built it.

They know a school is important.

Now their children have

TEACHING HELPS—page 121

CONCEPTS
1. The children in India learn many of the same subjects that children in America learn.
2. The methods of teaching, the classrooms, the books, and the writing materials used by the Indian children differ from those used by American children.

Recommended Procedure

Getting Started Write the lesson title on the chalkboard. Review what Japanese and Swiss children study in school *(pages 108, 109, 113, 116, 117)*, and talk about the subjects the children study in school.

Developing the Lesson Have the children read page 121 to find out what things Indian children learn in school. Record their answers. Then compare these subjects with those studied in Japan and Switzerland.

Read Sentence 5 aloud. Ask, "What does this sentence mean?" Discuss why it is important to study this subject in school.

Explain that few children have more than just a few years of schooling. Also point out that the people of India are working hard just to build schools for the people. It will be some time, however, before they can have good schools for everyone.

Discuss the pictures, bringing out points listed in the annotations.

Concluding the Lesson Guide a discussion of the concluding question, leading the children to conclude that slates are cheaper to use than paper, and that paper is scarce in India. Point out that paper is used in many of their schools, however.

Going Further If possible, have the children practice writing on a slate or a small chalkboard. Have them think of some advantages and some disadvantages of using slates.

Read stories to the children about school life in India.

EVALUATION
Prepare slips of paper on which you have written parts of sentences such as those enumerated below. Or write the sentence parts on the board. Have the children match the parts to make statements that are true about India. Note how well individual children contribute to the exercise.

1. Indian children   how to cook and sew.
2. The girls learn   is scarce in India.
3. Paper   write on slates.
4. The boys learn   how to make things.

What do children learn in schools in India?

The children learn to read.

They also learn to write.

What do they use to write on?

The children learn about health.

They learn how to stay well.

Girls learn to cook and sew.

Boys learn how to make things.

Why might Indian children use slates instead of paper?

Student objectives

The students should learn that:
If they are thoughtless, they can cause inconvenience to themselves, parents, teachers, and other students.

Vocabulary and concepts

forgot   sorry
brought   thank you

Student attitudes

Awareness that students should be responsible people
Awareness that individuals are responsible for their mistakes
Awareness that the statements "I'm sorry" and "Thank you" should be commonly used

Sue's father came to the school.
He brought the note with him.
"You're lucky," Sue's father said.
"You're lucky I could bring the note."

"Thank you, Dad," said Sue.
"I'm sorry that I forgot my note."

The other children were on the bus.
Sue ran to get on the bus.

Creating interest

Ask what would happen if children forgot to bring a note or their lunch from home. Write *forgot* on the board. Mention that it would have to be brought to them. Write *brought* on the board. Discuss what they might say when the note or lunch was delivered. ["I'm sorry; thank you"] Write *sorry* and *thank you* on the board.

Guiding reading and learning

Have the students read pages 42 and 43 to find out what almost happens to Sue. Then discuss the pictures. Suggest that sometimes it is inconvenient for father or mother to stop what they are doing and bring a note or a lunch to school. Explain that they do it because they care about their children. Sue's father didn't want her to miss the trip. Ask them if they think that everyone forgets something at some time. Conclude that all people do make mistakes and students should be understanding and kind when others make mistakes. Also tell them that **people**

Ready to go

Today is the day for the trip.
Mrs. Linder asked for their notes.

Sue said, "Oh! I forgot my note! May I call my father?"

Sue called her father.

should learn from their mistakes. Ask if they think Sue learned from her mistake.

Ask what we say to people who have done something for us or have helped us. Point to the words *thank you* on the board and explain that we say "thank you." Stress that we all must be responsible people. Then ask how they think Sue felt when her father brought the note. [Sorry, but happy that she could go on the trip]

Reinforcement and enrichment activities

1. Use role-playing situations that will help children accept responsibilities and learn to say, "I'm sorry," etc. Examples:

A child throws a ball and breaks a window. The child accepts the responsibility, tells father or mother, says "I'm sorry," and tries to figure out a way of repairing the window with allowance, etc.

A child runs through a pile of leaves raked up by a family member. The child says, "I'm sorry," and rakes up the leaves.

A child forgets and leaves a jacket outside. Mother sees the jacket, brings it in, and shows it to the child. The child says, "I'm sorry," and then "Thank you for bringing my jacket in."

A child forgets to give a pet dog water. It is a hot day and the dog is thirsty. A brother sees and fills the water dish. He reminds the child that the dog's water was forgotten. The child says "I'm sorry I forgot, and I thank you for giving the dog water."

2. Have the children keep a record of their responsibilities. (For maintaining good behavior in playground arguments, for taking turns for doing their jobs in class, etc.) A chart for classroom jobs could be hung in class and the jobs changed each week.

from *At School*. Virginia Finley, et al. of TIEGS-ADAMS; PEOPLE AND THEIR HERITAGE, © Copyright, 1983. by Silver, Burdett & Ginn Inc. pp.42-3. Used with permission.

This lesson develops children's understanding of themselves as inhabitants of Earth. It focuses on the Copernican view of the solar system and the controversy this view created.

The learning experiences in this lesson help to develop the skills of comparing, classifying, and conceptualizing. The lesson also fosters tolerance of uncertainty and respect for the natural environment.

The student should be able to:

Classify and compare the Ptolemaic and Copernican views of Earth.

Demonstrate tolerance of conflict by explaining why new ideas may arouse anger and controversy.

Conceptualize Earth's correct position in the solar system by drawing a picture.

student text pages 34–37

butcher paper, drawing paper, crayons (optional: props for play)

Copernicus, planet, Galileo

from *Who Are We?* Sara S. Beattie, et al. © The Houghton Mifflin Co. 1976. pp. T68-71. Used with permission. All rights reserved.

Discuss the two pictures on page 34. **Which one shows the idea you studied in the last lesson? What is that idea?** (Earth is in the center and the sun goes around it.) **How is the second picture different?** Ask students to explain as much as they can about the second picture. Tell students they will read to find out if their guesses were correct. (The Background Information on page T71 will be useful in your lesson preparation.)

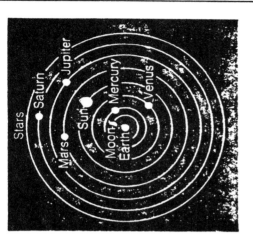

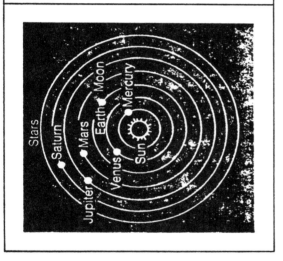

DOES EARTH MOVE?

About four hundred years ago, a scientist named **Copernicus** (ko-PUR'nik-us) wrote a book. Copernicus said Earth is *not* the center of everything. He said Earth moves around the sun. How is that different from what people thought before? Which picture shows Copernicus's idea? Which one shows what people thought before?

Copernicus said Earth is a **planet**. Planets move around the sun. Do you know the names of some other planets besides Earth?

You can see some of the planets in the sky at night. Planets may look like stars to you, but they are different. Both pictures on the next page show the same group of stars. This group of stars is called Leo. Do you see the new "star" in the second picture? It isn't a star at all! It is the planet Venus. It moved into Leo's part of the sky after the first picture was taken. Planets are sometimes in one part of the sky, sometimes in another.

At first only a few people heard about Copernicus's new ideas. But slowly more and more people began to read his book. Earth moves around the sun! It was an exciting idea, but it made some people angry.

About one hundred years after Copernicus died, a scientist named Galileo (gal-i-LAY'oh) made more discoveries. He began to think Copernicus had been right. And then people became angry at Galileo. Some people were so angry that Galileo was arrested. He was taken to a judge for trial.

pages 34–35 and to study the pictures on page 35. A more complete discussion of planets and the solar system can be found in Lessons 15–17. If the children express curiosity about other planets, you may want to present these lessons next. The only explanations necessary at this point, however, are a few basic facts about planets. Tell students: **Planets are much closer to Earth than the stars are. Often they look brighter. But planets do not make their own light. They only reflect the light of the sun. And planets go around the sun. That is why they sometimes appear in one part of the sky, sometimes in another.**

Ask students to look at the two photographs of the star-group Leo. Point out that the stars have stayed in the same place, while the planet has moved. Remind students that planets travel around the sun.

Tell the students to look again at the two drawings on page 34. Ask them to describe what they see in each one. Make two columns on the chalkboard, one called "Old idea" and the other, "New idea — Copernicus." As children describe each diagram, write down the characteristic in the appropriate column. When complete, the columns should include the following ideas:

Old Idea
Earth in center.
Earth does not move.
Sun, moon, stars and planets move around Earth.
Earth is the largest object.

New Idea — Copernicus
The sun is at the center.
Earth moves.
Earth and other planets move around the sun.
The sun is the largest object.
Only the moon moves around Earth.

Summarize the differences between the two systems. Then ask: *Why do you suppose it was so hard to tell which was true?* With students, construct a butcher paper tube with stars drawn on the inside. The tube should be about three feet tall, if possible. Let one child stand inside the tube and tell him or her to watch the stars in the "sky." Have the student turn round and round slowly while looking at the stars. (If you have a swivel chair, students will enjoy sitting in that and turning inside the tube.) Then tell the student in the tube to stand still and watch the "sky" while others slowly turn the tube around. *Did the sky look the same when you were*

Galileo's Trial

Judge: Who is this man?

Witness: His name is Galileo.

Judge: Why has he been arrested?

Witness: He is teaching ideas that are not true. His ideas are wrong and dangerous.

Judge: What ideas is he teaching?

Witness: He says the sun does not move around Earth. He says instead that the sun is in the center. Earth moves around the sun.

Judge (to Galileo): Did you really say that?

Galileo: Yes. I think it's true.

Judge: I do not feel Earth moving. Neither does anyone else. Where did you get such a strange idea?

Galileo: For many years I have studied the stars with a telescope.

Judge: And what is a telescope?

Galileo: It is a new tool. A telescope makes things look closer and bigger. With a telescope you can see things that are very far away.

moving and when the tube was moving? Let students take turns standing in the center.

Pick three students to read the parts of Galileo, the judge, and the witness. It is probably advisable to tell the three "actors" the day before, so that they can read the play through ahead of time. The judge might have a wooden mallet for a gavel, and Galileo a cardboard tube to represent a telescope. You may also have to give some explanation of the various roles of judge, witness, and person on trial. Comparison with some of the television shows featuring courtroom drama might help.

After students have read the skit, ask: *What other new idea have we read about that made people angry?* (Recall the story of Anaxagoras on page 24.) Discuss the question on page 37.

Concluding the Lesson   Tell the students to look back at the cartoon of the smug person on page 33. Ask: *If Earth is not the center of everything, how should this drawing be changed?* Have the students draw a new version of the cartoon, this time in accord with the Copernican view. Pictures should show the sun in the center with Earth going around it.

Return to the list of questions about the Earth which was drawn up at the beginning of this unit. Write the questions on the board again. *How many of these questions can you answer now?* Students should be able to give answers to the following responses:

What is Earth? Earth is a planet.

What does Earth do? It moves around the sun.

What shape is Earth? Round.

The question "Where is Earth?" can be answered in relation to the sun. But students will be able to give a more complete answer to that question by the end of the unit.

On student text page 38 you will find review exercises for Lessons 1–5. The suggested duration for this lesson (3 days) is intended to accommodate the use of these review exercises.

Students can work in groups to make mobiles representing the two different systems.

Students can make signs for "Sun," "Earth," "Stars," and other planets. Then each student can carry a sign and demonstrate the motion of his object in the Copernican system.

BACKGROUND INFORMATION

Copernicus (1473–1543) was a Polish astronomer. On the basis of his own carefully charted planetary motions, Copernicus formulated a heliocentric or sun-centered concept of the solar system. The heretical nature of this idea kept him from publishing his theories until shortly before his death.

Galileo Galilei (1564–1642), an Italian astronomer, became one of the strongest supporters of the Copernican theory. With the telescope he built, Galileo studied the skies and recorded numerous original observations. Galileo cited many phenomena which were best explained by the concept of an Earth which rotated and travelled around the sun. Galileo was forced to recant his heretical views. After his trial, he remained under house arrest until his death.

Witness: What difference does a telescope make? All the books say Earth is the center of everything. The people who wrote the books were wise. You should listen to them, Galileo.

Judge: How did your telescope give you these strange ideas?

Galileo: With the telescope, I can see the moon and stars and planets very well. All the planets move around the sun.

Judge: What does all this have to do with Earth?

Galileo: I think Earth is a planet, too. If that is true, Earth must move around the sun.

Judge: Earth is a planet? Just another planet? An ordinary planet? Not the center of everything? Nonsense! It can't be true.

Witness: See what I told you? He thinks Earth is just a planet. The man is crazy!

Judge: Galileo, we can't have you teaching this nonsense. Your punishment is to go home and stay there as long as you live. Never leave your house. That way, no one will hear these foolish ideas.

Do you think people forgot about Galileo's ideas after the judge sent him home?

The Health Department

Workers in the Health Department help to keep the people well. They try to keep disease germs from spreading in the city.

They test for germs in food. Germs can make people sick. The food in the city must be safe to eat.

Workers in the Health Department go to the wholesale market. They look at the fruits and vegetables. Fruits and vegetables must be clean. They must not be spoiled.

Workers in the Health Department inspect places where food is stored. Storage places must be clean. There must be no rats or insects in them. Rats and insects spread germs.

The workers go to food stores. They go to bakeries and to food factories. They go to restaurants, too. The food must be fresh. Refrigerators must be in good working order. Machines must be clean. The dishes in restaurants must be clean. People who work with food must be clean and healthy.

Many workers in the Health Department are doctors and nurses. Some of them work at health clinics. *Clinics* are places where people go for health care. Clinics are like small hospitals. There are eye doctors and dentists at clinics. There are doctors who care for babies.

Sometimes workers at the clinics give shots. Shots can keep people from getting sick.

Citizens go to the Health Department about their health problems. The workers listen to the people's problems. Then the workers decide what to do. Workers in the Health Department work to keep people in good health.

Guiding reading and learning

The following questions may be used during the discussion of the Health Department.

1. Why is the job of the Health Department so important? [Helps keep us healthy]

2. What are clinics? [Places where people go for health care]

3. How do health inspectors help us? [They check to see that the food we eat is clean and fresh and that the people who handle the foods are clean and healthy.]

Providing background

A one-year-old child today has a good chance of growing up if the child does not have a bad accident. This was not true a hundred years ago. Diseases then killed a great many children. Sometimes one disease killed many, many people. This was called an *epidemic*. Children then had only a fifty-fifty chance of growing up.

Today, disease is fought by means of inoculations, vaccinations, medicines, better health care, and better diets. Scientists know more about the causes of disease and how to prevent its spread. Doctors know more about health care and how to treat diseases. People know more about healthy diets and health rules. All these things help people of today live a much longer life than people of long ago.

From Teachers' Edition of *In Communities* of TIEGS-ADAMS: PEOPLE AND THEIR HERITAGE, © Copyright 1979 by Silver, Burdett & Ginn Inc. Used with permission.

City government
in East Bend

"Uncle Ben and Aunt Mary are coming to dinner tonight," Mrs. Birch said. "Before we eat we'll watch the mayor on TV. The mayor is going to talk about the new plans for East Bend."

Mr. Birch said, "The mayor will explain the need for the new plans. Some people might not like the changes. Some will have to move to new homes. Some business people will have to move to new buildings.

"The mayor will try to convince people that the new plans will be good for everybody."

The mayor is a busy city leader. She was elected by the citizens of East Bend. She talks to citizens every day. She talks to business owners. She talks to workers in factories and stores. She listens to the ideas of all of these people. She also gets many letters.

The people tell the mayor about problems of the city. The mayor works on problems with the city planners.

The mayor has the help of many workers. They do different jobs for the city. They work in different departments.

The city must pay all of these workers. It must pay for new things it needs. Most of the money comes from taxes. Taxes are paid by the people who live in East Bend.

All of the city workers help take care of East Bend. They make it a clean, safe, beautiful place in which to live.

From Teachers' Edition of *In Communities* of TIEGS-ADAMS: PEOPLE AND THEIR HERITAGE, © Copyright 1979 by Silver, Burdett & Ginn Inc. Used with permission.

Guiding reading and learning

Have students read to find what the mayor of East Bend is going to do on TV.

Have students look up the word *mayor* in a dictionary. See if students can guess what the duties of a mayor are. Find out from students if they know the name of their city mayor. Ask what kinds of things their city mayor does.

City government, like all forms of government in our society, is citizens working with the government. Therefore the vital role of citizens in supporting and guiding the government should be emphasized to the students.

Elicit from students the meaning of *citizen*. Discuss with the class the role of a citizen. Tell students that the city planners talk to the citizens of the city. Tell them the planners tell the citizens the plans they have drawn up for the city. The planners listen for ideas from the citizens. Ask how city planners can be helped by listening to the citizens of the city.

A key theme of this year's programs should be the privilege of citizenship in our democratic republic and our individual responsibility in this government. Each of us has a personal responsibility as a citizen to support our government and to work for change whenever it seems necessary to bring about the most good for all the people.

Ask students if they know how a mayor gets to be mayor. Discuss the fact that the mayor of a city is elected by the citizens of the city. Discuss why it is important for the citizens to decide who the mayor should be. Discuss the importance of citizen participation in the decisions of the city.

After students have read these pages, discuss why the mayor went on TV to talk about the new plans for East Bend. Ask the children if they think the mayor of East Bend is a good mayor. Have them explain why or why not.

City problems

East Bend grew into a city. Businesses and factories came to East Bend. Many people came to work. People built houses and apartment buildings.

No one had time to plan the way the city grew. Now there are many problems.

Some buildings in the city are old. Many of them are not safe.

In downtown East Bend the buildings are close together. The streets are narrow. There is not enough space for parking. There is no place for playgrounds.

56

Mothers and fathers talk about building new schools and playgrounds. They want parks and swimming pools.

Business people talk about parking problems. They say, "People must be able to park their cars downtown. If they can't find places to park, they won't come to our stores."

Business people want more highways, too. Highways bring people to the city.

Some people do not want new highways. "We'll lose our homes where new highways are built," they say. "It will cost us a lot of money to find new homes."

Lesson plan 56-61

Creating interest

Review and discuss with students the meaning of *problem*. [something to be worked out] Ask the children if they have ever had a problem. Were they able to do something about it? If so, how did they go about doing this? Discuss whether all problems can be solved.

Guiding reading and learning

Read aloud the first paragraph, having students listen to learn how East Bend grew. Then have students read the next three paragraphs to find out what problems this growth created.

The citizens of East Bend are working together to solve the problems of the city. Review with students the technique that can be used in problem solving.

1. State the problem clearly.
2. Make a list of possible solutions.
3. Gather and examine information about the problem and about the possible solutions.
4. Choose the solution that seems best.
5. Test the chosen solution to find out if it really solves the problem.

Discuss with the class the problems that East Bend has. Elicit from students possible solutions to East Bend's problems. One of East Bend's problems is narrow streets. Students might discuss whether this problem would be helped if some streets were made one-way.

Guiding reading and learning

Read these paragraphs aloud, having students listen to find out what various groups of people in East Bend wanted. After reading each paragraph, stop and ask what the people in that paragraph wanted. List these wants on the chalkboard. Then after the list is complete ask if students think that all of the wants can be taken care of. Help the children realize that some of these wants conflict. Encourage a discussion of why people have to get together and plan the best way to provide for these wants.

There will be a number of different approaches in this book to develop understandings about cities and city life. These different approaches are planned to gradually deepen and expand students' understandings of this major phenomenon of modern life. In developing these understandings, the approach should be positive, stressing opportunities and responsibilities as well as problems.

An American City With a Problem

An American city with a problem

CHAPTER UNDERSTANDING In urban areas people often have conflicting values, needs, and wants.

CONCEPTS interaction, needs, roles, values, wants.

SKILLS SYMBOLS

Activities involving map skills are designated by ●. Activities involving graph, table, and chart skills are designated by ■. Activities involving reading readiness, vocabulary development, and other language skills are designated by ▲.

EVALUATION STRATEGIES

The Introductory Lesson may be used as a pre-testing device. Post-testing may take place in Lesson 4. Activities 1 and 2, or during any of the Chapter Wrap-up Activities, particularly Activities 1 and 2.

Within the chapter, evaluation can occur during Lesson 1, Activity 3; Lesson 2, Activities 1 and 2; Lesson 3, Activities 2 and 3; and Lesson 5, Activity 2.

For purposes of formal evaluation, a short objective test is provided at the end of the Chapter Wrap-up Activities.

CHAPTER UNIFYING ACTIVITIES

1. Divide the class into three groups. Announce that each group will have its own secret assignment. The secrets will not be revealed until study of the chapter has been completed. Stress the idea that students should not discuss their assignments with anyone outside their own group. Item 5, page 225, contains synopses of three situations. Give one synopsis to each group. Let each group work out its own pantomime presentation of the situation and be ready to act it out later in the chapter.

2. A showing of the shortstrip "People, People Everywhere" from the *Towns and Cities* Media Kit would be an ideal lead-in to this chapter. A second showing, when the chapter has been completed, would effectively underscore the concepts presented in the text. If it is impossible to present the recommended cartoon strip, the students may make their own cartoon by drawing, frame by frame, the changes that would take place in their own classroom if it had to be shared with the rest of the school. Item 6.

Problems, problems

Picture TL: subway graffiti, New York; BL: crowded street, New York

from *Towns and Cities*. Ronald Reed Boyce, et al. © Addison-Wesley Publishing Co. pp. 102-113,115. Used with permission. All

OBJECTIVES

Hypothesize about city problems.
Observe the ghetto in New York.
Interpret what the New York City plan might mean to the people in the ghetto.

LESSON UNDERSTANDING Many of the people in the overcrowded New York ghettos would like to move out, but, for various reasons, cannot.

CONCEPTS environment, interdependence, needs, wants

DEVELOPING THE LESSON

1. *Hypothesizing.* Discuss: What is the biggest city in the whole United States? (After students have made their guesses, suggest that they read the first sentence on page 104. Call for a show of hands of all those who had correctly answered your question. Ask for guesses as to the second and third largest cities in the United States. Students can check their answers in the Student Resource Center, page 191.) Have students read the rest of page 104. Discuss: We have already talked about some problems that cities have but that a place like Forks does not have. Do you think that the problems all arise independently, or do you think most city problems result from one major problem? Why is overcrowding such a hard problem? (See also Activity 2 on Student Resource Center page 211.)

Alternative Activity: Have the class read page 104. Discuss: Does our community have any problems? Are they more like the problems of New York or the problem in Forks? Is overcrowding one of our problems? If not, is it possible that it may be a problem someday? In places where overcrowding is not yet a problem, what could be done to keep it from becoming one?

2. *Observing.* Write the word *ghetto* on the chalkboard and have students practice pronouncing and spelling it. Discuss: *Ghetto* is a very old word. It comes from an Italian word that means foundry, a place where metal or glass is molded. Long ago in Venice, Italy, there was a part of the city called the ghetto because there was a cannon foundry there—a place where cannons were made. Later it became the home of Venetian Jews, who were not allowed to live

problems, problems

New York City is the biggest city in the United States. There are many interesting things to do in big cities. But like all big cities, New York has many problems. The problem you will read about in this chapter is only one of New York's problems. As you read this chapter, think about why some city problems are so hard to solve.

Picture New York.

The problem in New York

Many poor people live in big American cities. One of the biggest city problems is what to do to help them. Some of the poor people live in crowded parts of the city called *ghettos*. Many of these people would like to live in other parts of the city.

These pictures show a ghetto in New York City. Why do you think people might want to leave the ghetto?

anywhere else in the city in those days. Why do you think crowded places like you see in the pictures on page 105 are called ghettos? (Elicit the understanding that people live in these areas because they too are not allowed to live anywhere else—either because they cannot afford to, or because they are made to feel unwelcome in other parts of the city because they are members of minority groups.) Have the class read page 105 and answer the question.
Alternative Activity: Ask the class to read page 105, examine the pictures, and answer the question. Discuss Ghetto conditions are certainly unpleasant. What kinds of problems do you think the people who live in the ghettos have? (Sickness spreads fast when people are crowded together. The buildings in the ghettos are old and dirty and full of rats. Studies have shown that when people or animals are crowded together, they tend to become violent, and there are many crimes of violence in the ghetto.) Do ghetto problems have any effect on the people in other parts of the city? (Elicit the understanding that sickness, crime, and violence spread and may affect anyone. Even the rats may invade other parts of the city.) Is it a good idea for ghetto dwellers to move to other places in the city? Why?

▲3. *Interpreting*. Have the class read pages 106 and 107. Explain that the picture on page 106 shows a housing project such as the one the New York City officials had in mind. The picture on page 107 shows part of Forest Hills. Ask: Why do you suppose the officials thought Forest Hills would be a good place for the apartment buildings? What are some other things, besides housing, that are done to help people? (monthly checks, food, money for medicine, etc.) Elicit the understanding that these different kinds of help are called *welfare* or *welfare services*. Write the word on the chalkboard and have students learn to spell it. Ask: Would being able to move out of the ghetto help people as much as food, medicine, etc.? Which kind of help would you prefer? Why?
Alternative Activity: Have the class read pages 106 and 107, and explain the photographs on those pages to them. Ask: Suppose you were living in one of the places shown on page 105

An American city with a problem

you heard that you and your
...ily were going to be able to move
...one of the buildings shown on
...e 106, in a neighborhood like the
... shown on page 107. Write a
...m or a paragraph or draw a
...ure of yourself that tells how that
...s made you feel. (Suggest that
...h student stand in front of a
...or, act out his or her reaction to
...news, and then describe it in
...ing or put it into a self-portrait.)

In 1966 the New York City officials made a plan. The *officials* of a city are the people who run the city's government.

The plan would help some of the people who lived in the ghetto. The officials decided to build some apartment buildings in other parts of the city. The rents in the apartments would be low. The poor people could afford to move into the buildings.

Picture low income housing, New York

In 1971 the New York City officials were looking for a place to build some of these apartment buildings. They chose a part of New York City called Forest Hills.

OBJECTIVES
Classify statements as facts or opinions.

Valuing Students are asked to evaluate the opinions of people who were opposed to having the apartment buildings in Forest Hills.

LESSON UNDERSTANDING Some people had good reasons for thinking the apartment buildings should *not* go in Forest Hills

CONCEPTS environment, needs, space, wants

DEVELOPING THE LESSON
1 *Classifying* Have the class read the first paragraph on page 108. Then ask for volunteers to read each of the quoted sentences on pages 108 and 109, making each one sound as if a resident of Forest Hills were saying it. The final paragraph on page 109 may then be read by the class in unison. Ask the class to recall what they learned about the difference between a fact and an opinion in the previous chapter. Ask for volunteers to read sentences of their choosing from the quoted sentences on pages 108 and 109, telling the class whether the statements are facts or opinions. Permit disagreement and discussion, but try to have the entire class agree on the classification of one statement before going on to the next (For example, on page 109, the first sentence is a fact, but the second sentence is an opinion.)
2 *Valuing*. Discuss: Let's go back over some of the things those people in Forest Hills said. First, what may have been some reasons for deciding to build the apartments in Forest Hills? (There was enough vacant land. There were a few apartment houses there already. There were only a few Puerto Rican and nonwhite families living in the area. That was important because it meant that the families in the new apartment building would not be moving from one ghetto into another. They would be becoming part of a largely middle-class neighborhood.) But what about the fact that no one explained the reasons to the people in Forest Hills—that they were not even told about the plan? Some of the Forest Hills people said, "That's not fair." Do you agree? Why or why

Ideas from Forest Hills

Many people in Forest Hills did not want the buildings in their neighborhood. Here are some of the things they said:

"Why did they decide to build those apartment buildings here? No one asked us if we wanted them. That's not fair!"

"Think of all those people moving into those big buildings! Our subways and schools will be even more crowded than they are now!"

"Most crime in New York is in the ghettos. If those people move here, there will be more crime here. I think we should help poor people, but I'm afraid of them."

"I don't believe in moving people out of the ghettos. We should spend that money to fix up the old buildings in the ghettos."

Some people in Forest Hills became angry. Some of them carried signs around the land where the apartment buildings were to be built. Some of them even threw mud and rocks.

not? Maybe the New York planners made another mistake. As you can see from the picture on page 108, the subways were already crowded. So were the schools. Do you think the planners should have done something else before they started to build apartments for several hundred more people? If so, what should they have done?

Alternative Activity: Ask the class to look again at the picture on page 109. Discuss: Instead of an "against" sign, might this man in Forest Hills have made a better point if he had carried a "for" sign? One might have been "Build more schools and subways first. Then invite the people."

Ask each student to think of and execute a "for" sign. Display a few of the best around the classroom

An American city with a problem

OBJECTIVES
Recall the purpose of the Forest Hills project. *Analyze* the arguments against the Forest Hills project.

Valuing. Students are asked to define the word *prejudice* and to identify their own prejudices.

LESSON UNDERSTANDING Some people had good reasons for thinking the apartment buildings should go in Forest Hills.

CONCEPTS needs, space, values, wants

DEVELOPING THE LESSON
1. *Recalling.* Have the class read the first paragraph on page 110. Discuss: Before you read what the people outside of Forest Hills thought, think about this: Does it make any difference that these ideas came from *outside* Forest Hills? Do you think people who do not live in Forest Hills have a right to have an opinion about what goes on inside Forest Hills?

Elicit as great a variety of opinions as possible, ranging from the feeling that only people who live in Forest Hills have a right to an opinion to the feeling that all parts of a city are interdependent, and therefore anyone has a right to an opinion about what goes on in any part of the city. Try to encourage the realization that on this matter, as with the different opinions inside and outside Forest Hills, no one point of view is valid and no one opinion is right.

Alternative Activity: Have the class read the first paragraph on page 110. Discuss: The New York City planners wanted to help a few ghetto families move to a middle-income neighborhood and be a part of it. Would a 24-story building be likely to bring that about? Why or why not? Do you think the people in Forest Hills would have been as much against having some low-income families for neighbors as they were to having a 24-story apartment house in their neighborhood? Why or why not?

▲2. *Valuing.* Say: In this chapter there is a long word that will be easier to understand if we take it apart. The word is *prejudiced.* (Put it on the chalkboard and teach the class to pronounce it.) The first part of the word, *pre,* is used in lots of words. It

Problems, problems

Ideas from outside Forest Hills

Other people had other ideas about the apartment buildings. But most of these people did not live in Forest Hills. Here are some of the things these people said:

"Many people in the ghetto are black. Almost everyone in Forest Hills is white. Those people in Forest Hills are just prejudiced against black people."

"People in other parts of New York will feel just the same way as the people in Forest Hills. Everyone thinks the apartment buildings are a good idea. But nobody wants them in his or her own neighborhood."

"People in Forest Hills are afraid of black people and poor people. But most of them don't know any black people or poor people. After the apartment buildings are built, the black people and the white people will get to know each other. Then they will like each other."

means "before." Preschool means before you start to go to regular school. Sometimes there are pregame rallies before football games. The second part of the word looks a lot like *judge*. (Put *judge* on the board.) And that is just what prejudiced means—judging something or someone before you know much about him, her, or it.

Ask a good reader to read aloud the final paragraph on page 110, making it sound as if a person were actually saying it. Then ask each student to rewrite the last sentence in that paragraph *without using the word prejudiced*.

Alternative Activity: Ask a good reader to read aloud the final paragraph on page 110, making it sound as if a person were actually saying it. Then ask students to make their own lists of two or three kinds of people or foods that they are prejudiced against—that they have decided to dislike even though they do not know such people or have never tasted the foods. Encourage a freewheeling discussion of the lists, during the course of which some students may try to convince others that their prejudices are in error.

3. *Analyzing:* Ask for volunteers to read aloud each of the paragraphs on pages 111 and 112, while the rest of the class follows the lines in the book. At the close of each paragraph ask the class to decide who has been speaking—ghetto dweller, suburbanite, city planner, or whoever.

Alternative Activity: Ask for volunteers to read aloud each of the paragraphs on pages 111 and 112, while the rest of the class follows the lines in the book. When the reading has been completed, ask for other volunteers to go back over the sentences and decide which statements are facts and which are opinions. For example, "Many people in the ghetto are black" is a fact, but "Everyone thinks the apartment buildings are a good idea" is an opinion.

OBJECTIVES
Hypothesize that other city problems are as difficult to solve as the problem in Forest Hills.

Valuing. Students are asked to come to their own conclusions about what should be done in Forest Hills.

LESSON UNDERSTANDING The needs and wants of the ghetto dwellers in New York conflict with the needs and wants of the people in Forest Hills.

CONCEPTS interdependence, needs, values, wants

DEVELOPING THE LESSON
1. *Valuing.* Ask the class to read the first paragraph on page 113. Discuss: What are the needs and wants of the ghetto dwellers? (better housing; safer and cleaner places to live; more money for food, clothes, and other necessities; jobs; education; etc.) What are the needs and wants of the people who live in Forest Hills? (to keep their neighborhood from becoming overcrowded; to keep their neighborhood safe by not letting criminals live there; in fact, to keep their neighborhood just as it is, as much as possible) Part of the problem in New York City is that the needs and wants of these two groups of people *conflict.* That means that one group could not get what it needed and wanted unless the other group did *not* get what it needed and wanted. In a case like this, do you think it would be better to force one side or the other to give in or to try to reach a *compromise,* in which each side gives up some of what it wants and gets some of what it wants? What might happen in this situation if one side or the other wins? What might be some of the problems of trying for a compromise? What kind of compromise might work for Forest Hills?
Alternative Activity: Ask the class to read the first paragraph on page 113. Then ask them to pretend that they are attending a meeting of the New York City housing board. Designate one part of the room to be people from Forest Hills; another, a ghetto group. Explain that not all members of each group need to agree with one another, any more than the New Yorkers and the Forest Hills residents would all see eye-to-eye. Encourage

Problems, problems

"They won't let criminals into the apartment buildings. They will check everyone who wants to live there. People in Forest Hills won't have to worry about more crime because of those buildings."

"I live in the ghetto now, but I would like to live in a place like Forest Hills. That part of New York is much prettier and safer than here. But I would be afraid to go there. Those Forest Hills people act dangerous. I'm afraid they would throw a rock through my window if I lived there."

Many people thought that there was no simple answer to the Forest Hills problem. But everyone thought something should be done. What do you think the people in New York City should do?

What are some other problems that American cities have? Why are city problems so hard to solve?

each student to make up his or her mind as to whether everybody should just forget the whole thing, build the apartments in Forest Hills as planned, build scattered low-cost houses in various parts of Forest Hills, house ghetto residents in army barracks until their ghetto homes can be completely rebuilt, or anything else they can think of. Each student should signify his or her wish to speak by raising a hand. No one should be permitted to speak for more than a minute. When several views have been presented, suggest that perhaps it would be more efficient to work as committees. Activity 1 on student page 115 may then be initiated.

2. *Hypothesizing.* Ask the class to read the second paragraph on page 113. Then have students examine the photographs on pages 112 and 113 in order to name other city problems—rats, crime, pollution, overcrowding, litter, and whatever else the students see in these pictures. Point out that some pictures may represent more than one problem. Ask each student to write and hand in a one-sentence caption for each picture. Discuss: Do you think any of these other problems in big cities might lead to conflicts, such as the one we have been reading about in Forest Hills? What about energy? Do you remember about the blackout in New York in 1965? Since then, the electric company in New York has wanted to build a new plant to generate more electricity for the city. The city needs this plant. But the plant will pollute the water near New York City, and most New Yorkers feel their water is already too polluted. What other similar conflicts can you think of?

An American city with a problem

Things to do

1 Your class can make its own decision about what New York should do about Forest Hills. Think about what all the people in this chapter have said. Then form a committee with other people who feel the way you do. With your committee, make a plan to solve New York's problem.

Your committee should make a list of reasons for being in favor of the plan you made. Everyone on the committee should try to add at least one reason to the list. Then choose one member of your committee to tell your reasons to the rest of the class. Try to make everyone else in the class feel the way you do.

When your class has listened to reasons for all the plans, take a vote. Which plan did most people in your class vote for?

2 Think of some good things about cities. Then draw a picture, make a collage, or write a poem that tells something you like about cities.

3 Take an opinion poll in your class. How many would like to live in a city? How many would like to live in a suburb? in a small town? on a farm? Compare your poll with the one on page 213. In what ways is your poll like that one? In what ways is it different?

HOW AM I LIKE ALL OTHER HUMAN BEINGS?

Look at the children in the pictures.
What is happening in each picture?
Do you know why?
Do ALL people do these things? Why?

This lesson develops children's understanding of themselves as individuals and human beings. It focuses on needs that each child has in common with all humans, with special emphasis on the need for food.

The learning experiences in this lesson help to develop the skills of inferring and comparing. The lesson also fosters self-awareness and respect for others.

The student should be able to:

Infer from pictures that eating, sleeping, and breathing fulfill basic human needs.

Compare his or her basic needs with other people's needs illustrated in pictures.

Exhibit increasing empathy with human beings who are often hungry by making statements about how those human beings feel.

student text pages 212–214

drawing materials

Have students look at the pictures on page 212. Ask: *What is happening in each picture?* Students may be able to tell you that one person is breathing under water with a snorkel, another is sleeping, and the third person is eating. Ask students: *What would happen to these people if they stopped breathing or didn't sleep or eat?* Elicit the idea that breathing, sleeping, and eating are essential to life and satisfy basic human needs. Have children answer the questions in the text. They should become aware that all people have these same needs because they are human beings.

T252   Unit 4, Lesson 1

Ask students to write down what they ate at their last meal. Ask them to star the items on their list that they enjoyed eating most, and to put an X next to the items they did not enjoy eating. Have the students share their lists with the rest of the class. Have students tell why they ate those things and not others. You will have a variety of answers here. Try to have them think about the nutritional value of food and the need to eat well-balanced meals. Allow students to express their feelings about foods they enjoy eating, some of which may be nutritionally poor and foods they dislike eating, some of which may be nutritionally high. Ask students: *How might you feel right now if you did not eat that last meal or ate very little of it?* If children ate only an hour or less before, they might not be experiencing much hunger; but if they ate several hours before, they might be hungry by now. Ask students: *Can you remember a time when you were very hungry and there was no food around?* Perhaps they went on a trip and forgot to take food and could not find a store or restaurant open. Ask students to describe these experiences if they had them. *How did you feel after you finally had a meal?*

Have students read the poem, "When I Am Hungry" on page 214. Ask students: *What do you think the child in the picture feels? Are the feelings similar to the feelings the poem describes?* Tell them to choose one or two lines of the poem that especially describe how this child feels. Have students then compare this child with the people eating on page 213. Ask: *Do you think there are people in the world as hungry or even hungrier than the child in this picture?* Make students aware of the many, many people in the world who do not get enough to eat. Involve the children in a discussion of what happens to people when they do not get enough to eat. Make sure students understand that people without proper food become sick, and they have little energy to work or play. Many people die from starvation. Then briefly discuss why people do not get enough food. You might want to begin by asking the children where and how they obtain food and then ask why all people cannot get food in the same way. Begin to help children understand some of the causes of extreme hunger in the world, such as drought, poverty, and overpopulation.

THE NEED FOR FOOD

I am like all other human beings because . . .
    I need food.

I eat.
I eat many different things.
I like to eat.

Why do I eat?
Why do I eat the things I do?
Why do I like to eat?

All of you from time to time have said, "I am hungry. I want something to eat." But are you really hungry? Do you really know what it feels like to be hungry?

213

WHEN I AM HUNGRY

When I am hungry,
I do not play.
I am not gay.
My world is gray,
When I am hungry.

When I am hungry,
I sing no song.
My day is long.
All things go wrong,
When I am hungry.

When I am hungry,
I think of food.
I remember food.
I dream of food.
I WANT food.
I NEED food,
When I am hungry.

Write a poem like the one you just read. Use the title "When I Am Tired" or "When I Am Cold."

214

Children may experience the feelings of being tired and cold more often than they feel hunger in some cases. Ask them to write a short poem on how these feelings of being tired and cold affect them.

Concluding the Lesson Have children draw a picture or write a story or a skit on the part they enjoy most about being human and needing food: helping to shop for food, helping to prepare food, eating food at home, eating at a restaurant. Have them draw a picture or write a story or skit about the part they like the *least* about being human and needing food. For example, they may dislike being hungry, eating foods they dislike, helping to shop for food, or preparing food. Have students share their work with other members of the class. Or if it seems more appropriate conclude the lesson by beginning an action project through which the class can contribute food or money to people in need of food. You can contact CARE or local welfare organizations for help in planning such a project.

PROVISION FOR INDIVIDUAL DIFFERENCES

Have students make a picture essay of some of their favorite foods, using pictures cut from old magazines.

Invite a representative from a community agency that helps people get food to explain what the agency does.

If there are health and nutrition charts in your school, have children look at them and report what the most nutritious foods are. Do they think these items are available to all human beings?

BACKGROUND INFORMATION

Some of the major reasons for worldwide food shortages are the rapidly expanding population and the resulting increase in the demand for food; the improper use of once-fertile areas which are now becoming depleted of soil nutrients essential for crops; changing weather conditions such as the drastic decline in rainfall in certain areas of the world, resulting in severe droughts; and the sky-rocketing costs of petroleum-based fertilizers, placing them out of the reach of poorer countries.

LINEAR MEASUREMENT

Materials You Furnish	Kit Materials	Notes and Suggestions	Recommended Student Grouping
Books, 1 per group Meter sticks, 1 per group New crayons, 1 per group Pencils, unsharpened, 1 per group Scissors, 1 pair per group	*Chart 1 *Chart 2 *Construction paper, 23 x 30 cm (9 x 12 in.), 1 sheet per student *Metric rulers, 1 per group	Yard sticks can be used instead of meter sticks. If sufficient number of meter or yard sticks cannot be obtained, some groups can use metric rulers.	Twos

Average time: 30 min.
Minimum time: 20 min.
Maximum time: 50 min.

INTERACTIVITY GOAL

The student will apply sensory skills to investigating the properties of objects.

CONTENT OBJECTIVE

The student will measure a variety of objects using a metric ruler and a meter stick.

SCIENCE SKILLS

The student will —
demonstrate the use of the metric ruler and the meter stick; measure lengths and heights of a variety of objects.

MULTIDISCIPLINARY ASPECTS

Language arts
Oral communication

Mathematics
Measuring

KEY VOCABULARY

length, long, longest, measure, meter stick, metric ruler, short, shortest, tallest

PURPOSE

This activity is designed to provide students with experiences in measuring.

TEACHER ROLE

Assist the students throughout their measuring tasks. Let them explore freely with their measuring instruments.

TEACHER PREPARATION

Obtain enough meter or yard sticks for one per group.

BEGINNING THE ACTIVITY

Group the students in twos. Distribute one sheet of construction paper, 23 x 30 cm (9 x 12 in.), to each pair of students.

TEACHING STRATEGIES

POSSIBLE STUDENT BEHAVIORS

EACH GROUP NOW HAS A SHEET OF PAPER. WHAT SHAPE IS THE PIECE OF PAPER?

Respond, "A rectangle," "A square," "I don't know."

YES, IT IS A RECTANGLE SHAPE.

from *The Elementary School Science Program.*
Biological Sciences Curriculum Study.
Colorado © J.B. Lippincott Co. pp. 72-74.
Used with permission.

*Equipment Kit Items   †Media Kit Items   Unmarked items are in the Consumable Kit

ARE ALL THE SIDES (point to the sides) THE SAME LENGTH?
  Respond, "No."

FIND THE TWO LONG SIDES AND POINT TO THEM.
  Students locate and indicate the long sides of the rectangle (the short sides of the sheet of paper).

HOW LONG DO YOU THINK THE SIDES ARE?
  Respond, "Real long," "I don't know," "A hundred."

LET'S USE OUR HANDS TO MEASURE THE PAPER. WORK WITH YOUR PARTNER TO FIND OUT THE LENGTH OF THE PAPER.

Demonstrate one or two ways to measure the paper by using hands. Remind the students to start at the edge of the paper when measuring.

Encourage individuality by permitting students to use their hands in a variety of ways (hand widths, thumbs to little fingers, wrists to finger tips, and so on) to measure the paper.

Some students may find it difficult to measure the paper. Ask a successful student to demonstrate his/her technique.

Paper-measuring time

Call on pairs of students to show and tell about their hand measurements.
  Demonstrate different measuring techniques.

THOSE ARE ALL VERY GOOD WAYS TO MEASURE!

WHY DID WE GET SO MANY DIFFERENT NUMBERS?
  Infer that hands are not all the same size, and that different approaches to the measuring also gave different answers.

▲Materials
Pencils

COULD WE USE PENCILS TO MEASURE THE PAPER?
  Respond, "Yes," "No," "I'm not sure."

I WILL GIVE YOU A PENCIL. WORK WITH YOUR PARTNER TO FIND OUT HOW MANY PENCILS LONG YOUR PAPER IS.

Demonstrate one or two ways to measure the paper by using hands. Remind the students to start at the edge of the paper when measuring.

Measuring time

Call on pairs of students to report their findings.

Accept all answers. Reinforce the correct response by saying:

GOOD. YOUR PIECE OF PAPER IS ABOUT TWO PENCILS LONG.

NOW WORK WITH YOUR PARTNER TO FIND OUT HOW LONG THE SHORT SIDE OF YOUR PAPER IS.
  Partners work together.

Move from group to group, giving assistance and encouragement.

Call on pairs of students to report their findings.
  Respond, "More than one," "Almost two."

Accept all responses.

GOOD. SUPPOSE WE WANTED TO MEASURE THIS (point to a bulletin board or bookcase that measures more than a meter). WHAT MIGHT WE USE?
  Responses will vary.

▲Materials
Meter sticks

Show the students a meter stick and ask:

COULD WE USE THIS?
  Respond, "Yes."

WHO WOULD LIKE TO USE THIS METER STICK TO FIND OUT HOW LONG THE _____ IS?

Select a pair of volunteers. Have the volunteers measure the object and report their findings.

Repeat the above strategy with another pair of volunteers.

▲Materials
Chart 1
Meter sticks

Hold up Chart 1 and say:

HERE ARE PICTURES OF FOUR OBJECTS. FIND ONE OBJECT HERE IN THE CLASSROOM THAT IS LIKE EACH PICTURE. THEN FIND OUT HOW MANY METER STICKS LONG IT IS. OR HOW MANY METER STICKS TALL. FIND OUT WHICH OBJECT IS LONGEST OR TALLEST. FIND OUT WHICH IS SHORTEST, TOO.

Place the chart in an area where students are able to refer to it.

Distribute a meter stick to each group. Then circulate around the room to be sure that students are making the measurements.

Measuring time

After the measuring is completed, encourage the students to discuss their findings. If time is left in the activity period, encourage more measurements of the students' own choices of objects.

Collect the meter sticks and place them at the Interest Center.

A good place to stop

▲Materials
Chart 2
Metric rulers

You may wish to begin this part of the activity by reviewing the previous lesson.

Group the students in twos. Hold up Chart 2 and say:

HERE ARE PICTURES OF FOUR OBJECTS IN OUR CLASSROOM. COULD WE USE A METRIC RULER (hold one up) TO MEASURE THE OBJECTS?

Respond, "Yes."

WITH YOUR PARTNER, MEASURE EACH OBJECT. FIND OUT HOW MANY RULERS LONG EACH OBJECT IS. FIND OUT WHICH OF THE FOUR OBJECTS IS THE LONGEST AND WHICH IS THE SHORTEST.

Place the chart in an area where students are able to refer to it.

Distribute a ruler to each group. Then circulate around the room to be sure that students are making the measurements.

Measuring time

After the measuring is completed, encourage the students to discuss their findings. If time is left in the activity period, encourage more measurements of the students' own choices of objects.

Collect the rulers and place them at the Interest Center.

B. Animals

B1. Studying Animals that Are Pets

Objectives: The child should be able to . . .
- **observe** and **identify** some animals that make good pets.
- **observe** and **describe** pets found at home and in school.
- **identify** and **describe** the basic needs (food, air, water, shelter) for pets.

Vocabulary
animals
pets
food
air
water
shelter

Materials
photographs of children's pets or pictures of pets that children would like to have

Teaching Suggestions

1. Initiate this activity by asking children to bring in photographs of their pets, pictures of pets they would like to have, or those they think might make good pets.
2. Have the children tell about their pet and reasons why it is a good pet.
3. Have them describe the features of the pet, its size, coat, name, color, what it eats, how it moves, and the sounds it makes while moving.
4. Have the children tell about the pet's house and how they, the children, care for their pets.
5. Encourage children to group their pictures of pets in as many ways as possible. For example, have the children group all pets according to color, size, etc. Attach pictures of pets to a large bulletin board labeled with appropriate categories.

Questions
- How would you describe your pet?
- What are some animals that make good pets?
- How does your pet move?
- How does your pet sleep?
- What does your pet eat?
- Can you think of a way to show the class how your pet can hear?
- Where does your pet live?

Extending Activities

1. Have the children act out what they think is their pet's favorite activity.
2. Play a game in which each child chooses a pet and imitates a way that pet moves, eats, and sleeps. Other children try to identify the animal.
3. Have the children tell a happy story about an event that happened to them and their pets.
4. Have some pet days during which a child and, if possible, a family member, bring a pet to school. Have the children show their favorite pets. Describe how the pets are similar or different. Have the children tell about where the pet sleeps at night and what it eats at home. Take pictures of the pets and display them in a pet booklet for the class.

from *Heath Science.* James P. Barufaldi, et al. Reprinted by permission of D. C. Heath and Company. © 1965. pp. 78-79.

OBJECTIVES

- *Identify* how a variety of things move.
- *Demonstrate* the meaning of the terms *roll, slide, bounce, swing,* and *spin.*

BACKGROUND

An object may be moved by the application of a force that is either a push or a pull. Different kinds of forces affect motion in different ways. Friction is a force that opposes motion between two rubbing surfaces. Friction causes moving objects to slow down or stop. Gravity is a force that attracts all matter toward the center of the earth. An object that slides or rolls downward on a hill is being pulled by the force of gravity.

LISTENING VOCABULARY

roll, slide, bounce, swing, spin

MATERIALS

Motivation masking tape **Core Activity** variety of objects, such as balls, marbles, chalkboard erasers, empty milk cartons, crayons, yo-yos, rolls of tape, tops

PICTURE PACKET

Photograph 7-1 of the Silver Burdett Picture Packet may be used as a motivation or a reinforcement for this lesson. Or it may be used in place of this lesson.

1 MOTIVATION

Give the children an opportunity to demonstrate different kinds of motion. Clear a large area of the classroom. Use masking tape to mark off on the floor a start line and a finish line, about 2 m (6 ft) apart. Have the children stand behind the start line. Explain that each child is to move from the start line to the finish line using one kind of motion. Each child should try to demonstrate a different kind of motion from that used by previous children.

2 CORE ACTIVITY

Purpose To identify how a variety of things move and to demonstrate the meaning of the terms *roll, slide, bounce, swing,* and *spin.*

PROCEDURE

Have pairs of children sit opposite each other about 1 m (3 ft) apart on the classroom floor. Give one child in each pair a round object, such as a ball or marble. Ask that child to push the object across the floor to his or her partner. Ask: **How does the object move?** (It rolls.) Now have the other child of the pair push the object across the floor and tell how it moves.

Distribute to one child in each pair a flat-sided object, such as a book, chalkboard eraser, or empty milk carton. Have the children repeat the procedure used for the round objects. Elicit that the flat-sided objects slide. You may wish to have the children classify into two groups the objects that roll and the objects that slide. Have them name some other familiar objects that roll or slide.

from *Science.* George G. Mallinson. Silver Burdett Company. © 1978. pp. 72-73. Used with permission. All rights reserved.

Show the children a variety of objects that move in different ways. Include objects such as crayons (which can roll or slide), balls (which can roll or bounce), yo-yos (which can swing or go up and down), rolls of tape (which can roll or slide), balls attached to strings (which can swing, roll, or bounce), and tops (which can spin or slide). Distribute the objects to the children and allow them to manipulate the objects to find out how they move. After all the objects have been explored, have the children use them to demonstrate for the class the meaning of the terms *roll, slide, bounce, swing,* and *spin.* Elicit that other objects move in these ways. For example, a door swings back and forth, a merry-go-round spins, a sled slides, etc.

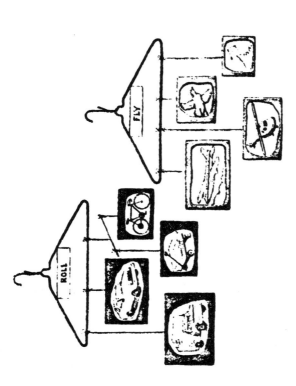

ACTIVITIES

● You may wish to read aloud the poem "If You Were a Wheel" on page 123.

● Have groups of children use wire coat hangers to make mobiles that show objects that move in different ways. Have them cut out from magazines pictures of objects that move in different ways and then group them on the mobiles according to type of movement.

● Adapt the game "May I?" so that the children can act out different types of motion. For example, give commands to roll, slide, bounce, swing, or spin as the children move toward the finish line.

BOOKS FOR YOU TO READ ALOUD

Bendick, Jeanne. *Why Things Work.* New York: Parents Magazine Press.

Branley, Franklin. *Gravity Is a Mystery.* New York: Thomas Y. Crowell Co.

BOOKS FOR THE CHILDREN TO LOOK AT

Podendorf, Illa. *Things Are Made to Move.* Chicago: Children's Press.

Simon, Seymour. *Everything Moves.* New York: Walker G. Co.

---

3 REINFORCEMENT AND EXTENSION

COPY MASTER

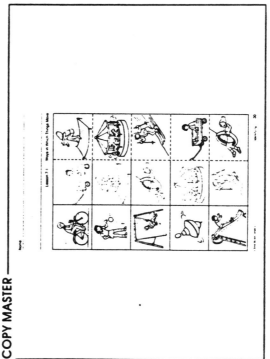

Distribute Lesson 7-1 copy master. Have the children cut out the pictures in the last column. Then have them look at the first picture in the first column and identify the type of motion shown. Direct them to find the cutout picture that shows the same type of motion. Have them paste this picture next to the first picture that it matches. Repeat this procedure for the remaining pictures.

Guiding the Learning

Pages 82-85 will help the children discover what makes water come out of the air. Use question **1**. List their ideas on the chalkboard.

Focus attention on the tin can pictured on page 82. Ask question **2**. Encourage the children's questions and accept their ideas. Ask questions **3** and **4** as they discuss other ideas. List the ideas. Ask question **5**.

Produce the materials for the children's experiment. Discuss what the first sentence on page 82 tells them to do. Then ask what the second sentence tells them to do. Have a child add several drops of red food coloring to the ice water.

Show the piece of construction paper so the children can see that it is dry. Place the can on the sheet of paper. Have several children feel the outside of the can. Have a child pour the colored ice water into the tin can. As the children observe, ask, **What do you see happening?** Choose the same children to feel the outside of the can now. They should observe that there are many drops of water on the can and that they are making the paper wet. Show the other children the sheet of paper so they can see what is happening to it.

Ask questions **3** and **4** again to verify their observations. Relate their observations to the tin can pictured on page 82. The children may need help in making the association between the cold can cooling the warm air around it and the water coming out of the air.

83 Suggested Questions

> **1. How do you know that water comes out of the air?**
> **2. How do you know that the lemonade in the picture is cold?**

Purposes

To help the child: observe what happens to a glass of very cold lemonade; obtain information by experimenting.

Concepts

Air is around the glass.
When air is cooled, some of the water comes out of the air.

Have the children recall that there is some water in the air all of the time even though they cannot see it. They can see water when it comes out of the air and collects on the can.

Extending the Learning

Experimenting With Different Kinds of Containers. Collect two tin cups, two glass jars, two plastic jars. Have the children add tap water to one set of containers and ice water to the other set. Add two drops of food coloring to each. **Does each container have drops of water on the outside? Do some have more than others? Where did the water come from?** Some children might use a thermometer to determine the temperature of the air around each container before the tap water and ice water are poured. Record the temperature. Observe that the air is warm. They might also record the temperature of the ice water and tap water. The children will observe no drops of water on the containers filled with tap water. The temperature of the tap water and the temperature of the air around the containers are almost the same. The coolness of the ice water and the warm air around the containers cause water to come out of the air or condensation to take place.

Book:

Wyler, Rose, and Ames, Gerald, *Prove It!* (see page 89T, **Book**)

> **3. What do you see on the outside of the glass?**
> **4. Where did the water come from?**
> **5. How can you find out?**

Materials: *glass; can of lemonade concentrate; pitcher; ice cubes; paper cup for each child*

Guiding the Learning

Before introducing page 83, ask question **1**. The children's responses should reflect their experiences with the tin can on page 82.

102T

from *Discovering Science 1.* Albert Piltz, et al. Charles E. Merrill Publishing Co. © 1973. pp. 82-83, T101-T102. Used with permission. All rights reserved.

Suggested Questions

1. What have you learned about water?
2. What do you see on the outside of the tin can? drops of water

3. Where do you think the water came from? **82**
Did it come from inside the can?
4. What color is the water inside the can? red
5. What can you do to find out whether your ideas are correct? experiment

Purposes

To help the child: obtain information by experimenting; observe what happens to a can filled with ice water; check his ideas through experimenting and observing the picture on page 82.

Concepts

There is water in the air.
You cannot see it.
Water comes out of the air.

Materials: *2 empty coffee cans; pitcher of ice water; small bottle of red food coloring; sheet of white construction paper*

Put ice water in a tin can.
Put red food coloring in the water.

Observing

Look at the outside of the can.
What color is the water on the outside of the can?
Did it come from inside the can?
Where do you think it came from?

Inferring

82

Can water come out of the air?

Look at this glass of lemonade.
The lemonade is very cold.
Is water on the outside of the glass?
Where did the water come from?
How can you find out?

Inferring
Conceptualizing

83

Looking and Learning

TODAY'S BASIC SCIENCE: Book 1

Four inter-related activities should be developed as the children proceed with the unit. These activities are reading, discussion, observation, and experimentation. The child is not called upon to read his science book, but it should be made clear to him that he can learn things about science by reading books.

The pictures offer many opportunities to explore incidental areas of science (clouds, shadows, life at the seashore). Keep in mind, however, that the main objective is to introduce the first-grade pupil to the scientific method. He will apply this method to his future work in science.

LESSON PLANS

Pages 6-7—Encourage your pupils to study the picture and to relate the activities on the beach to the unit title: *Looking and Learning*. Bring them around to the conclusion that we can learn by *observing* (looking) and *doing experiments*.

Responsive children in your class will have many observations to make about the picture. They will see things that not even the artist himself had pictured. There are also many predictable observations that should be brought out in your discussion. Among them are:

1. Several children are playing on the beach. Others are in the water.

2. The children on the beach cast shadows.

3. The girl in the foreground (page 7) is looking at a shell. (Could it be a mussel shell?) The girl sits beside a starfish, but she seems to be ignoring it. Has she possibly looked at the starfish and then put it aside? Has she examined other shells?

4. The girl in the green bathing suit is looking at a crab. The crab is moving along the beach.

5. The girl in the yellow bathing suit is doing an experiment. She has dug a hole in the sand. Sea water fills the hole. The girl is observing (looking at) the sea water.

6. The three boys are looking at a horseshoe crab.

7. The boy at the left of the picture is wearing underwater goggles. All the children in the water are wearing life preservers.

8. Birds are flying along the beach.

9. Sailboats are moving along with the wind.

10. A lifeguard is watching the child who is swimming alone.

11. The sky is clear.

12. Waves are rolling onto the beach.

Listen carefully to the children's observations about the pictures, then ask them questions about what they see. Build a classroom discussion around the observations and the evolving questions. A discussion might proceed in this way:

1. How many shadows do you see? Where must the sun be to cast the shadows in this way? (To the left.)

2. Have you ever used underwater goggles? What is it like when you look at things under water?

from *Today's Basic Science 2*. John Gabriel Navarra, et al. © Harper & Row, Publishers. 1967. pp. 6-7, T1-3, 8-9. Used with permission. All rights reserved

2

3. Have you ever been on a beach? What are the waves like at your beach? What causes the waves?

Science Background — Winds cause most of the waves on the ocean or on a lake. A calm day usually means few waves and not much wind. A disturbance in the water may also produce waves. A motorboat, for example, may roll a wave onto the shore.

4. How does a life preserver work? (Air in the life preserver makes it float.)

5. From which direction is the wind blowing? (From the right of the picture.) How can you tell? (By the sails on the sailboats.)

6. Does the sky always look the same day after day at the beach? What does the sky look like in the picture?

7

What the Scientist Does pages 6-19

Materials for Teaching

apple	chart paper	paper (blank sheets)
bird feeder	flashlight	paper clips
butterfly	hand lens	potato
carrot	magnet	turnip

Ready References

Science Today for the Elementary-School Teacher, by John G. Navarra and Joseph Zafforoni. Chapter 1, "Scientific from the Moment of Birth;" Chapter 2, "Science in the Elementary School;" Chapter 13, "Measuring Growth in Science." Harper & Row, Publishers, 1960.

PREVIEWING THE UNIT

Attacking Vocabulary

This opening unit of *Book 2, Today's Basic Science,* introduces the second-grade pupil to eight new words. Most of these words are science words. They are defined within the context of the text, experiments, and observations. The words are:

science	observes	record
scientist	butterfly	outside
experiment	lens	

Generalizations

- Scientists learn things by observing.
- Scientists learn things by doing experiments.
- Scientists learn things by talking to others.
- Scientists learn things by reading.
- Scientists learn things by keeping records.
- Scientists find out about things.

A second-grade pupil is curious. He asks questions about his environment, and is eager to learn about the things around him.

from *Today's Basic Science 2.* John Gabriel Navarra, et al. © Harper & Row, Publishers. 1967. pp. 6-7, T1-3, 8-9. Used with permission. All rights reserved

This is a book about science.

You are going to learn about science.

You will do things that a scientist does.

What do you think a scientist does?

Scientists Find Out

Scientists observe and do experiments.

Scientists read and talk to others.

Scientists write things down and keep records.

Scientists find out about things.

They find out by observing things.

They find out by doing experiments.

They find out by reading books.

They find out by talking to others.

They find out by keeping records.

Learning About Science

How can you learn about science?

You can observe things.

You can do experiments.

You can read science books.

You can talk about things.

You can keep a record.

At the age of seven, the second grader possesses a scientific attitude. This attitude, to be sure, is immature and underdeveloped, but it is a reflection of the child's instincts for knowledge and of his desire to discover things for himself.

The seven-year-old can make discoveries independently. He can approach problem-solving situations with a degree of imagination and ingenuity. Yet, his investigative techniques are neither refined nor orderly. Some understanding of the scientific method will help him to go further and to learn more than he does in his unguided approach to a problem.

The first unit of *Book 2, Today's Basic Science,* summarizes the scientific method. The unit sets forth the major components of the scientific method—observation and experimentation. It also points up the step-by-step segments of observation and experimentation. Among these important steps are reading, discussion, and record-keeping.

Recording data, talking things over with others, and searching through books for answers (collateral reading) are skills too often neglected in science education at the primary level. These are important techniques of scholarship that should not be overlooked. The child will use them often as he advances from grade to grade.

LESSON PLANS

The ideas set forth here are suggestions. They should be looked upon as one approach to teaching the unit. Build upon these suggestions. Take an idea, then develop it fully. Fit it into the needs of your class and into the level of your particular group.

Pages 6-7—Here we have an introductory illustration. It introduces the pupil to the topic of the unit—the scientist and what he does. It leads the second grader into a fully developed presentation of the scientific method.

Have the children read the text on page 7. Then work up a discussion of the text and of the illustration. Ask, "What do you think a scientist does? Where does he work? What tools does he use? What does he try to do? Does he make things?"

List the ideas which the children have put forth. Summarize their notions of what a scientist does. Then refer once again to the picture on pages 6 and 7. Explain that the picture tells us something about the scientist and what he does. Ask the children to compare their ideas with what they see in the picture.

The illustration is designed to stimulate discussion. It helps you to "draw the children out" and to get them to re-

2

veal their understanding of a scientist and his work. A good technique is to listen to the children and then at appropriate times to ask, "What do you mean? I'm not sure I understand what you mean." Such remarks will elicit further discussion and clarification of the children's notions.

Remember, the picture is presented to help the child develop and clarify *his* ideas. However, the following analysis may serve to focus your attention on certain key factors:

Generally, the picture is meant to develop the notion that the scientist is concerned with all of nature—the universe and all it contains. The earth pictured on page 7 is symbolic of this. The scientist stands and *observes* the world as a part of the universe.

The scientist works with living things. Thus, biology is symbolized by the plant with its diagrammatic leaf and root system. The scientist digs into the past and is concerned with the development of life. Thus, we see the skeletal system of a prehistoric animal. The double circle to the right of the scientist contains microscopic plants and animals.

Three cups on an *anemometer* (an instrument that measures wind speed) symbolize an interest in the atmosphere. The propeller suggests *aerodynamics* (the forces of air and gases) along with an interest in aviation (airplanes and flight). Then there is the symbol of the atom in the lower right-hand corner of page 7. It suggests the study of matter and atomic energy.

Note the compass in the upper left-hand corner of the page. The instrument may be unfamiliar to second graders, but it can arouse their interest. The compass symbolizes mathematics as a part of science. It also suggests that scientists work with models and plans. Does the compass give your pupils **any ideas?** Perhaps they would like to draw circles with a compass.

Pages 8-9—The scientist employs five techniques in his work. These techniques, or steps in his method, are observation, experimentation, discussion, recording data, and reading. All these activities are pictured here.

Have the children read the text under the first picture. The key word is *looking*. Explain that this scientist looks through a telescope. Ask the children to list other ways that scientists look, or *observe* (through microscopes, with their eyes alone, by taking photographs).

At this point, explain also that scientists use all their senses in making observations. A scientist observes with his senses of touch, taste, hearing, and smell, as well as with his sense of sight. Something can be heard but not seen. A scientist may see an object, but he may not fully understand it unless he tastes it, smells it, or feels it.

Experiment—You will need pieces of raw potato, raw apple, raw carrot, and raw turnip. Cut the pieces into cubes. Show the pieces to the pupils. Ask them to identify each piece. How can they be sure of their identifications? (By tasting.)

(In presenting the experiment be sure to caution the children against putting strange objects into one's mouth. The purpose of the experiment is not to suggest tasting as an indiscriminate way of working. Rather, it is to demonstrate that we can learn things by observing with such senses as taste, smell, hearing, and touch.)

The lower picture on page 8 depicts a scientist doing an experiment. Have

3

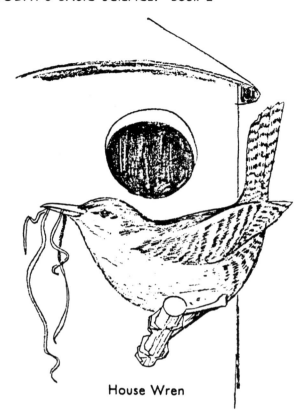

House Wren

Page 13—Refer to the text at the top of the page. Then have a boy or girl read the two lines of text orally. Call attention to the illustration. Ask, "Why is the man making a telephone call? Do you suppose he is talking to another scientist?"

Explain that scientists are at work in all parts of the world. A scientist at Cape Kennedy, Florida, may want to discuss a problem with another scientist in California. The two men can soon get together by using the telephone. Help the children to understand that we have many avenues of communications.

Refer to the "You Talk to Others" panel. Be sure your pupils understand that they, too, can learn things by talking to others. Ask, "Do you know some-

one who can tell us about birds? Do you have some questions you would like to ask someone who knows all about birds?"

Perhaps there is an ornithologist in your community. Or maybe some amateur bird watchers would have much to contribute to a classroom discussion. If possible, invite someone who can speak with authority about birds to appear before the class. Urge the children to question this person.

The picture at the lower right on page 13 suggests that the children may have additional interests and problems which may be profitably explored by talking to other people. Who would have an answer to the children's questions?

Page 14—This page highlights the importance of record keeping. Have the children discuss the different records they have made as they worked with this unit (lists of the ways a scientist observes, pictures of laboratories, an insect chart). Have them look at each record. Discuss the records.

Direct attention to the "You Make a Record" section. Have the children observe birds for one week. Ask them to make a record of the birds they see. Each child's record should include the name of the bird, its size, the shape of its body, the shape of its head, a description of its beak, and the color of its feathers.

Page 15—Get across to your class that the scientist's investigation leads to a conclusion. *The scientist finds out.* All the processes of science (observation, experimentation, interpretation, etc.) help to establish a conclusion. The scientists pictured on this page are Thomas Edison, Gregor Mendel, and Jonas Salk. Discuss.

8

Page 16—This page summarizes the way the children can learn about science. Have your pupils review the things they have observed, the experiments done, the books read, the discussions they have had, and the records they have made. Plan a bulletin-board display that will tell others how we have learned in each of these ways.

Pages 17-19—Have the children read the text on these pages. Then help them develop plans to make a bird-feeding station. They will need to select a site for the station. It might be on the ledge outside the window or it may be a more elaborate station placed within easy observation distance of the classroom.

These *Being a Scientist* pages involve the pupil in a review of the basic processes introduced in the opening unit (observation, experimentation, reading, record-keeping, discussion, forming conclusions). A similar review follows each unit of the book. Always teach processes along with your teaching of science content (principles, concepts).

Perhaps this unit has awakened a youngster's interest in birds. Be alert to any special interests a boy or girl might show. Encourage your pupil to pursue these interests. A study of birds can become a year-round activity.

EXTENSION AND EVALUATION

The *Being a Scientist* pages in *Book 2, Today's Basic Science,* serve as end-of-the-unit extensions. These pages suggest experiments and exercises that summarize the major concepts and generalizations introduced in the unit. They give the pupil an opportunity to work independently and to demonstrate his understanding of the basic principles involved.

Each *Being a Scientist* summary is introduced to the class as a discussion page. Thus, the restraints of a primary vocabulary are avoided. In this instance, the basic science content takes precedence over a reading lesson or a drill in reading comprehension.

The teacher may want to present additional problems and exercises to the class orally or possibly in written form. Suggested experiments, experiences, and tests follow:

Going Further

1. Ask another boy or girl to work with you in this experiment. Go to the window. Your friend, too, goes to the window. What do you see through the window? Observe closely. Write down the things you observe. Compare your list with your friend's list.

2. Read a book about birds. Perhaps you would like to read *Birds in Your Back Yard,* by Bertha Morris Parker. Report to your class on what you read.

9

Rocks of the Earth

Rocks—different sizes, shapes, colors, and textures—are very much a part of children's environment. Children step on them and play with them. At an early age children like to gather and show "pretty rocks" found in the country, at the beach, or in the mountains. Collecting, a characteristic of childhood, is a way of recording before having the ability to write. These early experiences provide a rich background upon which children build more concepts.

In Area 1, "Rocks of the Earth," children will begin to observe likenesses and differences among rocks by seeing, touching, smelling, and experimenting. Knowing the names of rocks is secondary at this level; however, children can begin to observe and test in a simple way some of the physical properties—color, hardness, luster—of the minerals which make up rocks. Children may want to identify rocks in their collections in terms of observations and discoveries. The emphasis need not be on differentiating between rocks and minerals. As children mature, they will learn that rocks are made up of one or more minerals.

Suggested Questions

2
pupils'
page
number

1. What are the rocks like that you have found?

2. What are the rocks like that are pictured on page 1? How are they different from the rocks you have found?

3. Do all the rocks in the picture on page 2 look alike? How are they different?

4. Can you pick up or move all the rocks you find? Why not?

5. Where can you look for rocks?

Purposes

To help the child: find out that rocks are different sizes, shapes, and colors; realize that rocks are found in different kinds of places; look for rocks in his community.

Concepts

Rocks are different sizes, shapes, and colors.
Rocks are found in many different places.

Materials: *a variety of rocks (may be brought in by children or teacher)*

Guiding the Learning

Children enjoy sharing and telling about rocks which they have found. This may be the time to

help children find out many interesting things about rocks. Naming rocks is not necessary at this time. At a later time the children will discover ways to classify some of the rocks they have gathered. You might ask several children to tell where they found rocks and the circumstances surrounding their finding the rocks. Ask question 1. You might use some ideas given by the children as a basis for dictated or written stories. Each child might want to write a sentence telling where he found his rocks and place it on the table along with his rock.

Direct the discussion about rocks so that eventually it will lead to the opening photograph on page 1. Along with question 2 you might ask, **Does this picture look like a place near where you live? Has anyone visited a place like the one in this picture?** Discuss the

13T

appearance of the rock formations. Bring out the idea that these are very large rocks.

Draw attention to the picture and the text on page 2. Ask question **3.** During the discussion have the children point out the variation in the shapes and sizes of the rocks in this picture, point out examples of smooth rocks, jagged rocks, large rocks, and small rocks. Ask, **Do you think all the rocks shown in this picture are the same kind? What do you think the girl in the picture might be pointing to across the water? Have you ever climbed over big rocks or played on them? Have you ever found rocks in places like this?**

Give the children time to express ideas and to recall experiences. Discuss questions **4** and **5.** Encourage children to continue to look for interesting rocks.

Extending the Learning

Looking for Pictures. Have the children look in magazines and books for pictures of interesting rocks or rock formations. Then let them tell others what the pictures show. Inquire about shapes, colors, sizes, and locations of the rocks. After the pictures have been discussed, the children may want to group the pictures of rocks on the bulletin board according to the shapes or some other features of the rocks.

Look for rocks.

What sizes and shapes of rocks can you find?

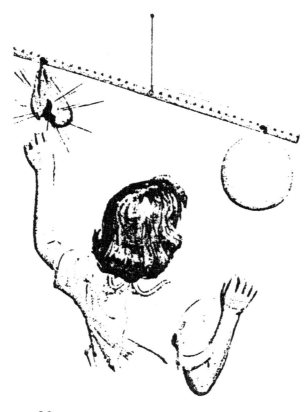

Air Has Weight

Most things have weight. Air has weight, too. We can do an experiment to show that air has weight. The experiment will help us to see that something invisible has weight.

EXPERIMENT

You will need: Yardstick, string, 2 balloons, 2 thumbtacks, drill.

Drill a hole in the center of the yardstick. Tie a string through the hole. Now hang the yardstick from a stand. Fill two balloons with the same amount of air. Tack a balloon to each end of the yardstick. Now prick one of the balloons. What happens?

The yardstick is no longer balanced. The balloon with air in it is heavier than the broken balloon. Air has weight.

26

from *Today's Basic Science*. John Gabriel Navarra, et. al. © Harper & Row Publishers. 1967. pp. T16-17, 26-27 Used with permission. All rights reserved

A Conclusion

Scientists use the word <u>conclusion</u> when they tell what they have found out by doing an experiment. The experiment you have just finished shows that air has weight. Air has weight is called the conclusion of this experiment.

Scientists check their conclusions. You will want to work as the scientist does. The best way to check your conclusion is to do another experiment.

We Try Again

EXPERIMENT

You will need: Basketball, air pump, scale.

Weigh an empty basketball. Then pump it full of air. Weigh it again. The ball with air weighs more than an empty ball. Air has weight.

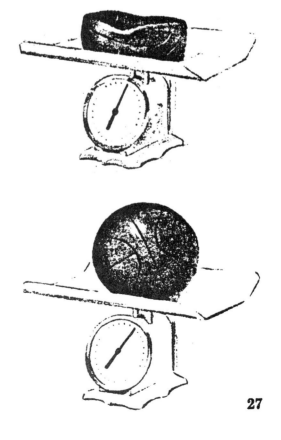

You have checked your conclusion by doing an experiment. Scientists work in this way. They check their experiments.

27

Perhaps some of your pupils will be unsuccessful in doing the experiment. That is, the water may continue to drip through the funnel into the bottle. If this happens, check the seal around the funnel. There must be no way for air to enter the milk bottle.

Now, have a boy or girl try the experiment described at the bottom of the page. Let several children do the experiment. The "feel" of the air pushing up as the inverted glass is forced below the water is an important aspect of this experiment.

For purposes of discussion, the text here includes an explanation of the experiment. Ask one of the children to read the explanation *after* the experiment has been tried. Then review the concept that air takes up space. *Air is real.*

Vary this experiment by inverting the glass over a small floating object (cork, wood chip) Force the glass down through the water. The object will clearly show that the water does not enter the glass (except for a slight amount caused by the compression of the air).

Page 25—The experiment described here is one that every child and teacher should try. It provides convincing evidence of the tangibility of air. In addition, it is an experiment that will give your pupils a great deal of pleasure. They will look upon it as "fun."

Have the instructions read aloud by one of the children. Ask, "Now, what equipment do we need for this experiment?" List the equipment on the chalkboard. In doing so, you will be emphasizing the necessity for careful preparation in the planning of experiments.

Instruct a boy or girl to do the experiment. Tell the others in the class to observe his work closely. Place the aquarium, drinking glasses, a waterproof apron, and a sponge or paper towels on a low table. Leave the equipment out for a day or two. This will allow ample opportunity for each child to try this experiment.

Page 26—The scientist defines matter as something that has mass and takes up space. Your third graders have done experiments showing that air occupies space. Now teach them that air has mass.

Science Background — Like all matter, air is composed of atoms and molecules that have mass. Gravity pulls each of these particles toward the center of the earth. The tighter air molecules are packed together, the greater is the pull of gravity on them in a given volume. Therefore, air in an inflated balloon can be used to demonstrate that air has mass.

Ask a boy or girl to read the instructions for doing the experiment. Assemble the equipment. Suspend the yardstick from a light fixture. Or you might put two chairs together to form a rack. Lay a curtain rod across the backs of the two chairs. You then can suspend the yardstick from this crosspiece.

Check to see that the balloons are identical in size and weight. That is, be sure the yardstick is balanced. You may have to make several adjustments before you get an equal volume of air into each balloon.

Tell a child to prick one of the balloons. Use a pin. Your pupils will be attentive. They will be waiting for the "pop" of the balloon. Remind them to observe the results closely.

16

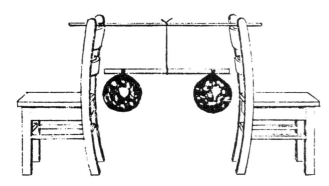

Ask the children if they are satisfied that this experiment shows in an accurate manner that air has mass. Evaluate their reactions. Some of the children may feel that part of the pricked balloon blew away. This could be true. Others may feel that the balloons slipped on the yardstick as the balloon was broken. Still others may be satisfied with the experiment.

Make use of this opportunity to encourage the children to check their conclusions. Try the experiment again. This time (1) allow the air to seep from one of the inflated balloons or (2) start with deflated balloons and inflate only one of them.

Encourage the children to discuss their earlier reactions in view of the additional evidence that they have collected. Emphasize the importance of critical thinking.

Page 27—Write the word *conclusion* on the chalkboard. Read the top half of the page with the children. Then perform the experiment set forth at the bottom of the page.

This experiment demands careful observation. Be sure the scale you use is graduated in ounces. The inflated basketball will weigh only ½ ounce more than the deflated basketball.

Try the experiment several times. Be sure your pupils note the slight difference in weight. The difference amounts to very little, but it brings out a significant concept: *Air has mass.*

Have one of the children read the text at the bottom of the page. Do your results agree? That is, have you checked your conclusion?

Page 28—The experiments presented here and on pages 29-30 teach another important concept: *Air presses.*

Ask a boy or girl to read the text at the top of page 28 orally. Call attention to the diagram of the earth. Do your pupils understand the significance of the arrows? (Air presses on the earth from all directions.)

Cite some everyday examples of how air presses from all sides. Air presses upon the top of a desk. It also presses from beneath the desk. Air presses against the classroom window from outside. It also presses from inside.

Have the children read the remainder of the page silently. Then have a child try the experiment over a sink or a pan. Do the experiment with a glass three fourths full of water. Then try it with a glass completely filled.

Turn the glass upside down. Keep the file card in place. The water still remains in the glass. Air presses from all directions.

Science Background — The air beneath the card pushes up on the card. The water in the glass pushes down on the card, but this downward force is less than the upward push of the air. The downward force is reduced further if the glass is only half full of water.

17

Resources for Teaching Critical Thinking

Critical Thinking Videotape Library

Videotapes are one of the most important developing resources for critical thinking in-service education. They can be used in a variety of ways: 1) as discussion starters, 2) as sources of information on the nature of critical thinking, 3) as models of critical thinking, and 4) as models for classroom instruction. All of the following videotapes have been developed as low-cost resources. No attempt has been made to achieve broadcast quality. An order form follows the tape descriptions.

Critical Thinking in Science

Professor Richard Paul, Chemistry Professor Douglas Martin, and SSU student Eamon Hickey discuss ways in which critical thinking may be applied in science education. The following issues are raised: "To what extent is there a problem with science education being an exercise in rote memorization and recall? Is there a conflict between preparing science students to become critical thinkers and preparing them for specialized scientific work? To what extent is science being taught monologically? Does monological instruction alienate students from the overall goal of becoming educated thinkers?" This tape is an excellent discussion-starter for in-service use.

Critical Thinking in History

In this videotape, Professor Richard Paul is joined by History Professor Robert Brown and SSU student Eamon Hickey to discuss the relation of critical thinking to the interpretation, understanding, and construction of history. The following issues are discussed: "What is the place of value judgments in history? To what extent is history written from a point of view or frame of reference? Can students come to understand history from a critical vantage point? How would history be taught if this were the goal? To what extent should history be used to inculcate patriotism? What is it to learn how to think historically? Have teachers been adequately prepared to teach history from a critical vantage point? What can be done to facilitate historical thinking rather than memorization of 'facts'?"

Dialogical Practice. I

One of the most important skills of critical thinking is the ability to enter into and reason within opposing viewpoints. In this videotape, Sonoma State University students Stacy Golding-Ray and Jean Hume practice dialogical reasoning, using the Israeli-Arab conflict as the subject.

Dialogical Practice. II

In this videotape, Sonoma State University students Hub Lampert and Dave Allender practice dialogical reasoning, using the issue of abortion as the subject.

(Both of these dialogical practice tapes are excellent illustrations of what it is for students to integrate a host of critical thinking skills and dispositions into their spontaneous thinking.)

Critical Thinking: The State of the Field

In this welcoming address to the Third International Conference on Critical Thinking and Educational Reform, Professor Richard Paul addresses the following issues: "What fundamental changes are necessary to give students the incentive to develop critical thinking skills? How does the very nature of belief pose difficulty for critical thinking? How does traditional intra-disciplinary education provide an obstacle to independence of thought? How is critical thinking fundamental to all forms of reference and how can we use it to think across and beyond disciplinary boundaries? How is the field of critical thinking developing so as to cut across subject matter divisions? What are the social and institutional barriers to the development of critical thinking as a field and as an educational reality?

Socratic Questioning In Large Group Discussion (4th Grade)

Professor Richard Paul leads a 4th Grade class discussion, using Socratic questions. Issues such as the following are discussed: "What is your mind? Does it *do* anything? Where does your personality come from? Is thinking like an American kid different from thinking like an Eskimo kid? Do you choose to be the kind of person you are going to be? Can you be a good person and people think you're bad? How do you find out what's inside a person?"

Socratic Questioning in Large Group Discussion (6th Grade)

Professor Richard Paul leads a 6th Grade class discussion, using Socratic questions. Issues such as the following are discussed: "Who does the 'our' in the textbook title *Our World* refer to? Are people easy or hard to understand? Are all members of a group alike? Do some groups think they are better than other groups? Are there any groups of people that you think are bad? If you had to list the qualities of most Americans, what would they be? If you had to list the qualities of Germans, what would they be? Italians? Russians? Now imagine all of you are Russian boys and girls: how would you describe Americans?" The students' stereotypes and biases are probed. When contradictions begin to emerge, the students struggle to reconcile them or go beyond them.

Socratic Questioning in Large Group Discussions (7th and 8th Grades)

Professor Richard Paul writes a definition of critical thinking on the board --"Critical thinking is seeing throught the surface of things, events, and people to the deeper realities"-- and then leads the class to probe the definition by Socratic questioning: "Can anyone give an example of a person you met that you thought was one way whom you later came to think was very different? Have you ever seen a toy advertised on TV that you later saw was very different from the way it appeared on TV? Do people ever try to make things look different from the way they are? Is it common or not common for people to try to trick other people? How can we check to see if people or things are really the way they appear to be? Do we always know what we really want? What we are really like? Are all people around the world basically alike or basically different? How could we check? How could we find out if we are right or wrong?"

Learning How To Think About Thinking

Professor Paul leads a small group discussion whose purpose is to shed light upon the process of learning how to think about one's thinking. The issues used to illustrate the problem are "What is egocentrism? What is sociocentrism? What is the relation between these tendencies of mind and critical thinking?" All the students involved have had at least one course in critical thinking.

The Attributes of a Critical Thinker

Professor Paul leads a class discussion about the attributes of a critical thinker. The class is introductory. Professor Paul uses Socratic Questioning and other techniques to facilitate student analysis, synthesis, and evaluation of the subject at hand. This tape can be used to illustrate both 1) initial student grappling with the idea of becoming a critical thinker, and 2) discussion techniques that facilitate student insight.

Student Insights into Metacognition

Professor Paul leads a discussion focused on a class's early experiences with metacognition. The students analyze the problems which they experienced in thinking dialogically on isssues chosen by them. In the assignment discussed, the students constructed arguments on opposing sides of an issue. Some surprising insights and problems are articulated.

Four-Part Workshop on Critical Thinking

Part One: Introduction to the Concept

In this introductory talk to an audience of public school teachers, Professor Richard Paul addresses the following issues: "What is the nature of critical thinking? How has it been defined and how useful are definitions? What are some of the characteristics and character traits of a person who thinks critically? What kinds of macro-abilities and micro-skills would critical thinking instruction foster?
Professor Paul emphasizes fairmindedness, reciprocity, intelligent skepticism, and multilogical thinking. He explains the intimate relation between critical and creative thinking.

Part Two: Dialogical Practice

In this videotape, Professor Paul explains the nature and importance of dialogical thinking and dialectical discussion. Dialectical exchange is modelled and the difference between it and 'debate' is explained.

Part Three: Reciprocity

This tape focuses on a second macro-ability essential to strong-sense critical thinking, *reciprocity*, the process of entering into points of view that are in opposition to our own and reasoning within them. The teachers in the audience play the role of students and use the Lebanon hostage crisis as an occasion for learning how to reason sympathetically within an 'alien' and 'unpopular' point of view. A discussion is held on the importance of skills in reciprocity. The audience selects an unpopular point of view for two of Professor Paul's students to 'reconstruct' and model. It is emphasized that there are no 'dangerous' or 'forbidden' ideas, only ideas well or poorly justified. The importance of freedom of thought is discussed.

Part Four: Socratic Questions

Socratic questioning is designed to foster the habit of reflective thinking rather than the habit of looking to a teacher, a book, or a formula for a ready-made answer. A Socratic questioner probes deeply for reasons, clarifications, explanations, and evidence, helping us to see what grounds or lack of grounds we have for our beliefs. In this tape, the process of Socratic questioning is discussed and modelled. Background information is essential to its understanding. "Pitfalls" are discussed.

Proceedings of the Fourth International Conference on Critical Thinking and Educational Reform

Critical and Creative Thinking -- Sharon Bailin

Critical and creative thinking are both frequently cited as goals in education, yet they are often conceived as very different kinds of goals requiring different and even antithetical kinds of pedagogy. Teaching critical thinking often consists in teaching isolated techniques of reasoning, while fostering creativity is connected with encouraging intuition and the spontaneous generation of ideas. Ms. Bailin argues that both tendencies are misconcieved as they are based on false opposition between critical tnd creative thinking.
Ms. Bailin attempts to show that the two are really intimately and inextricably interconnected, and outlines the educational implications of pursuing critical and creative thinking as joint and inseparable goals.

Coaching Teachers Who Teach Critical Thinking -- John Barell

If we wish students to engage in critical thinking in the 'strong sense,' how do we nurture this intended outcome through teacher-supervisor-coach interactions? Assuming experienced teachers are aware of the nature of critical thinking and find it difficult to engage students in this process, how do we help them become more flexible, empathic analysts and problem solvers? A model coaching process will be demonstrated and related to research on staff development, teacher growth, metacognition and achievement motivation.

Critical Thinking and Women's Issues -- Corrinne Bedecarré, Bernadine Stake

Bernadine Stake and Corrinne Bedecarré explore a variety of women's issues related to critical thinking instruction including sex equity in the classroom, social factors in learning, sex roles, thinking styles, built-in biases, male norms, moral issues, etc.

Problems with Teaching How to Use Arguments to Decide What to Believe --
J. Anthony Blair

Professor Blair recommends using arguments to inquire critically and systematically into whether we should believe a claim when that claim is important, controversial and one we want to adopt or reject. But it is easier to describe this method than to teach it successfully in the classroom. And it is especially difficult to get students to exercise the reciprocity of 'strong sense' critical thinking when examining a claim which they strongly favor or oppose beforehand. Members of the audience describe their own experiences and difficulties, and discuss together ways of getting students to look at the arguments for and against a claim in a truly open-minded, critical way.

Effective Design for Critical Thinking Inservice -- Chuck Blondino, Ken Bumgarner

A team approach has been used effectively in the State of Washington to institute and improve the teaching of critical thinking in elementary, secondary, and higher education. Central to this team is effective networking that exists between and among the educational service districts (ESDS) and the curriculum and instruction leadership of the state office. Employee and curriculum organizations as well as parent, citizen and business associations have joined in this team effort focused on the teaching of thinking skills at all levels. Organizing and networking techniques employed are discussed along with approaches taken to garner support of the educational groups, citizen organizations, and outside enterprises.

Advocating Neutrality -- Linda Bomstad, Harry Brod

There is a controversy over the preferred method of teaching critical thinking: Should an instructor treat competing viewpoints neutrally or advocate certain viewpoints over others? Professor Bomstad argues that there are weak and strong senses of advocacy. Weak advocacy may involve giving greater or more careful development to unfamiliar or minority viewpoints, but it does not involve a teacher prescribing these views as such. Strong advocacy is advocacy *simpliciter*; it does involve a teacher recommending or prescribing some views over others. Professor Bomstad contends that weak advocacy is compatible with neutrality in the classroom and that it often serves, in fact, the goal of neutrality as well as the goal of critical thinking in Richard Paul's strong sense. Strong advocacy, on the other hand, is assailable on a number of moral grounds, and it hinders critical thinking in the strong sense. Professor Brod offers an opposing point of view.

Critical Thinking and the History-Social Science Curriculum, 9-12 -- Jerry Cummings, Ira Clark

Using the Model Curriculum Standards for Grades 9-12, History-Social Science, the presenters and audience discuss and develop classroom activities and strategies for getting students to enlarge their views through critical thinking skills.

Bridging the Gap Between Teachers' Verbal Allegiance to Critical Thinking and their Actual Behavior -- M. Neil Browne, Stuart Keeley

Faculty and administrators regularly rank critical thinking as a preeminent educational objective. They claim it is the core of what teachers should be doing. Unfortunately, their talk is rarely supported by their teaching behavior. An initial obstacle to transforming verbal devotion to critical thinking into classroom performance is the mistaken belief that the discontinuity between prescription and practice is illusory. Professors Browne and Keeley summarize research done by themselves and others concerning the extent of critical thinking activity in secondary and post-secondary classrooms, and discuss strategies that offer promise for actually integrating critical thinking into the classroom. Especially important is the need to addresss the dominance of the 'coverage model' in shaping teaching practice. The presenters include suggestions for dialogic conversation with those who are motivated by the 'coverage model.'

Teaching Critical Thinking Across the Curriculum -- John Chaffee

Professor Chaffee explores an established interdisciplinary program which teaches and reinforces fundamental thinking skills and critical attitudes across the curriculum. The program is centered around *Critical Thought Skills,* a course specifically designed to improve the thinking, language, and symbolic abilities of entering college students. The course has been integrated into the curriculum through an NEH funded project of faculty training and curriculum re-design. In addition to reviewing the structure, theoretical perspective and evaluative results of the program, special attention is given to exploring practical approaches for developing thinking abilities.

Language Arts and Critical Thinking for Remedial and Bilingual Students --
Connie DeCapite

This workshop focuses on two specific components. Initially, Ms. DeCapite discusses the benefits of using critical thinking skills to help low-achieving or ESL students develop language, reading, and writing proficiency. The second part of the workshop focuses on how to develop and implement a language arts program consisting of activities utilizing critical thinking strategies and interdisciplinary materials.

A Conception of Critical Thinking -- Robert H. Ennis

On the assumption that a liberally educated person should be able to think critically in handling the civic and personal problems of daily life, as well as those of the standard subjects as taught in school, Robert Ennis offers a conception of critical thinking that bridges all of these concerns. Starting with the idea that thinking critically is reflectively and reasonably going about deciding what to believe or do, he suggests a number of dispositions and abilitites that might well constitute a critical thinking set of goals for the school, K-U.

How To Write Critical Thinking Test Questions -- Robert H. Ennis

Dr. Ennis offers suggestions on how to frame questions that test critical thinking skills.

The Human Image System and Thinking Critically in the Strong Sense -- James B. Freeman

Dr. Freeman reviews what the concepts of image and image system mean and discusses what light they shed on the strong sense of critical thinking and problems in teaching students to think critically in the strong sense. How, if at all, can we train students to be more consciously aware of their image systems? Will being aware of themselves as image formers or image producers help students to take a more critical stance toward the beliefs, attitudes, and values that comprise their images? Can we speak of rational as opposed to irrational image systems? Do images in any way mirror the world or are they merely subjective products? What in particular is the role of self-image and world image, or self-world image, in the human image system? How is it connected with egocentricity and sociocentricity? Can answers to these questions contribute to being stronger critical thinkers in the strong sense?

Egocentricity: What it is and Why it Matters --Lenore Langsdorf

Rather than treating egocentricity as a distortion of our reasoning, process, Professor Langsdorf explores, first, some consequesnces of egocentricity's being just as intrinsic to reasoning as perspective is to vision. She then explores some differences between reasoning with language and seeing with eyes. On the basis of this understanding of what egocentricity is and why it matters, she concludes with a consideration of some strategies for doing for our ego-centered reasoning what films and paintings do for our eye-centered seeing.

Philosophy For Children -- Thomas Jackson

Professor Jackson presents a brief introduction to the Philosophy for Children program followed by a 'hands-on' demonstration of how the program actually works. Participants then read from a section of the novel, *Pixie,* raise questions from the reading, group these questions, and work a follow-up exercise together.

Critical Thinking in Math and Science --Douglas Martin, Richard Paul

A discussion on the sense in which routine and non-routine mathematical and scientific thinking presuppose critical thinking. Consideration is given not only to the 'ultimate' nature of such thinking, but to the forms that thinking takes (or ought to take) as students approach it at various levels of 'ignorance' and incomplete understanding.

Moral and Practical Reasoning: Differences, Relations, Applications -- John D. May

In the first part of his presentation, Dr. May covers the following topics: how moral propositions differ from prescriptive ones; how the two affect one another in everyday practical reasoning; how mini-exercises can help students to identify components of practical arguments (normative, functional, warranting, prescriptive) to identify tacit elements and to spot flaws, to clarify their own moral and naturalistic beliefs, and to weigh practical significance of flawed arguments.

Dr. May continues with a discussion of Aristotle's Flautists, using a brief statement on justice as a vehicle for promoting strong-sense and other kinds of critical thinking. The session concludes with a demonstration of a multi-stages teaching module suitable for use in college and/or high school courses.

Projects for Integrating Critical Thinking -- Ogden Morse, Geoffrey Scheurman

The projects discussed help enable teachers to foster the deliberate teaching and integration of thinking skills with the presentation of normal content material. The project offers several avenues to aid teachers in developing units of study and integrating them into specific subject areas. Mr. Scheurman discusses the Wyoming Critical Thinking Project. Mr. Morse discusses a model he developed for transferring critical thinking theory into practical application in the classroom.

Varieties of Critical Thinking Tests: Their Design and Use -- Stephen Norris

Critical thinking tests can serve different purposes. They might be used to examine, for example, critical thinking skills or critical thinking dispositions, or to examine either several aspects of critical thinking or only a few aspects. In addition, the information provided by a critical thinking test might be used to make decisions about individual students, to assess the critical thinking curricula, to evaluate teachers, or to compare the quality of schools.

Dr. Norris argues that not all types of critical thinking tests can serve equally well all of the purposes for which such tests might be used. A systematic matching of type of test to the intended use can help make currently available critical thinking tests more effective. The bottom line in all cases, no matter what type of test is used and no matter what the purposes for using it, is that the reasons be known for students' responses to the tasks on the tests.

Teaching Critical Thinking in the Strong Sense in Elementary, Secondary, and Higher Education --Richard W. Paul

In his opening address to the Fourth International Conference, Richard Paul argues for the importance of teaching critical thinking at all levels in such a way as to foster the critical spirit and the application of that spirit to the foundations of our own beliefs and actions. He argues that it is inadequate to conceive of critical thinking simply as a body of discrete academic skills. The synthesis of these skills and their orchestration into a variety of forms of deep criticism is accentuated. He comments on the application of strong sense critical thinking to personal and social life as well as to academic subject domains. In this perspective, the strong sense critical thinker is conceived of as having special abilities and a special commitment to becoming an integrated and moral person.

Workshop on the Art of Teaching Critical Thinking in the Strong Sense -- Richard W. Paul

In this workshop, emphasis is placed on strategies which enhance strong sense critical thinking abilitieis and skills. First, the distinction between weak and strong sense critical thinking is explained. Then, exercises are used to explain and demonstrate how one can use the macro-abilities of critical thinking (Socratic quesitoning, reciprocity, and dialogical reasoning) to orchestrate micro-sikills in achieving 'strong sense' objectives.

Critical Thinking's Original Sin: Round Two -- David Perkins, Richard W. Paul

At the Third International Conference on Critical Thinking and Educational Reform, Richard Paul and David Perkins debated the psychological sources of closed-mindedness and superficial thinking. Paul contended that deep motivational factors such as egocentricity are the culprit. Perkins contended that powerful cognitive factors such as the avoidance of cognitive load lead to one-sidedness and oversimplification. Here, the two review, broaden, and deepen the debate. To demonstrate the spirit of fair thinking, however, each argues the other's side.

Knowledge as Design in the Classroom -- David Perkins

This workshop introduces participants to the basic strategies of "knowledge as design," a systematic approach to integrating the teaching of critical and creative thinking into subject-matter instruction. The key notion is that any piece of knowledge or product of mind -- Newton's laws, the Bill of Rights, a sonnet by Shakespeare -- can be viewed as a design, a structure adapted to a purpose. By examining the purpose of Newton's laws, the Bill of Rights, or a sonnet, analyzing structure, and assessing how and how well the structure serves the purpose, students can achieve genuine insight into such products and into the way knowledge works in general. By redesigning existing designs (for example, make up your own Bill of Rights) and devising new ones, students can learn the art of inventive thinking.

The Possibility of Invention -- David Perkins

"How can something come out of nothing?" is a fundamental question not only for physicists pondering the origins of the universe but for psychologists, philosophers, and educators pondering the nature of creative thinking. How can a person invent something genuinely new, or is it so that nothing we invent is really new? This presentation explores the basic 'logic' of invention, arguing that there are fundamental patterns of information processing that can be found in human thought, and some of them even in computers and biological evolution.

The Role of Thinking in Reading Comprehension -- Linda M. Phillips

Dr. Phillips discusses the intimate relation between critical thinking and reading comprehension, using case studies to illustrate how the same passage of text is interpreted differently by a critical reader and an uncritical reader. Thinking should not be separated from reading, she concludes, and reading well is thinking well.

Critical Thinking at the Community College -- John Prihoda, Richard Paul, Vincent Ryan Ruggiero, and David Perkins

This is the 'opening' session of a special program on critical thinking for community college personnel. John Prihoda defines some of the issues from a community college perspective and describes the program plan. Richard Paul discusses some of the history of the critical thinking movement and indicates some of the approaches being taken at the community college level. Vincent Ruggiero describes some of the methods and materials being used in critical thinking instruction. Dr. Prihoda comments on the administrative inplications of the critical thinking movement.

Teaching Thinking Strategies Across the Curriculum: The Higher Order Thinking (H. O. T.) Project: Elementary Level -- Edys Quellmalz

Dr. Quellmalz describes the Higher Order Thinking (H. O. T.) Projects currently underway in San Mateo County, Sacramento County and the San Juan Unified School District. The projects involve teachers in a collaborative effort to develop and monitor students' higher order thinking skills in school subjects. In the instructional component, teachers examine textbooks and other classroom resources in order to design activities that will involve students in sustained reasoning about significant concepts and problems typically encountered in academic and practical situations. Following an overview of the projects, teachers describe lessons developed and discuss samples of student work.

Moral Argument as a Means of Introducing Critical Thinking Skills to Elementary School Students -- Michael Rich

An important way to foster critical thinking skills in elementary school students is through the use of moral arguments. Dr. Rich suggests that teachers begin by examining the arguments that children actually have; not only arguments heard on the playground, but also arguments that arise between students and the teacher in the classroom. This approach has many benefits, the most important of which is the opportunity to practice critical thinking skills in the "strong sense." There are, however, some pitfalls as well. Through the use of examples taken from the classroom, Dr. Rich attempts to show how to reap the benefits of the use of moral arguments without falling prey to pitfalls.

Why Not Debate? Strong Sense Critical Thinking Assignments -- Dianne Romain

After defining strong sense critial thinking values such as fairmindedness, truth, and autonomy, Dr. Romain argues that student debates tend to emphasize some of these values. She presents a dialogue paper assignment, small group projects, and guidelines for class discussion that encourage strong sense critical thinking values.

Introducing Affective Awareness -- Vivian Rosenberg

This presentation is based on the assumption that Critical Thinking in the 'strong' sense is more than simply constructing, criticizing and assessing arguments. It involves 1) understanding how our minds work; 2) developing insight into different ways of thinking about problems and ideas and 3) developing strategies to analyze different kinds of problems and ideas. To illustrate how affective awareness can be taught in the classroom, Professor Rosenberg describes a program in which students are directed *consciously and systematically* to focus on feelings -- to identify how they feel as they deal with ideas and problems, and to understand how others feel. She concludes that affective awareness is a teachable skill, and that it can -- and should -- be taught and practiced in critical thinking courses.

Can Critical Thinking Be Taught? A Teaching Strategy for Developing Dialectical Thinking Skills -- Joel Rudinow

Rudinow discusses how Socratic techniques can be applied in issue-oriented small-group discussion settings to encourage students to engage in reflective self-criticism and to reason sypathetically within alternative frames of reference.

Mini Critical Thinking Course

At the Fourth International Conference on Critical Thinking and Educational Reform, several authors of critical thinking texts and other experienced critical thinking instructors were asked to speak on particular aspects of critical thinking. The series of lectures, presented as a mini-course in critical thinking, is now available in video format.

Using Arguments to Decide What to Believe -- J. Anthony Blair

Faced with contentious claims, there is a tendency to respond with immediate reaction, and also to consider only a few of the pros and cons. Moreover, the reflection that goes into such an examination when it does occur is seldom thorough or tenacious. What seems needed are some easily-understood and readily-applied methods that will extend and deepen the critical examination of contentious claims. The method suggestd by Dr. Blair is a systematic collection and examination of (1) the pros and cons of a contentious opinion or claim, (2) the merits of those pros and cons, (3) the overall strengths and weaknesses of the best case for the claim. Dr. Blair describes the theory of the method, then participants are given a chance to apply it and see how it works in practice.

Critical and Creative Problem-Solving -- John Chaffee

Solving problems effectively involves an integrated set of critical and creative thinking abilities. This workshop introduces a versatile problem-solving approach which is useful for analyzing complex problems in a creative and organized fashion. Participants work through a sequence of problems, individually and in small groups, and are given the opportunity to discuss and critically reflect on the learning process. In addition, participants explore ways of incorporating problem-solving approaches into the courses that they teach.

Learning About Good Arguments Through the Fallacies -- Edward Damer

This session is devoted to the treatment of a selected number of informal fallacies. Since a fallacy is defined as a violation of one of the three criteria of a good argument, the emphasis is upon the ways in which an understanding of the fallacies can help one to develop abilities to construct good arguments and to detect bad ones.

Argument Diagramming -- James Freeman

The purpose of diagramming is to display perspicuously what supports what, or what is claimed to support what, in an argument. Professor Freeman presents the four basic argument structures -- convergent, serial, divergent, and linked -- and points out how these structures may be motivated by very straight-forward questions which could easily arise in concrete situations where two people are deliberating some issue. He then applies his own diagramming procedure to display the strucutre of various sample arguments.

Stimulating Thinking About Thinking with Logical Puzzles -- John Hoagland

This is a practical workshop on using logical puzzles in ordinary language (no symbolism) for teaching critical thinking skills. Participants work one relatively straightforward puzzle, then solutions are shared. This brings an awareness of the challenges and some of the skills brought into play. Next, a second puzzle is worked together by the grid method. Then this solution is studied from the vantage points of the logical relations of consistency, inconsistency, implication, and contradiction. Finally, a method of teaching these relations along with examples and sample problems is treated.

Information and the Mass Media -- Ralph Johnson

Professor Johnson makes the following assumption: That in order to be a critical thinker, one must have the following things: first, certain intellectual and logical skills and the propensity to use them appropriately; second, a basis of knowledge and information; third, vigilance against ego- and ethno-centric bias. Professor Johnson concentrates on the second of the above-mentioned items, specifically on how the critical thinker deals with information and the mass media. The idea would be to give the students a crash course in how the critical thinker uses the mass media in such a way as to benefit from their strengths, while avoiding being seduced into thinking we know more than we do. He outlines the elements that go into being a RACON: a reflective and aggressive consumer of the news.

Practical Reasoning -- Carol LaBar, Ian Wright

Critical thinking includes reasoning about what ought to be done, as well as what to believe. This sort of reasoning, sometimes called practical reasoning, involves two logically different kinds of reasons: 1) motivating reasons in the form of value standards which the agent accepts, and 2) beliefs about the degree to which the actions under consideration will fulfill the value standard. These two different kinds of reasons lead to a conclusion about what ought to be done; that is a practical judgment. This session focuses on the practical syllogism and the use of principle 'tests' as a way of assessing the value standard.

The Nature of Critical Thinking Through Socratic Interrogation -- Richard Paul

Professor Paul interrogates the audience Socratically in order to elicit collective insights into the nature of critical thinking. This parallels the first couple of sessions of his introductory course in critical thinking in which Professor Paul uses a similar strategy for getting his students to begin to come to terms with some of the basic issues.

Disposition: The Neglected Aspect of Critical Thinking -- Vincent Ruggiero

All the understanding of creative and critical thinking and all the skill in applying that understanding to problems and issues will profit students little if they lack the *motivation* to think well. This fact has led a growing number of authorities on thinking instruction to urge that classroom instructors give special atention to the *dispositions* that underlie effective thinking. This workshop identifies these dispositions and suggests ways for instructors to assist students in developing them. It also examines the obstacles to such development and ways in which they can be overcome.

Epistemological Underpinnings of Critical Thinking -- Harvey Siegel

To be a critical thinker is to base one's beliefs, opinions and actions on relevant reasons. The notions of 'reason' and 'rationality' are, however, philosophically problematic. Just what is a reason? How do we know that some consideration constitutes a reason for doing or believing something? How do we evaluate the strength or merit of reasons? What is it for a belief or action to be *justified*? What is the relationship between justification and *truth*? Dr. Siegel examines these epistemological questions, and explores their relevance for critical thinking.

Order Form

Center for Critical Thinking and Moral Critique
Sonoma State University
Rohnert Park, CA 94928
(707) 664-2940

Please send the videotapes indicated below:

____ Critical Thinking in Science

____ Critical Thinking in History

____ Dialogical Practice, I

____ Dialogical Practice, II

____ Critical Thinking: The State of the Field

____ Socratic Questioning in Large Group Discussion -- 4th

____ Socratic Questioning in Large Group Discussion -- 6th

____ Socratic Questioning in Large Group Discussion -- 7th and 8th

____ Learning How to Think About Thinking

____ The Attributes of a Critical Thinker

____ Student Insights into Metacognition

____ Workshop in Critical Thinking Instruction, Part I: Introduction

____ Workshop in Critical Thinking Instruction, Part II: Dialogical Practice

____ Workshop in Critical Thinking Instruction, Part III: Reciprocity

____ Workshop in Critical Thinking Instruction, Part IV: Socratic Questions

____ Critical and Creative Thinking

____ Coaching Teachers Who Teach Critical Thinking

____ Critical Thinking and Women's Issues

____ Problems with Using Arguments to Decide What to Believe

____ Effective Design for Critical Thinking Inservice

____ Advocating Neutrality

____ Critical Thinking and the History-Social Science Curriculum, 9-12

____ Bridging the Gap Between Teachers' Verbal Allegiance to Critical Thinking and Their Actual Behavior

____ Teaching Critical Thinking Across the Curriculum

____ Language Arts and Critical Thinking for Remedial and Bilingual Students

____ A Conception of Critical Thinking

____ How to Write Critical Thinking Test Questions

____ Egocentricity: What It Is and Why It Matters

____ Philosophy for Children

____ Critical Thinking in Math and Science

____ Moral and Practical Reasoning: Differences, Relations, Applications

____ Projects for Integrating Critical Thinking

____ Varieties of Critical Thinking Tests: Their Design and Use

____ Teaching Critical Thinking in the Strong Sense in Elementary, Secondary and Higher Education

____ Workshop on the Art of Teaching Critical Thinking in the Strong Sense

____ Critical Thinking's Original Sin: Round Two

____ Knowledge as Design in the Classroom

____ The Possibility of Invention

____ The Role of Thinking in Reading Comprehension

____ Critical Thinking at the Community College

____ Teaching Thinking Strategies Across the Curriculum: The Higher Order Thinking (H. O. T.) Project: Elementary Level

____ Moral Argument as a Means of Introducing Critical Thinking Skills to Elementary School Students

____ Why Not Debate? Strong Sense Critical Thinking Assignments

____ Introducing Affective Awareness

____ Can Critical Thinking Be Taught? A Teaching Strategy for Developing Dialectical Thinking Skills

____ Mini-course: Using Arguments to Decide What to Believe

____ Mini-course: Critical and Creative Problem Solving

____ Mini-course: Learning About Good Arguments Through the Fallacies

____ Mini-course: Argument Diagramming

____ Mini-course: Stimulating Thinking About Thinking With Logical Puzzles

____ Mini-course: Information and the Mass Media

____ Mini-course: Practical Reasoning

____ Mini-course: The Nature of Critical Thinking Through Socratic Interrogation

____ Mini-course: Dispositions: The Neglected Aspect of Critical Thinking

____ Mini-course: Epistemological Underpinnings of Critical Thinking

****

Rates: **Purchase** -- $38.00/videotape, 4-9 tapes, $30.00/videotape
10 or more, $25.00/videotape

            Rental ---- $20.00/videotape

            Postage and Handling -- $2.00 for first tape, add .50 for each additional tape.

            California residents add 6% sales tax

Make Check or Money Order Payable To: SSU Academic Foundation
(U. S. dollars only; no stamps or foreign monies)

Please Mail Order Form and Payment To: Center for Critical Thinking &
Moral Critique, Sonoma State University, Rohnert Park, CA 94928

****

NAME _____

INSTITUTION _____
(if necessary for UPS delivery)

STREET ADDRESS _____

CITY, STATE, ZIP _____

Note: Please do *not* give Post Office Box Numbers. UPS will not deliver to them.

PURCHASE_____ RENTAL_____ TOTAL ENCLOSED _____

Critical Thinking Audiotape Library

_____ 1) Richard Paul **Teaching Critical Thinking in the Strong Sense in Elementary, Secondary, and Higher Education**

_____ 2) Stephen Norris **Varieties of Critical Thinking Tests: Their Design and Use**

_____ 3) John Prihoda, Richard Paul, Vincent Ryan Ruggiero, David Perkins **Community College Program: Critical Thinking at the Community College**

_____ 4) Richard Lichtman **The Media and Critical Thinking**

_____ 5) Lenore Langsdorf **Egocentricity: What it is and Why it Matters**

_____ 6) Ralph Johnson **Seminar on Teaching Critical Thinking**

_____ 7) Joel Rudinow **Teaching Critical Thinking the Hard Way**

_____ 8) Gus Bagakis **The Myth of the Passive Student**

_____ 9) Leonard Gibbs, M. Neil Browne, Stuart Keeley **A Randomized Evaluation of a Critical Thinking Program for Faculty and Students at the University of Wisconsin -- Eau Claire**

_____ 10) Dianne Romain **Faculty Development in Critical Thinking**

_____ 11) Frank Williams **Computer Assisted Instruction Lessons for Informal Logic and Critical Thinking**

_____ 12) Vincent Ryan Ruggiero **A Holistic Approach to Thinking Instruction**

_____ 13) Joseph Williams **Solving Problems in Writing**

_____ 14) Ralph Johnson **Mini Critical Thinking Course: Information and the Mass Media**

_____ 15) Sharon Bailin **Critical and Creative Thinking**

_____ 16) Gerald Nosich **On Teaching Critical Thinking**

_____ 17) Edward Damer **Can a Creationist Be a Critical Thinker?**

_____ 18) Debbie Walsh **The AFT Critical Thinking Project: The Hammond, in Pilot**

_____ 19) Corrinne Bedecarré **Lecture on Teaching Critical Thinking in the Strong Sense Using Women's Issues**

_____ 20) Edys Quellmalz **Teaching Thinking Strategies Across the Curriculum -- The Higher Order Thinking (H. O. T.) Project: Secondary Level**

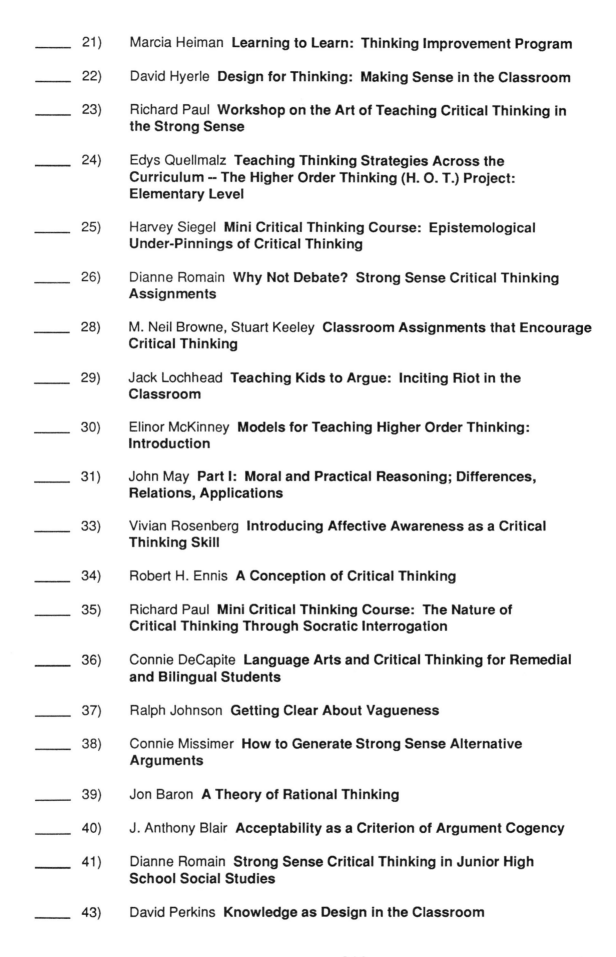

_____ 21) Marcia Heiman **Learning to Learn: Thinking Improvement Program**

_____ 22) David Hyerle **Design for Thinking: Making Sense in the Classroom**

_____ 23) Richard Paul **Workshop on the Art of Teaching Critical Thinking in the Strong Sense**

_____ 24) Edys Quellmalz **Teaching Thinking Strategies Across the Curriculum -- The Higher Order Thinking (H. O. T.) Project: Elementary Level**

_____ 25) Harvey Siegel **Mini Critical Thinking Course: Epistemological Under-Pinnings of Critical Thinking**

_____ 26) Dianne Romain **Why Not Debate? Strong Sense Critical Thinking Assignments**

_____ 28) M. Neil Browne, Stuart Keeley **Classroom Assignments that Encourage Critical Thinking**

_____ 29) Jack Lochhead **Teaching Kids to Argue: Inciting Riot in the Classroom**

_____ 30) Elinor McKinney **Models for Teaching Higher Order Thinking: Introduction**

_____ 31) John May **Part I: Moral and Practical Reasoning; Differences, Relations, Applications**

_____ 33) Vivian Rosenberg **Introducing Affective Awareness as a Critical Thinking Skill**

_____ 34) Robert H. Ennis **A Conception of Critical Thinking**

_____ 35) Richard Paul **Mini Critical Thinking Course: The Nature of Critical Thinking Through Socratic Interrogation**

_____ 36) Connie DeCapite **Language Arts and Critical Thinking for Remedial and Bilingual Students**

_____ 37) Ralph Johnson **Getting Clear About Vagueness**

_____ 38) Connie Missimer **How to Generate Strong Sense Alternative Arguments**

_____ 39) Jon Baron **A Theory of Rational Thinking**

_____ 40) J. Anthony Blair **Acceptability as a Criterion of Argument Cogency**

_____ 41) Dianne Romain **Strong Sense Critical Thinking in Junior High School Social Studies**

_____ 43) David Perkins **Knowledge as Design in the Classroom**

_____ 75) D. G. Schuster **Tracing the Essence: A Questioning, Restructuring Approach to Understanding Scientific Material**

_____ 76) John Hoaglund **Mini Critical Thinking Course: Stimulating Thinking About Thinking with Logical Puzzles**

_____ 77) Paul Lyons **Critical Thinking and Critical Consciousness**

_____ 78) Connie Missimer **Doing Battle with Egocentric Proclivities without Dying on the Plain of Relativism**

_____ 79) Peter E. Kneedler **California State Department of Education Program: Overview of K-12 Critical Thinking Assessment in California**

_____ 81) Paul Connolly **A Natural Process Approach to Critical Inquiry**

_____ 83) Greg Sarris **Toward Socratic Learning and the Third World Student**

_____ 84) Donald Lazere **Overcoming Fragmentation in Teaching Critical Thinking**

_____ 85) Linda M. Phillips **The Role of Critical Thinking in Reading Comprehension**

_____ 86) John Barell **Coaching Teachers Who Teach Critical Thinking**

_____ 87) James Freeman **Mini Critical Thinking Course: Argument Diagraming**

_____ 89) Diane F. Halpern **Critical Thinking Across the Curriculum: Practical Suggestions for Promoting Critical Thinking in Every Classroom**

_____ 90) Peter Kneedler **California State Department of Education Program: Evaluation of Critical Thinking in California's New Statewide Assessment of History and Social Science**

_____ 92) Jenna Brooke **Teaching Critical Thinking in the Secondary History Classroom**

_____ 93) James Freeman **The Human Image System and Thinking Critically in the Strong Sense**

_____ 94) Ogden Morse, Geoffrey Scheurman **Panel: Projects for Integrating Critical Thinking**

_____ 95) T. Edward Damer **Mini Critical Thinking Course: Learning About Good Arguments Through the Fallacies**

_____ 96) Jane Rowe **Reshaping the Elementary School Curriculum to Infuse Teaching for Thinking**

_____ 97) Carol LaBar, Ian Wright **Necessary Distinctions in Critical Thinking**

_____ 123) Peter Blewett **Learning is a Crystal: A Project Method for Teaching Critical and Creative Thinking in the Social Sciences**

_____ 124) George Collison **Teaching deductive and Inductive Thinking Using computer Simulations as Instructional Tools**

_____ 125) Dennis Rohatyn **The Contemporary Relevance of Stephen Toulmin's** *The Uses of Argument*

_____ 126) Mark Battersby **Teaching Critical Thinking in the High School: A College Instructor's Confession**

_____ 127) John D. May **Moral and Practical Reasoning: Differences, Relations, Application. Part II**

_____ 128) Joseph Ullian **Thoughts Pertaining to Rationality, Relativism and Problems of Classification**

_____ 129) Judith Collison **A Program for Teacher Education in Reasoning Skills**

_____ 130) Elinor McKinney **Models for Teaching Higher Order Thinking, Demonstration**

_____ 132) Margaret Hyde, George Willy, John Chaffee **Teaching Critical Thinking Skills: A Telecourse Approach**

_____ 134) David Perkins **The Possibility of Invention**

_____ 135) John Chaffee **Teaching Critical Thinking Across the Curriculum**

Cost per tape: $7.50

Name_____Phone_____

Address_____

City, State, Zip_____

Total # Tapes Ordered_____Total Cost_____

Make checks payable to **SSU Academic Foundation.** Please mail form to **Center for Critical Thinking and Moral Critique, Sonoma State University, Rohnert Park, CA 94928**

Note: Please do **not** give Post Office Box numbers. U. P. S. will not deliver to them.

Annual International Conferences on Critical Thinking

Every year in the first week of August, the Center hosts the oldest and largest critical thinking conference. In 1986, the conference had over 100 presenters, nearly 200 sessions, and 900 registrants. The conference is designed to meet the needs and concerns of the widest variety of educational levels. Practitioners, administrators, professors, and theoreticians regularly attend the conference. Many registrants have responsibilities for curriculum design and inservice or particular subject matter concerns: math, science, language arts, social studies, humanities, fine arts.... Others are principally concerned with asessment issues, or remediation, or preservice education. Still others want information about the relation of critical thinking to reading, writing, speaking, or listening. Or again, some are especially concerned with the relation of critical thinking to citizenship, to vocational or professional education, or to personal development; while others are eager to explore the relation of critical thinking to the classic ideals of the liberally educated person and the free society, or to world-wide social, economic, and moral issues. The conference discussions and dialogues that result from bringing together such a large number of committed 'critical thinkers' with such a broad background of concerns are not only truly exciting but also rich in practical pay-offs.

Please send me more information on the Center's Annual Conferences on Critical Thinking:

Name_____

Address_____

_____

_____

Special interest (grade levels, subject, etc.)

_____

_____

CRITICAL THINKING HANDBOOK: 4-6

A Guide for Remodelling Lesson Plans
in Language Arts &Social Studies

by Richard Paul, A.J.A. Binker, Marla Charbonneau, & Karen Jenson

This latest handbook enables teachers to learn how to remodel already available lesson plans to include critical thinking. Like the K-3 Handbook, this handbook describes 31 remodelling strategies and gives examples of original and remodelled lessons. The authors' remodels simultaneously show how to use the strategies and refer the reader to the section in which the strategy is explained at length, making the book clear and easy to use. Readers need not have formal training in critical thinking in order to understand and use this book.. Each strategy is designed to promote one aspect of critical thought from fostering independent thinking to evaluating assumptions. The authors also suggest ways to apply the strategies outside of traditional lesson plans. An excellent adjunct to teaching, pre-service, and in-service.

Purchase Price: $18/each
     10 or more: $16/each
     20 or more: $14/each
     50 or more: $9/each

Shipping: $3 for first book, add $1 for each additional book
    Foreign Orders: $7 for first book, add $2 for each additional book

California residents add 6% tax

**Make Check or Money Order
Payable to:**
    SSU Academic Foundation
    (U. S. dollars only, please)

Mail to:
    Center for Critical Thinking & Moral Critique
    Sonoma State University
    Rohnert Park, CA 94928

Information About the Center for
Critical Thinking and Moral Critique

Sonoma State University

The Center conducts advanced research, inservice education programs, professional conferences, and disseminates information on critical thinking and moral critique. It is premised on the democratic ideal as a principle of social organization, that is, that it is possible

> so to structure the arrangements of society as to rest them ultimately upon the freely given consent of its members. Such an aim requires the institutionalization of reasoned procedures for the critical and public review of policy; it demands that judgments of policy be viewed not as the fixed privilege of any class or elite but as the common task of all, and it requires the supplanting of arbitrary and violent alteration of policy with institutionally channeled change ordered by reasoned persuasion and informed consent.*

It conducts its research through an international network of fellows and associates, as follows:

Honorary Fellows

Max Black, Professor of Philosophy, Cornell University, Ithaca, NY

Robert Ennis, Director, Illinois Thinking Project, University of Illinois, Champaign, IL

Edward M. Glaser, Psychologist, Founder, Watson-Glaser Critical Thinking Appraisal, Los Angeles, CA

Mathew Lipman, Professor of Philosophy, Founder and Director, Institute for the Advancement of Philosophy for Children, Montclair, NJ

Israel Scheffler, Thomas Professor of Education and Philosphy, Harvard University, Cambridge, MA

Michael Scriven, Professor of Philosophy, University of Western Australia, Nedlands, Australia

Research Associates

J. Anthony Blair, Professor of Philosophy, University of Windsor, Ontario, Canada

Carl Jenson, Associate Professor of Communications Studies, Sonoma State University, Rohnert Park, CA   (Continued)

*Israel Scheffler, *Reason and Teaching* 1973, Bobbs-Merril Co., Inc.) page 137

Ralph Johnson, Professor of Philosophy, University of Windsor, Ontario, Canada

Don Lazere, Professor of English, California Polytechnic State University, San Luis Obispo, CA

Perry Weddle, Professor of Philosophy, California State University, Sacramento, CA

Ian Wright, Professor of Education, University of British Columbia, British Columbia, Canada

Joel Rudinow, Assistant Professor of Philosophy, Sonoma State University, Rohnert Park, CA

Teaching Associates

Robert Ennis, Center Fellow

Carl Jensen, Center Research Associate

Don Lazare, Center Research Associate

Richard Paul, Director

Dianne Romain, Assistant Professor of Philosophy, Sonoma State University

Douglas Martin, Associate Professor of Chemistry, Sonoma State University

Joel Rudinow, Center Research Associate

Research Assistants

A.J.A. Binker, Sonoma State University

Karen Jensen, Bellevue High School, Bellevue, Washington

Director

Richard W. Paul, Center for Critical Thinking and Moral Critique and Professor of Philosophy, Sonoma State University

The work of the Center includes an annual international Conference on Critical Thinking and Education; Master's Degree in Education with emphasis Critical Thinking; Supplementary Authorization Program in the teaching of critical thinking (under the Single Subject Waiver Credential Program of the State of California); inservice programs in the teaching of critical thinking; Research Intern program (for graduate students in the field of critical thinking and moral critique); a resource center for the distribution of tests, documents, position papers; and research in the field of critical thinking and moral critique and in the reform of educaiton based upon the teaching of reasoning and critical thinking skills across the curriculum. Other recent contributors include the historian Henry Steele Commager and George H. Hanford, President of the College Board.

Center for Critical Thinking and Moral Critique

Sonoma State University

Rohnert Park, CA 94928